PEOPLE AND PLACES

People and Places

RICHARD COBB

Oxford   New York
OXFORD UNIVERSITY PRESS
1985

Oxford University Press, Walton Street, Oxford OX2 6DP

London New York Toronto
Delhi Bombay Calcutta Madras Karachi
Kuala Lumpur Singapore Hong Kong Tokyo
Nairobi Dar es Salaam Cape Town
Melbourne Auckland
and associated companies in
Beirut Berlin Ibadan Mexico City Nicosia

Oxford is a trade mark of Oxford University Press

British Library Cataloguing in Publication Data
Cobb, Richard
People and places.
I. Title
082   PR6053.01/
ISBN 0-19-215881-3

Library of Congress Cataloging in Publication Data
Cobb, Richard, 1917–
People and places.
I. Title.
PN5123.C44A25 1985   824'.914   84-27238
ISBN 0-19-215881-3

Set by Rowland Phototypesetting Ltd.
Printed in Great Britain by
Biddles Ltd., Guildford and King's Lynn

For
Tim and Alexandra Hilton

CONTENTS

ACKNOWLEDGEMENTS

Acknowledgements are due to the editors of the following periodicals in which some of these essays first appeared: *Balliol College Annual Record, The Cambridge Review, Guardian, The Listener, The New York Review of Books, Spectator, Times Literary Supplement, The Welsh History Review.*

INTRODUCTION

Going to see M. Lageat

He was rather small, very neat and stocky in his dark blue suit, white collar, and sober tie. He could have been the manager of a provincial branch of the *BNP* or the *Crédit Lyonnais*, at least on first appearance, for the red ribbon in his lapel, shown to full advantage against the dark blue background, and his air of alertness, suggestive of sudden, swift movement, held in check, but ready to spring at the slightest sign of warning, pointed to something rather more active. His very pale blue eyes, expressionless, unblinking, but very attentive behind his steel-framed glasses, never left my face throughout the time it took me to read out to him, translating as best I could—it was not too difficult, for there was quite a lot of French in it in any case, and most of the quotes and slang words were in that language—as I went along, the long straggling proof of the review that I had written of his book and that was to come out the same week (I dropped in a copy with the huge doorman four days later) from start to finish. He remained completely still throughout my reading. There was something menacing about his stillness; or perhaps I was imagining things, my friend, Claude Dubois, who had brought me along and had introduced me, having previously filled me in with some unconventional biographical details, such as that he thought that he might at times have acted as a killer at the behest of the Resistance and that he had a ready hand with his revolver (he added that he still carried one, and had a larger one within easy reach in his villa in the Brie).

When I got to the end, there was a slight pause. It was rather like reading an essay out to one's tutor and then waiting for him to make some sort of comment while he fiddled with the bowl of his pipe. Then he broke into a sudden, warm smile, and I knew that it was all right; there was really no reason why it should not have been, for I had said most flattering things both about the author and about his book. Well, they weren't *meant* to be flattering, my admiration had been quite genuine and I had at once warmed to his anarchic personality and to his marvellously Parisian use of language. Like a great many people totally lacking in physical courage, I had also been drawn to a man who apparently had always shown himself outstandingly brave, whether in the ring, on the street, in the rough and tumble of the markets, or in operations vaguely connected with the Resistance, and who had been throughout life a stickler for matters of personal honour. He rang a bell at the side of his desk, and a huge blond man with very short curly hair and china-blue eyes—he was a Hungarian all-in wrestler who doubled up on the premises as a quietly persuasive bouncer—came in with a bottle of champagne in an ice-bucket and three glasses. Speaking for the first time, he commented that, for an Englishman (*un rosbif*), I seemed to have quite a remarkable knowledge of French, even of Parisian *argot*. As if to provide further value to the compliment, he voiced it in an accent that was almost theatrically Parisian. He gave me a card with the name and address of the establishment and on the back of which he had written, in a sloping hand and in green ink, that I was to be admitted gratis at all times, whether alone or accompanied, and that, in the case of his own absence, I was to be offered the full *honneurs de la Maison*. I still have the card, so perhaps some day I shall use it in order to find out what these extend to. They did seem at the time to suggest possibilities both inviting and, no doubt, judging from the general appearance of those hanging around the place, even during this slack Tuesday afternoon period, voluminous. My host, who had been, among other things, a market-porter, a boxer and a gymnast, seemed to be the only small person around a place in which it was made clear, from the posters and the publicity and the living reality of both, that female well-rounded and large bottoms (*valseurs*) were very much at a premium.

My friend, Claude Dubois, who had helped Robert Lageat, 'Robert des Halles', write his book of reminiscences, had been very insistent that I meet the author, tempting me by pointing out that he was one of the last surviving genuine Parisians, a true child of the old Central Markets, of the IVème *arrondissement* and of the Passage Pecquay. I think it was the last that had tempted me most, having spent so much of my time, in the Thirties,

Forties, and Fifties, exploring the *Passages*, covered or uncovered, the *Cités*, the *Villas* and the *Impasses* of that secret city. He had reassured me that M. Lageat was quite approachable, provided one handled him the right way; and this, he went on to say, he was well able to do. I did feel the need of some reassurance on this point, for Claude had supplemented, for my benefit, some of the information that the author had provided in the book itself. There had, in particular, been the business about the accessibility and apparently frequent use of the revolver, indeed of *several* revolvers, of different sizes, but all of the same make: FNB Herstal (perhaps a fairly rare case of 'Belgian being Best'). Claude had added, lowering his voice so that his wife and his five-year-old twin sons could not hear, that, only a few weeks previously, M. Lageat had displayed his revolver for the benefit of some neighbour in the Brie whose garden abutted on his own and who had proved troublesome and lacking in understanding, but who, as a result, had come round to a more reasonable appreciation of the proprieties of neighbourliness. He had also filled me in a bit on the subject of the dark, uncertain frontiers that, during the black Occupation nights, had often provided the furtive meeting-places of *Résistants*, black-marketeers, members of *le Milieu*, and *Occupants*: such-and-such a large *café-billard*, long-since destroyed, its front abutting on the entrance to the Métro station Strasbourg-Saint-Denis, but with an unobtrusive back entrance on to the rue Sainte Apolline. I had already learnt something of such discreet points of encounter from my friend Louis Chevalier, in his fairly recent capacity as the historian of the Paris Night (a bright page of Paris history, velvety black, bright silver and a pallid yellow, that has now been turned for ever) and who, as a child, staying with relatives in the Boulevard de Sébastopol, had had as playmate and fellow-explorer of the *passages* of the Xème *arrondissement* the son of the *concierge*, a person who, in adult life, was to distinguish himself as a minor *caïd* in the milieu of the rue du Faubourg-Montmartre, before being guillotined as a result of a *crime d'honneur* on emerging from a long stage in the *Centrale* of Melun: a predestined victim, Louis had commented, over supper in the Balza, of inflated pride: *L'Orgueil, voilà ce qui l'a perdu*. His former playmate had felt the insistent need to punish—and to be *seen* punishing—his one-time girlfriend who, during his period in prison, had gone off with another man. So, no sooner had he been released than he had made for the Faubourg-Montmartre, tracked the girl down to one of her usual ports of call, and shot her dead.

Louis Chevalier had also been quick to realize, in terms of the rapidly shrinking social history of Paris and of Parisians, the unique importance of Robert Lageat as a monument to a Parisian past that was already in the process of being totally erased. He had willingly provided an Introduction to the book. I had long known Louis Chevalier, a convinced bachelor who had done his military service in the French Navy, as one of the last of the disappearing breed of night-walkers of the Paris streets; indeed, some ten years after him, I had covered many of the same night itineraries, and I was very much aware of the odd items of information that he had been in the habit of obtaining in the course of these lonely prospectings between midnight and four in the morning from café-owners, *garçons de café* (wonderful recorders of regular timetables and leisure habits), prostitutes and friends of his in the Quai des Orfèvres. It had been through Louis Chevalier that I had originally met Claude Dubois, who had himself come into a good deal of unusual information about some of the more secret itineraries of the city—especially during the night hours—from his own father, a retired *agent de ville* who had at one time been on the regular night patrols as an *agent cycliste*.

Claude had added that there was no time to be lost. Robert Lageat, it is true, though then aged seventy, was still in excellent trim, thanks to daily early morning sessions with the dumb-bells. And it looked as if he might be around for a good many more years; but he was already tending to repeat himself, telling the same story again and again, or losing the sequence of what he was saying. Already most of his friends—including the three *Grands Argotiers*—had passed on; and M. Lageat's memory was beginning to fail. Claude had told me that M. Lageat's son, Jacqui, who was now nominally in charge of the establishment, was not up to his father, he had had things come too easily to him, and he completely lacked the old man's adaptability, drive, intrepidity, quick reactions, tenacious friendships (once they had stood the pretty severe tests that he had put them to) and as sudden and extremely dangerous flashes of anger. The son was but a pale reflection of a very remarkable and potentially rather sinister father. I did not need much more persuading after such skilled advocacy, both from one of my oldest friends in Paris, and from one of my most recent. I only hoped that I would stand the test and that M. Lageat would take my interest in himself and in his unique background as a friendly one. I could not help feeling that if I made the wrong impression, he might be a very dangerous man to put out. Anyway, as I have said, all went swimmingly; and though I have only made use of his bizarrely illustrated card to call on him from time to time, when we have both been in Paris, without putting it to the test for whatever other delights it might be made to provide, I have certainly managed to retain his friendship and benevolent attention—the bucket and the champagne bottle would duly arrive, after a quarter of an hour or so—at the cost, it is true, of having to listen, with an air of eager expectancy, to a discourse that I had heard again and again. The novelty provided by the bizarre décor, by a small army of gentle giants and one or two vaguely sinister dwarfs (these had not made an appearance on my original visit) both of which seemed to have escaped from some minor, rather dusty medieval court, by the air of natural deference that surrounded the man himself, and by meeting, yet again, someone who, though loquacious, seemed to retain curious areas of reticence (I could see that it would be imprudent to press him too far on some of the missing or uncompleted chapters) soon wore off, perhaps after my third or fourth visit. But I still managed to appear an eager and attentive listener, even if I called more out of politeness than in an effort to find out more.

I have been listening to elderly people most of my life, certainly from the age of ten or twelve; and I think I can always give a convincing impression of attentiveness, even when the record has quite clearly got stuck. This is an occupational risk faced by anyone who is concerned to learn about a fairly recent or remote past from the jumbled and muddled wealth of personal testimonies. Old people tend to repeat themselves, just as the judicial and police documents that illustrate French social history tend to repeat themselves, often providing, by their very repetition, a comparative scale of values that may be of great use to the historian who has acquired an ear attuned to such litanies. I even ended up by finding something reassuring about Robert Lageat in the predictability of what he was likely to come out with. I would know what would be coming next and how the story would end. My visits to the spare, red-faced man in the blue suit and wearing the steel-rimmed spectacles had become a habit, almost a rite. I was also concerned thus to put to the test, time after time, a friendship that might, from the outset, have seemed entirely improbable. In the past, particularly in the late Thirties and the second half of the Forties, I had been drawn to one or two fairly unassuming *petits truands*, minor black-marketeers, people who dealt in counterfeit American-style hundred franc notes, and fairly prudent law-breakers, like my friend Maurice Chauvirey, certainly anything but a trigger-man, and a natural coward like myself. Indeed, through the experiences of Maurice, I could relive some of the discomforts and hazards of the Occupation period, particularly in respect of his encounters with German soldiers embarking, under his interested guidance, on 'Paris by Night' (to include the rue de Lappe, as well as the Place Blanche), and of his difficulties with the so-called Resistance people in his home area of the Haute-Saône. Maurice had entirely human proportions, was anxious to keep out of serious trouble and to remain uncommitted. What I liked about him was his redeeming prudence. But M. Lageat belonged in quite a different category. Before 'going straight' and making his peace—no doubt at a price—with *La Tour Pointue* he had certainly operated at least on the fringes of gangsterism, and his methods of debt-recovery had been anything but gentle, involving as they did one or other of his FNB Herstal revolvers. But it was not just that I really *liked* the man and was gratified by his friendship. I have spent much of my life flattering people; and in French one can get much further in flattery (the language lends itself admirably to that agreeable exercise) than in English; and it amused me to see just how far I could go without arousing suspicion. M. Lageat was a simple man, especially in his pride of achievement, and I very soon spotted in him an almost ideal target for some of my more ambitious excursions into fairly florid flattery.

Robert Lageat is the last surviving monument to something now almost totally lost; the sheer inventiveness of Parisian popular speech, the sharp, alert language of the more plebeian former residents of the central districts of the capital—and M. Lageat was that fairly unusual being, a Parisian of four or five generations, tracing his family back to constant employment in or near the Central Markets to the beginning of the nineteenth century; the warm and extensive sociability, accompanied by an ever-ready violence, of the old market quarter, the survival of the street and the *impasse* as a form of closely watched and, on the whole, kindly, neighbourliness, the changing pattern, within a given and very circumscribed, highly specialized area—fruit, vegetables, meat, and prostitution—of the hours, both by night and by day, but mostly by night, beginning at 2 a.m., and ending round eight (there had been little room for sleep in either): in short the total identification of people with place, just as he could give a name to every small street, square and *passage*, he could place, at each stage in each, and through the night hours (some would cut off at five in the morning, some would only start trading at three) this or that stall-holder, identified by name or nickname, accent, speech defect, appearance. M. Lageat would be inconceivable outside the limits of the IVème and the Ier, the areas in which he grew up and first worked, though he later became acclimatized to the IXème and the Xème (boxing rings, gyms, cinemas, music-halls) and has more recently put down deep roots in the XIème, just as Albert Simonin would be inconceivable beyond the limits of La Chapelle pre-1914, during the First World War and in the Twenties and the early Thirties. Simonin died in the early 1980s, Lageat is still alive. By the time of his death, the former would have found La Chapelle unrecognizable and completely alien. M. Lageat has long since abandoned the Passage Pecquay and 'La Quincampe' to an invading army of antique-dealers and young professional couples with two children and one dog (a poodle) each; and he now spends most of his time away from Paris, *à la campagne*, the old, old dream of every native-born Parisian, in a semi-fortified villa on the edge of the grainlands of the Brie.

But he has not abandoned Paris. In a perhaps rather desperate attempt to prove to himself—and to others—that something of the past of *le Paris populaire* of the 1920s and the 1930s (that, in particular, portrayed, in striking black and white, by flash bulb, in the extraordinary inside-looking photos of Brassai) has survived, he acquired and has held on to one of the last, and certainly the largest and the most lavish of the old *bals-musette* of the rue de Lappe, the Balajo, named after its founder, Monsieur Jo, at the near end of the street. The street, very dark and narrow, rather sinister, still looks much as it did in 1937 or 1938, though the crowds have thinned, especially at night, and there are far fewer bright neon lights and wider gaps of anonymous and vaguely threatening dark. The sailors have disappeared, and so have the pale girls in blue silk with the big black question marks of hair sticking to their low foreheads. There are two or three other similar establishments, smaller and more modest, their little orchestras perched in tiny balconies overlooking the narrow dance-floor, little more than a passage, and corresponding much more closely to the sort of places photographed by Brassai in 1930 or 1931, noisy, hot, and sweaty centres of once-popular entertainment to which I was in the habit of taking delightfully fearful American ladies, during their 'Paris by Night' in 1936 or 1937. An air of stale crime, used-up violence and spent savagery still hangs over the narrow street, little more than a gulley. It can still even take concrete form, as Claude Dubois has recently reminded me, when telling me, with some satisfaction—as if to indicate that the old place was still living up to its past reputation—of the knife attack on M. Lageat's gigantic blond bouncer, who had been left on the sticky, glistening *pavé* in a very poor state of health before being carted off to Lariboisière.

The Balajo was a cut above this sort of establishment. Instead of being long and narrow it was vast and circular, with a domed ceiling painted in very dark blue and lit only by silvery shining stars, as if it had been a planetarium bizarrely enlivened by rather listless accordion music. The place had been entirely redecorated, in 1937 or 1938, in a style wonderfully evocative both of the interior fittings of the liner *Le Normandie* and of the French house in *L'Expo 37*. With the *lycée* Claude-Bernard, the interior of the Balajo is probably one of the best examples of the optimistic pretentiousness—a massive use of gold and silver filigree, a propensity to sculpted winged horses—of the official styles favoured by the very last years of the Third Republic. The style, surviving in its rare perfection in this odd corner of Paris, seemed altogether appropriate both to the present owner of the place, a man who had really begun to make his way in the late Thirties as a gymnast and an entertainer, and who still dressed in the conventional manner of the period—*complet veston*, white shirt and tie—and to his regular clientele. I asked him who were his most faithful customers, and he told me that they were ladies of a certain age (*des dames d'âge mûr*), that is between forty and fifty-five, shop-assistants, secretaries, typists, *standardistes*, twenty-five or thirty years on, who came there to recapture the fast, eager steps of their twenties, to dance with attentive young men (rewarded with bottles of cheap champagne, and no doubt provided with other inducements) to the swift accordion music of a *java*, in the vast, largely empty circular semi-darkness, redolent of sweat and cheap perfume, through the long afternoon sessions in the week. Wednesday and Thursday afternoons, he explained to me, represented the peak period, attendance falling off in the evening. Lately he had taken to closing the place at the weekend. It seemed an odd pattern of leisure, the very reverse of what had happened in the Thirties, when the *bals-musette* had filled up to almost unbearable capacity on Saturday nights, which seemed to make sense, if only in terms of the old 1900 favourite: *Samedi soir, après le turbin, l'ouvrier parisien . . .* The calendar of nostalgia could be decidedly mysterious. Why should Parisiennes in their middle years want to spend Wednesday and Thursday afternoons dancing to accordion music in an enormous, dark, half-empty ring? Was there a special loneliness that clung to afternoons mid-week? M. Lageat did not know the answer; that was the way it was, he said. I asked him if the Balajo drew on a provincial clientele. Not as far as women were concerned, he said, though plenty would come in from the *banlieue-est*. But he did get occasional male sexagenarians from places as far away as Montbard, Dijon, Beaune, and Lyon; the rue de Lappe was, after all, in the catchment area of the Gare de Lyon.

I thought there was something a bit sad about the place, a bit like a Luna Park that had lived beyond its allotted days, going into a slow decline. It seemed well enough kept, in so far as one could pick out details in the dim light, though I did notice that some of the red velvet seats that stood along the outer walls and that looked as if they had been borrowed from Le Rex or one of the other big cinemas of the Boulevards, had marks of stitching where the material had suffered rents and that looked as if it had been done a long time back. The general effect was one of somewhat fatigued grandeur; and this was further borne out by the listless faces of the accordionists and the other members of the dimly-seen orchestra. They were playing a *java* all right, but their hearts did not seem to be in it, and it was not the sort of *java* that would have sent young couples whirling round like dervishes. I wondered what Raymond Queneau would have made of the rather used-up ambience, suggestive as it was of stale perfume and of very old, lingering lust. It was a backward-looking sort of establishment—indeed this was its undoubted charm as an almost perfect period piece—but it did not seem to offer much hope for the future. At best, it looked as if it might soldier on for a few more years of Wednesday and Thursday afternoons. I could not help wondering whether it represented a viable investment, and whether its owner was not himself, like his establishment, a captive of past successes. Certainly, he seemed to radiate material success; but then that was part of his personality, he was a plucky little chap in every respect, *très crâneur*, he had been in one form or another of show-business for a good many years, and even his more dramatic exploits in the Resistance (I learnt of these from Claude, not from M. Lageat) had many of the characteristics of a piece of pretty bad theatre—and he was certainly not at all the sort of person who would have been prepared to admit, even to himself, that he had taken on something that was already well on the way down. There was something touchingly defiant about the bottle of champagne—and very good champagne—in its bucket of ice so readily proferred, and poured out with such ceremony. The measure of his ambition could well have been that of forty years back. To have been the owner of the Balajo in 1937 or in 1938 would indeed have been a *titre de gloire*, placing the title-holder at the very head of a rather dubious, and, indeed, dangerous hierarchy, as reigning king of the rue de Lappe, and a leading personality in the *quartier de la Bastille*. Rather a fragile, transitory eminence, certainly, in an area where reigns could be terminated abruptly and bloodily, but offering even greater prospects in the favourable conditions of 1940 with the arrival of an almost limitless German clientele—not that M. Lageat would have gone for *that*. But I could not help feeling that the position was not exactly a prize one in 1980, or that M. Lageat (always referred to as such, with a slight lowering of the voice, by the blond giant, by his own son, Jacqui, and, indeed, by my friend Claude—it would have been unthinkable, even among ourselves, and in his absence, to have referred to him as 'Robert') was an object of envy and wonder throughout the length and breadth of the XIème *arrondissement*.

My own feeling was that the place might just about last out its owner's lifetime, but that his son was not particularly enthusiastic at the prospect of taking on the succession of an establishment that, having seen better days, had been granted something of a charmed extra life, as an unexpected, and, indeed, in its very perfection, magnificent relic of a no longer recent past. M. Lageat and the Balajo (and I think it is significant that not only has Mme Lageat never been associated with it, but has never even set foot in its dim, rather musty interior) are well mated, a perfect coupling of period to period, the keeper of the temple and the temple itself constituting two absolutely intact monuments to the almost lost Paris of the 1930s. It is not just for himself, for the warmth of his personality, for his rich vocabulary, for his unbelievably Parisian accent, for his friendliness, it is not just for the bizarrerie of an establishment in which ladies well on in their middle years whirl around in the penumbra, some wearing hairstyles of another age, black velvet *bandeaux*, short skirts, and little-girlie buckle-shoes, it is also, in a similar journey back into the past, in search of my largely and quite happily forgotten self that I make my regular pilgrimages to that strange Temple of Fame, giving nothing away, apart from its flickering neon-sign, from its bleak outside, rich, if a bit blowsy, and in a sort of tattered, wonderfully out-of-date perfection from its aquarium-like inside: a link, almost physical, and recognizable, right down to the smallest detail: perhaps the *Suze* advertisement on the ashtrays, with the year 1937, when I was twenty. It is the *year* that matters to me, not the attempt—impossible in any case—to rediscover myself at that uncertain, gauche, and very frightened age: *anything* rather than having to have all that over again, the dreadful pre-War years of fear, of *waiting*, of constant anxiety and constant enquiry. I am a traveller in the past for the sake of the past. Unlike *ces dames d'âge mûr*, I have no desire to go back in time, especially to that unhappy age. But 1937, which had a sort of brash optimism about it, did not deserve what was to follow: the agonizing 1938, the awful 1939, the hideous 1940.

I have reached the by no means unhappy age of sixty-seven. It is an age that brings its own inevitable priorities. Opening *The Times* in the morning, as one sits down to breakfast, one turns, with perhaps an agreeable sense of expectancy, to the obituary page. The fare is varied: possibly yet *another* granddaughter of Queen Victoria, or an obscure member of the Habsburg dynasty, or the last survivor of the young Sarajevo Bosnians, or a former Headmistress of the Godolphin School, Salisbury, or a Bishop of a diocese in Southern India. Only too often one finds oneself in familiar territory; and, in recent years, on a number of occasions, I have contributed to that all-important page myself, or have added to obituaries written by others: 'RCC writes:' is the usual formula. So, in a collection of this kind, and with an author of this age, there is inevitably a strong sense of loss: Jack Gallagher, Arthur Marder, David Williams, Albert Soboul (about whom I also wrote in *The Times* and telephoned to the *Morning Star*), Raymond Queneau, all I counted as friends, though the last only as a correspondent over the years, unfortunately never having met him. Georges Lefebvre I would not have the audacity to describe as a friend, he was not an easy person to get at all close to. I could have added others: the Breton novelist, Louis Guilloux, whom I did indeed meet, and who, beyond the grave, paid me the unusual compliment of referring to me with affection in the second volume of his *Carnets*, published a year after his death; my friends Alun Davies, Richard Spilsbury, Murray Senior and Janet Heseltine (editor of the *Oxford Book of French Prose*), whose obituaries I wrote for *The Times*; the historian, Jean Meuvret, whose unforgettable personality I attempted to evoke, shortly after his death, in a paper published in *Le Bulletin de la Société d'Histoire moderne*; another historian, this time of the French Revolution, my faithful Leningrad correspondent Yakov Moissevich Zakher, who wrote to me regularly, after his release from a prison camp (where he had spent the previous twenty-five years) in 1956, and whose *notice nécrologique* I provided for the *Annales Historiques de la Révolution française* at the time of his death in the

1960s; my Merton contemporary, the poet Christopher Lee, to whose memory I dedicated a recent book; and, finally, Wilfred Willett, about whom I have written briefly in a book published in March 1985 by his daughter Marjorie. Perhaps I am already in some danger of earning for myself the nickname given to one of my Turin friends, a man much given to funeral orations: *il necrofilo*. Happily, others included in the present collection, Christopher Hill and Robert Lageat, are still very much alive. The first section of the book, 'People', is thus rather more than a Garden of Remembrance.

If there are indeed hints of the graveyard, it is in the second section, entitled 'Places'. I have written about a Brussels now mostly lost. No trace now exists of the old Montagne de la Cour, also known as the Mont des Arts. The arts have indeed abandoned the hill, which has itself disappeared under massive and unsightly new buildings. The small streets of the Marolles have gone, and with them the narrow pavement, on a steep incline, outside Chez Bastiaan on which, in the hot months, the locals could be seen squatting on the ground to play mysterious card games, interrupted every now and then when the cards themselves slid down towards the Lower Town. It is with a similar sense of loss that I have attempted to evoke a Paris that, in the Thirties, and even in the Fifties, still retained human proportions and a ready sociability based on the storey (*le palier*), the street, the quarter, and the *café d'habitués*. The successors of the dreadful Le Corbusier have seen all such humble and consoling virtues right off the premises. Aberystwyth, or rather the University College that gave the little place much of its charm and animation, has mostly moved up the hill to a new site. I don't suppose anyone watches the Promenade any more, for there is no longer anything much to watch, save the wheeling gulls and the big black cormorants as they re-emerge with silver fish shining in their long yellow beaks. The road that Les Broadhurst and I took on his Army motorcycle from Brussels to Valenciennes is now an *autoroute* that skirts all the little towns and villages that we went through on the Belgian National Day of 1945 and that affords little view of the rich cornfields of the Hainaut or anyting else apart from the huge advertisement boards. I have not returned to Bayeux since 1947. I believe the quiet little town is much as it was, but *La Renaissance du Bessin* has not lived up to its name, for it no longer exists, and the dusty unmade road from Barbeville has been widened and surfaced to allow for the heavy traffic taking relatives and tourists to the neat war cemeteries that line it on both sides. I was told recently that Roubaix had become a jumble of high-rise blocks and that the rue aux Longues Haies had been destroyed as a result of 'slum clearance'. *People* have not changed much, but *places* certainly have, and everywhere for the worse. If one wishes to preserve memories that were happy, it is advisable not to go back.

In conclusion, a very grateful word of thanks to my OUP editor, Mrs Judith Luna, who has borne with my dilatoriness with exemplary patience.

Wolvercote, 14 January 1985

Jack Gallagher in Oxford

'Wait till Jack comes', they would say, 'he's quite a character', 'he will liven things up'. This was in the autumn of 1962, when I was first in Balliol. But Jack did not come; like the Cheshire Cat in reverse movement—and, later, I used to think that with his round face, his round glasses and his unblinking eyes, he looked rather like the Cheshire Cat (others were to describe him as the Living Buddha); and he was indeed from Cheshire—he was always about to be there, but never quite there. No one, the Master of Balliol included, had any idea where in fact he *was*. Nor had he ever written to anyone to accept his Professorial Fellowship. It was an early training in what later one would come to regard as one of Jack's principal characteristics: his elusiveness. This was later illustrated, once he had moved into his rooms in the tower, above the library, by the lines of supplicants—Indian ladies in saris, the Lord Mayor of Addis Ababa, an assortment of Africans and Thais, and a clutter of undergraduates, waiting patiently, and with suitable oriental resignation, on the spiral staircase, all the way down from his closed door to the level of the Library. Was he in? Was he in Oxford? Would his door open? One could only wait. Jack too Moved in a Mysterious Way. He was fortunate, too, in respect of Balliol that the College was connected by an underground passage, little known to outsiders, to neighbouring Trinity, so that Jack, from his observatory in the Senior Common Room, on seeing the then current Chairman of the Examiners, could make a rapid escape into Trinity Garden, and thence walk nonchalantly through Trinity Lodge into the Broad, until scouts had reported to him that the danger had passed and that the way was clear for him to return. Sometimes, if he were reading a magazine, he would ask me to stand look-out and report to him the stealthy approach of the long-suffering Chairman, who, soon used to Jack's wiles, sometimes took to approaching the Common Room obliquely, *en rasant les murs*, in the hope of escaping detection. Of course, Jack was long overdue with the papers that he was supposed to be setting or be marking. It was hardly surprising that, in the course of his nine years in Oxford, he developed a strong affection for Trinity Garden, a long rectangle of safety, up and down which we would walk, denouncing Enthusiasm, or planning our futures. It was the same with mail; when Jack turned up, all at once, and hardly ever at the beginning of the term, the Head Porter would hand him his post: an enormous pile of beige envelopes. 'Put them in the bin, Bert', he would say. Sometimes it was as abrupt as that. At other times, he would say: 'Just look through quickly to see if there are any scented lilac envelopes, then put the lot in the bin.' Once he asked my wife to see if there were any lilac scented envelopes, but, of course, there never were. The Balliol porters have retained a sort of amazed and awed respect for Jack's manner of dealing with accumulated administrative correspondence.

Then, all at once, it was reported, on good authority, that Jack had been *seen*, not in Balliol, but in Queen Elizabeth House, a sort of seamen's home for transients. This was where I first saw him: a bedroom with twin beds, three tin trunks spilling out printed blue books marked Top Secret, Ten Copies Only, Restricted, for the Attention of the Vice-Roy, and with such titles as 'Report on Terrorist Activities in West Bengal', 'Report on Civil Disobedience in Bihar', 'Enquiry into the Attempted Murder of the Governor of Sind', mixed up with socks, shoes, and shirts. It looked as if the room had been assailed by very rough seas. Jack, round-eyed, was sitting on one of the beds. I introduced myself (it appeared that, from whatever mysterious quarter he had just come, reports had reached him concerning *me*, for he gave me a most charming, warm smile, and in his quiet, and pleasant voice, asked if I would like a drink. There was a bottle of *Black Knight*, Delhi whisky, on the top of the chest-of-drawers). The room really did look like a cabin.

After a spell in the seamen's home, Jack was finally installed in Balliol, first at the top of the Library tower, later in a penthouse flat at the top of the new building. I think he favoured heights as likely to discourage the more importunate of his visitors. They also offered him a clear view of approaching supplicants, giving him time to pull up the drawbridge if the enemy were sighted. He liked heights too because they gave him ready access to the

College roof, used at regular intervals for his splendid and
sometimes alarming parties. It was always something of a surprise to me that, in the course of these, none of his guests ever fell
off the roof, crashing to the ground, though one, having put a
burning cigarette in the face of one of Jack's pupils—he was also
one of mine—was, on Jack's quiet orders, expelled *celerissimme*
down the spiral staircase. Jack was a marvellous host; but he
would not tolerate bad manners. On the other hand, he had
derived considerable pleasure at the antics of some of his guests: I
can recall one of his former Trinity pupils whose bearded head
suddenly fell sideways into his plate of nuts from which position
it stared at us with glaucous eyes. Jack made some remark about
his guest thinking he was John the Baptist. Later the same guest
wandered off dazedly up and down the spiral staircase leading to
High Table. One of Jack's fantasies—and he was rich and ingenious in these—was that we should organize a Widmerpool
Dinner to which would be invited a careful selection of the biggest
boors and the rudest dons that could be provided by the Common
Rooms of both ancient Universities. This remained a project. But
a number of Jack's guests, most from Trinity, behaved, to Jack's
observant delight— one could tell this by the steady stare from
behind the round spectacles and the attentiveness of his immobile, Buddha-like face—in a manner either dramatic or wholly
incoherent. I can remember one who spent the rest of the night in
a vain search for his car, scouring the whole of central Oxford for
the missing vehicle, asserting, piteously, that it was yellow.
When it was found, at midday the next day, parked by some
laboratories, it turned out to be grey.

Nothing gave Jack greater pleasure than for a solemn occasion
to go wrong and for pomposity to trip up in its own robes. One of
the stories most often repeated from his extensive Cambridge
lore—and our sister University, in Jack's accounts, always
appeared much more accident-prone than the apparently staider
institution further west—concerned the Inaugural Lecture of a
newly-elected Regius Professor of Moral Theology. The Professor, led in to the Senate House, preceded by the beadles,
reached the dais, pronounced the single word 'I' and then fell
down dead drunk. Jack returned to this account again and again
with loving detail. Then there was another recurring theme on

the subject of a Cambridge Professor whose marriage turned on and off *par éclipses*, the legitimate wife alternating with a recurrent mistress—a beautiful Slav; when the Professor was in one of his periodical returns back to his wife, the couple could be seen, parading in an open barouche—sometimes it was a victoria, sometimes a landau, sometimes a white Rolls—up and down King's Parade. It was in character that Jack adored W. C. Fields and took enormous satisfaction in old-fashioned music-hall acts involving glasses and trays of drink flying through the air and as regularly being retrieved by a nimble waiter clad in a long white apron. There was something child-like in his pure enjoyment of the sight and sound of breakage, an enjoyment that I fully shared. The breakage was sometimes imaginary. On one occasion, I had brought in as a guest a young historian with a nose of Cyrano-like proportion; the nose was in scaffolding, following some major construction work on it. Jack passed me a note: 'Would you tell your guest that his nose has fallen into my soup?' In fact the nose was still on, beneath its elaborate superstructure.

Jack also showed a devastating readiness in his allocation of nicknames to those of whom he did not wholly approve, who were too solemn, too convinced, or took themselves too seriously. A colleague for a brief time in Oxford—his departure from Oxford was no doubt accelerated by Jack's presence there—a specialist in Indian history, was constantly referred to as the Grand Eunuch. A young research fellow whose surname reiterated his Christian one, was always addressed as Humbert Humbert, and indeed introduced as such to other guests. Balliol contained at one time both Ghenghis Khan and Robespierre. Jack's persecutor, the Chairman of the Examiners, was named, for some reason, the Minstrel Boy. There was also a Barnsley Boy. An English Fellow from Merton—a splendid figure always clad in loud checks, and with a voice like a fog-horn—was described alternatively as Micawber or W. C. Fields. There were mysterious figures from Cambridge referred to as Hot Lips, Wet Leg, Boyo, Daddy, Rhino, Electric Whiskers. Jack himself was generally evoked as the Living Buddha; and, though he was not especially big, as Big Jack. He was a large man who somehow helped to fill any room in which he was sitting. In a group, such as at a College Meeting, he would be the first person one would pick out, his broad, solid and still presence as reassuring as that of some eighteenth-century Bishop of Peterborough, a Learned Theologian and of Moderate Piety, an Enemy of Enthusiasm. There was something very eighteenth century about Jack, he was certainly an Enemy of Enthusiasm, and he was the most English Irishman I have ever met. His presence was reassuring, because it radiated calm, carefully concealed kindliness, and immense good sense. It was hard to imagine that Big Jack, in what he liked to describe as his 'formative years', had once managed to insert himself through the turret of a tank. It was only fair that, in his descriptions of myself, for the benefit of others, he would refer to the Scavenger, to Ghandi, and to Lazarus. Others have said that, when seen together at table during Consilium dinner, we made as extravagant a pair as Laurel and Hardy. We certainly made a pair, especially at those convivial occasions, engaged as we were in a sort of double act of impudence and irreverence, extravagance and fantasy. We always took care to sit well away from the main table, and among the more raffish and pleasure-loving members of the College. Our presence at the end of the peripheral table was marked by a fine array of bottles. When I first met Robbie Robinson—sliding down the banisters of Staircase XXII, with a bowler hat over his eyes—Jack introduced him as a bookie friend of his, warning me at the same time to keep a firm hold on my wallet. (Later, indeed for years, Jack made a point of announcing to all and sundry that I had stolen his large black overcoat, though I would have been completely lost in it. By a twist of irony that would have greatly appealed to Jack, after his death I was offered his large black overcoat, not in jest, but in all seriousness, by one of his dearest and most devoted friends.) Jack, to complete his role, needed a partner who would also be a foil. One of the younger Fellows of Balliol described the double impact of Jack and myself on the more puritanical elements of Balliol as the sudden arrival on the sober scene of 'those two wicked old men', unrepentantly and shamelessly calling for More Drink, More Wine. If Robbie was—and is—in the habit of dividing the world between 'the sort of chap I would not mind flying with' and 'not the sort of chap I would go flying with', Jack liked to tell a story in which Robbie and he decided to fly from Cambridge to Colchester in order to eat oysters. Flying over a

5

town, Robbie had said: 'Look, that is Colchester'. But, once they had landed, it turned out to be Peterborough. Robbie at the time was a Flying Proctor. In a much more important sense Gallagher & Robinson constituted a partnership of lasting value to historical scholarship. Though fundamentally a lonely man, and perhaps even a melancholy one (the allusion both to the scented lilac envelopes that never came and to Alexandra, the beautiful Greek girl, encountered on an island during Jack's three weeks idyll of Missing Believed Killed, a recurrent figure in Jack's reminiscences late in the evening, no doubt indicated something that had been lost a very long time back) Jack loved the company of his own choice. I recall, with delight, a supper party at the Vine, in London, on Jack's birthday, which as he liked to point out, was on 1 April, made all the more memorable by the presence of the recently resigned Foreign Secretary, George Brown, quite magnificently and noisily drunk, at a corner table. Jack was not fortunate in the devotion of his close friends; he *deserved* them. And he needed them to bring him out. It was as if he had managed to surround himself with a small group of loyal retainers, extending from the Lodge to the inner fastnesses of Trinity, so that, when Jack moved, went on a journey, or on holiday, it involved a small *état-major*. Jack was not merely an Imperial historian, there was something Imperial about Jack. I often thought how suitable was the parting gift of the Fellows of Trinity on Jack's elevation to his Oxford chair: a group photograph of the Master of Trinity, George V and some marvellously stoned officers, at the manoeuvres held in Cambridge in 1910 or 1911. In Balliol, Jack withdrew into a tower, an object of some mystery; in Trinity, one felt that the whole College was built around him. Here indeed was the splendid palace of the Living Buddha.

Jack had breakfast fantasies, supper fantasies, and post-midnight fantasies. At breakfast, we would be invited to take a seat in the Great Train as in sedate slowness it steamed past Alpine fields thick with bright spring flowers, girls with straw-coloured hair in plaits, and very blue eyes, and dressed in grindels or brindels, approaching the train and smilingly holding up to its windows baskets of multicoloured fruit and gourds of rough peasant wine. The blue and gold carriages would pass on slowly, amidst a shower of rose petals, a beautiful Romanian spy, her long lashes reaching halfway down her cheeks, posted at each window, would survey the happy, yodelling Alpine scene. Outside, sleet would be falling over the Garden Quad, while, opposite, Tommy Balogh plunged into the pink pages of the *Financial Times*. Breakfast was decidedly the time that took Jack on long Balkanic wanderings; it was then too that he evoked the Inaugural Lecture of the newly appointed Professor of Macedonian History at the University of Niš, a lecture entitled 'The Macedonian Problem'. First sentence: 'The Macedonian Problem is one of great complexity.' BANG. The Professor, his recently and lavishly endowed chair and his audience are blown sky-high, like Stambulisky in Sofia cathedral. A breakfast variant on the 'I' lecture of the Regius Professor of Moral Theology. It would still be sleeting; and the electric toaster had gone wrong again giving forth clouds of thick, acrid smoke. Young resident research fellows and visitors staying in guest rooms would bury themselves in their papers. One of the evening fantasies would be the battle of Jutland—Jack liked to read Arthur Marder, tucked up in bed in the tower, on stormy winter nights, while the west wind howled outside—twelve hundred men sent to the bottom in one blast, as the magazine blows up—laid out on the floor of the Senior Common Room, the Grand Fleet steaming at thirty knots, the high smoke stacks emitting a long trail of thick black smoke low over the dark oily waters, the German Fleet represented by Hartmut Pogge von Strandmann, wearing for the occasion a spiked helmet. The post-midnight fantasy would often be sparked off by a vengeful record of Serge Ginsbourg's on the subject of *la petite putain* whose little bottom almost burst from its tight envelope and in which the singer, to *un air de java*, evoked with affection *le petit père Ronsard*. But it could also take the form of excursions back into past memories of the Trinity Footlights. Jack was as partial to political music-hall as to the pointed and joyous cruelty of the *chansonniers*.

Jack had a healthy dislike for puritans, the politically convicted, radicals, revolutionaries, fanatics, ranters, and ravers. He distrusted legislation, believed that nothing could ever be solved by laying down rules to meet hypothetical situations, and hated theorists and generalizers. In Balliol, his was always the voice of calm pragmatism; and by his cool patience and gentle persuasion he often managed to prevent the College from taking some inconsidered step into sheer foolishness. He was a natural conservative in the best sense, and his presence often preserved the College from some act of singular folly such as might be inspired by the old, dangerous and rather arrogant notion that 'Balliol must lead the way', no matter where the way might lead: such, for instance, as the suggestion, put to a College meeting, that the unfortunate Rudi Dutschke should be admitted as a graduate student (in politics?). On this occasion, the College was saved from much potential trouble, not by Jack, but by Dutschke himself, who declared a preference for Cambridge. Jack was too much of a Trinity man ever to have made a true Balliol one; but he brought to the College the temperate wind of East Anglian common sense. However, while he undoubtedly enjoyed his years in Oxford, it would not be quite true to say that he enjoyed *all* his years in Balliol. Indeed, shortly before being elected to the Cambridge chair, he had been engaged, with backing in important circles, in engineering his physical transfer to Christ Church. The Cambridge election saved Oxford from what could have been a major and interesting constitutional row, and one that Jack would have enjoyed.

Undoubtedly what he enjoyed most in Oxford was the warm friendship both of Anne Whiteman, very much a kindred spirit, and of Hugh Trevor-Roper, whom he greatly admired for his concern for graduate researchers and for his good sense, as well as the possibility of building up a powerful group both of undergraduates and research pupils. He used to say that his Oxford pupils were the best that he had ever had; and, from the start, although a professorial Fellow, he readily undertook a great deal of undergraduate teaching for the College, starting the new Special Subject: the Making of the Ententes, which, because he taught it, soon became enormously popular. At Jack's Nuffield seminar, what was most impressive was not so much the papers read, excellent though many were, as the urbanity with which Jack presided over these meetings, and the throw-away comments with which he would conclude them: small pieces of pure gold and great elegance, for the possession of which the jostling crowds would eagerly scramble. A chance suggestion of Jack's sent one of his pupils, Patrick Tuck (who later gave me a small

Buddha as a reminder of our mutual friend) off on an investigation of French policies in Siam in the late nineteenth century. A
remark by Jack at a Balliol guest night induced one of my pupils,
Peter Carey, to go off and study the possibly remote effects of the
French Revolution on Java, resulting in Peter becoming a leading
specialist of Indonesian history. It was Jack, too, who induced
Chris Bayly, a Balliol man, whom he always described as the best
pupil he had ever had in either University, to work on the
organization of the Congress Party at a provincial level, in this
case, that of Allahabad. Jack distributed wealth like a monarch on
a royal progress, with languid ease and elegance. Ideas flowed
from him apparently without effort, and at any hour of the day or
of the night. This was not just because he was endowed with a
very acute historical imagination and a natural facility of expression (his Ford Lectures were literary gems as well as being extremely witty), but also because he had travelled widely in India
and Africa, as well as in Europe (much of it *aux frais de la princesse*
while in the Armoured Corps), and because he was very well
read, especially in French. I was greatly surprised—and flattered
—to discover that he had read my own works in French, and that,
through such writers as Jean Galtier-Boissière he had acquired a
pungent knowledge of Paris slang. The schoolboy who had been
preached to by rough Irish fathers on the subject of 'that
notorious atheist Jean [as in Jean Harlow] Jakes Rewso', in
Birkenhead, had travelled a very long way since his days in that
city's Institute. His understanding of the particularities of French
colonialism was based as much on observation and sympathy as
on reading. He liked to evoke his time on the *north* bank of the
Congo Estuary, sitting on a café terrace, drinking his Ricard, and
staring across at *Léo* (Léopoldville), while his French companions
went on about *ces salauds de Belges*. One Balliol man he recommended to work on Faidherbe; another, on the tribal history of
Senegal. The principal monument that Jack has left as a historian
can best be traced in the ideas that he communicated to some
hundreds of pupils, in both Universities. His felicity of expression was more often verbal than written; and it is typical of his
courage and dedication that he insisted on lecturing when in
great physical pain, in the last stages of his accumulated illnesses.
Much of his conversational charm was injected into his lectures.

Jack's basic loyalty was to Trinity. Of Trinity he always spoke, in Oxford, with pride, describing how, in the days of G. M. Trevelyan, the Master would sit as in feudal splendour, while the emissaries from other Colleges would come and pick up the crumbs dropped from the Master's table, once the list of the College's choices had been read out. He loved to evoke this imperial scene. As a lonely man, without family—his father, a railwayman, died in his eighties in Jack's second year in Balliol —he was more attached than most both to institutions and to friends. It was fitting that he should have returned to Trinity, for this was his home. There, during his long series of illnesses, he was protected by the devotion of friends who included porters solicitous in the watchful protection of his privacy. In Trinity, his hospitality could acquire a suitably grand scale, even to the extent of offering to visitors the Judge's suite and the bed marked with a golden 'V' and a golden 'A' on red (when I slept in it, I was careful to sleep on the 'A' side). And in Trinity, in his rooms on the ground-floor of Great Court, he died in March 1980. The whole College followed his coffin as it was borne to the Lodge. It was the saddest sight I have ever seen. And yet, such was the strength, the warmth of his personality, I can see and hear Big Jack as if he were in his room in the tower, or standing, holding the beer mug engraved with his name, in Balliol Buttery, or talking to the barman of the JCR bar in Trinity, or sitting under the terrifying portrait of a cruelly Asiatic Henry VIII. Big Jack will live on in scores of grateful memories of those lucky enough to have known him and to have experienced his warmth, his humour, his elegance, his generosity and his elaborately concealed kindness. For he was a shy man who did good, as if he were pocketing the sugar or the silver spoons, by stealth, when he thought no one was looking.

Arthur Marder

Arthur J. Marder, who was Eastman Visiting Professor at Balliol from 1969 to 1970, and Professor of Modern History at the University of California, Irvine, till his retirement in 1977, died at his home in Santa Barbara on Christmas Day 1980, in the presence of his wife, Jan, and his two children, after a long illness which he bore with characteristic stoicism and patience. Equally characteristically, knowing that he had only a few months to live, he had continued working almost to the day of his death, completing, in February 1980, the first volume of a study of Anglo-Japanese naval rivalry in the 1930s and 1940s, the second volume of which he had almost finished when his death put an end to his prodigious output of books and articles. With editorial assistance in order to fill in the gaps, it was published in 1982. In October of the previous year his widow, Jan, was invited to be the guest of honour at the annual dinner of the British naval historians, held at the Garrick Club, and to be called henceforth the 'Arthur J. Marder Dinner', an entirely suitable tribute to the outstanding historian of the Royal Navy at the height of its power.

Arthur received many other tributes, both from this country and his own. He was a Corresponding Fellow of the British Academy, a Fellow of the American Philosophical Society, and, in 1971, he was elected to an Hon. D.Litt. by Oxford University, and appointed an Honorary CBE. When the fifth and last volume of his major work, *From the Dreadnought to Scapa Flow*, appeared in 1970, which was also the year that he left Balliol, he was entertained by the First Sea Lord and the Lords of the Admiralty to an official banquet held in his honour in the painted hall of Greenwich Palace, a tribute which gave him enormous pleasure. No other American historian, nor indeed any British one, has ever been so honoured. But then no other historian has ever even approached his truly amazing expertise in every detail of naval history, including the technical intricacies of gunnery, armoured

plating, the positioning of smoke-stacks in relation to the magazines, as well as in the human element of high command,
training, and recruitment.

Like many historians who in the course of time established an
international reputation in some specialized and yet vital field of
history, Arthur chanced on the history of the Royal Navy almost
by accident. As a young graduand of Harvard, under the guidance of the great diplomatic historian, Langer, he had intended to
work on Anglo-German diplomatic relations in the years between
1900 and the outbreak of the First World War. This involved him
in a close study of the Haldane Peace Mission, including efforts to
reach an Anglo-German understanding on the scale of mutual
naval expansion. In his own words, it was at this stage that,
discovering, to his surprise that the subject was virtually untouched and that the field was wide open, he got 'hooked' on
British naval history. His first work on the subject, *The Anatomy of
British Sea Power*, was published when he was thirty, to be closely
followed by a work on Admiral Sir Herbert Richmond, entitled
Portrait of an Admiral (there were to be many more portraits of
Admirals in the next thirty-five years or so). He then edited three
volumes of the correspondence of Admiral John Fisher; and it
was as a result of his unique familiarity with that forceful and
redoubtable eccentric that he conceived the vast project of a
full-scale study of British naval policies and achievements, in
peace, then in war, that resulted in his magisterial five-volume
work. Any other man might have then felt that he was due at least
a pause, if only to *cultiver son jardin* (Arthur did this too, with the
same meticulous concern for detail; I can recall him on his hands
and knees, in April 1972, when I stayed with him in Newport
Beach, weeding out by hand an immaculate front greensward)
and to savour his triumphs. But this would be to misunderstand
the compulsive energy of a man who put so much of his life into
writing. He was soon busy with books on Churchill and Sir
Dudley North and on the disastrous Dakar expedition ('Operation Menace'); and when I last saw him, it was clear that the
smoke-stacks of the Japanese Imperial Fleet were just beginning
to emerge above the Pacific waves. I asked him once why he had
never worked on the greatest navy of all time, that of the United
States in the Second World War; his answer was twofold: that

others had got in there first, and that he did not find American admirals particularly interesting.

His stupendous achievement was strongly aided by a disposition that contained an irresistible mixture of dogged persistence, enormous determination, and a gentle, but forceful charm, a combination that was revealed, again and again, by his ability to coax from Admirals' widows their husbands' official papers, private diaries, and correspondence. These operations were planned with minute precision: first, the ladies were identified, then located, then written to (and, if they did not reply, Arthur would write to them again, or would enrol in his support some other previously visited widows) and, once he had established contact, he would turn up: quiet houses, the furniture covered in pretty chintzes, in Devon, Cornwall, Dorset, Hampshire, or even in Scotland. The vital stage, so he told me, was usually reached over tea, accompanied by elaborate buns and thin-cut sandwiches, more rarely, over sherry. Almost always, the result was the same: Arthur would head for the nearest station with a suitcasefull of unpublished material. I do believe he was repulsed once or twice. But almost always the Admirals' widows (in French they would have been Amirales), perhaps after some initial token resistance, coughed up. Arthur was not a man easy to put off course, once he had spotted his quarry. Also I think that these ladies were genuinely touched by the interest taken by this soft-spoken American in the careers of husbands long since dead: and Vice-Admirals, Rear-Admirals, Commanders and Captains were stalked by him with the same relentless interest as the more august prey: men with gold braid halfway up their arms. It must also have been very hard to turn away a historian who was so exquisitely polite: an old-fashioned, ceremonious politeness and consideration that must have owed something to Arthur's Bostonian origins. It was an urbane charm that was addressed quite artlessly to all who came in contact with him, and who had nothing in the way of family papers to offer.

Arthur Marder has received tremendous acclaim from all the specialists in the field of British naval history, including his principal critic and friendly rival, Captain Roskill (how we miss the blast and thunder of the great guns of those two historians, as they pounded away at each other in the correspondence columns

of the *Times Literary Supplement*!). But those in no way versed in
the complexities of naval history found themselves captivated,
'hooked', by his skill at narrative. Of course he often had a
tremendously exciting story to tell; and his great friend Jack
Gallagher used to say that Arthur's volume on Jutland was best
savoured when one was tucked up cosily in bed, as the east winds
howled around his bedroom in the tower of the library staircase.
Like a preceding Eastman Professor, Garret Mattingley, Arthur
was peculiarly gifted at rendering naval history immensely exciting.

The Arthur that we came to know in Balliol seemed far removed from the exalted personage of the immense public reputation that had preceded him like a light cruiser scouting squadron.
He was quiet, gentle, and rather stately. In any room, he was a
presence, even before he opened his mouth. He loved Oxford
and loved Balliol. What he most enjoyed were public occasions,
the more elaborate the better. He seldom missed Thursday Guest
Nights, which he invariably enriched by his urbanity and by his
eagerness to communicate; and he was deeply shocked, even
outraged, when the College, in one of its intermittent bouts of
self-punishment and pleasure-hating, decided to suppress free
wine at Consilium Dinner. He did not protest publicly about this
act of uncouth puritanism; he was far too conscious of his status
as a *visitor* to the College ever to make such a public stand. But, in
private, he did not hide his feelings of outrage. It was not what he
would have expected of Balliol, or of Oxford, nor would it have
happened in the wardroom of a battleship. He complained
quietly, but in measured and stately tones. His own enjoyment in
College life was matched by the enjoyment that Jan and he had in
entertaining Fellows and their wives and University colleagues at
Eastman House. Lunch or dinner there was an elaborate exercise
in courtesy and sheer enjoyment. Arthur's gravity would combine quite admirably with Jan's warmth and easy friendliness. In
this, as in all their life together, they were ideally suited, com-
plementing each other in a way that made their company delightful, rewarding, and memorable.

During his year at Balliol, every Wednesday and Friday at
midday, an unusually large crowd of historians could be seen
emerging from the underground lecture-room beneath the new

Senior Common Room. They would be followed, after a pause, by the figure of Arthur himself, gowned and senatorial, carrying in one hand a long wooden pointer, in the other a cluster of rolled up maps, rather as if they had been emblems of rank and as if he had just been disposing of Europe and the world, the oceans and the continents. This was in fact just what he had been doing, as he gave regular lectures on the Special Subject: the Making of the Ententes (despite being 'hooked', he had never lost his taste for the intricacies of diplomatic history). The fame of these lectures gradually percolated throughout the University, so that, by the end of the Hilary term, Arthur had an audience treble the size of that with which he had started. Most of us have experienced the reverse process. He also did a considerable amount of under-graduate teaching for the College. Later, in 1972, I was able to sit in on his admirably informal, yet gruelling, undergraduate semi-nars at Irvine. Arthur knew how to listen, to wait, so as to bring out the best in even his most reticent pupils. He had about him something of a confessor; and he was very good at putting the shy and the awkward totally at ease. The informality of his seminars disguised the amount of trouble and preparation that he had put into them. He was not a man to improvise. He put the same careful planning into his teaching as he did into the preparation of his books. He did not see spontaneity as a virtue, regarding it rather as a form of carelessness. He was never careless.

Up to the time of his death, he followed what seemed to me a relentless working day. He did most of his typing sitting up in bed, his notes scattered all over the counterpane. He only got dressed when he had reached his own stern quota of typewritten pages. Then he could relax, in the protected family atmosphere that was, along with his prodigious industry, his greatest source of strength. He had been very lonely, a dedicated bachelor scholar, until, in a happy moment, he had met Jan North; and Jan provided him with the company of two adolescent children to whom he acted as an understanding, patient, and very loving father. It was a welcome sight to see him emerging from the bedroom sanctum and to hear him plan the rest of the day. He could be most relaxed; indeed, he needed to be, in order to keep up the relentless momentum of his writing. He found relaxation in his family, in his beautiful tropical garden, and in golf. He was also a very good cook, especially skilled in Chinese meals. There was something Chinese about his gravity and stillness.

Though most of his work rode, tossing, on the grey, cruel waters of the North Sea and the Atlantic, he spent most of his academic life on the coast of the Pacific: first, for many years, at the University of Hawaii, then in Newport Beach, near Irvine, and ultimately, in Santa Barbara. He liked the sun, loved the orange groves of his luxuriant garden and felt most at ease in light, tropical, informal Pacific Coast clothes. Perhaps this was the only contradiction about a man who devoted himself to a heavily braided personnel, muffled up against the bitter winds and weather of the German Sea. After all, though a scholar of rare singleness of purpose, there was no need for him to identify completely with his chosen subject.

Yet, perhaps, if only unconsciously, he may have done. When I was staying with him, I was put up on a folding bed in his study – or what had been his study, for, as I have said, he worked in bed. On the wall, there were various nautical objects, including several naval clocks, compasses, and barometers. Over the bed there was a large framed caricature of Arthur himself, immediately recognizable by his domed bald head, his round glasses and observant, unblinking, intelligent eyes: those of a mandarin, rather than washed-out pale naval eyes, scanning the horizon. Arthur was dressed up in the uniform of an Admiral of the Fleet, and he held in one hand a telescope, in the other, an Admiral's elaborate hat. It was the work of one of his Californian colleagues. I could not help feeling that the drawing was something more than a caricature, if only because Arthur jokingly drew my attention to it, and that it was indeed a portrait of Arthur himself, as, in rare moments of fantasy—and no man was less given to fantasy than this stern, unblinking historian—he may momentarily have willed himself into the position occupied by so many of his distinguished, but often quarrelsome (Admirals seem to quarrel among themselves even more than Generals) characters, on the bridge of a great battleship. Certainly, as the Greenwich banquet illustrated, the Lords of the Admiralty recognized Arthur as one of their own.

Christopher Hill as Supergod

'*Come* in', with the emphasis on 'come', warm and inviting, but with a hint, too, of menace. Christopher is sitting, slumped deep in an armchair, his head well into his shoulders, filtering the narrow glint of a look both enigmatic and benign (it is *meant* to be enigmatic, but it cannot help being benign). The candidate comes in nervously, and is directed towards a straight chair underneath my stuffed woodcock, in its glass palace, standing against a background of quite convincing-looking reeds. 'Now, Mr ****, tell us what History you have been doing at school.' And, seven times out of ten, it will be: 'Tudors and Stuarts', so it will be Christopher's round. 'What would you like to talk about?' 'Queen Elizabeth.' Then, with real warmth, and even a sort of perilous apparent *naïveté*, the eyes widening and taking on a kindly expression: '*Tell us* about Queen Elizabeth', as if he really wanted to hear all about her, Christopher conducting the rest of the proceedings gently, patiently, invitingly, with a warm charm in the voice, as if offering a guest the full range and freedom of a copious drinks tray: 'Help yourself, take a *large* glass', occasionally interjecting a mild objection, and, because of all that, dangerously. In short, no doubt, though in my old room, in Front Quad, the View from the Pupil, no. 19 staircase; but, having never been a pupil, the nearest that I would be likely to get to Christopher-as-Tutor, impenetrable, infinitely wise, very forbearing, an artist of the pregnant silence and the long pause, and occasionally murderous, though this aspect would not be revealed at interviews for awards and College entrance.

Before I had ever met Christopher I rang him up at his home, and the message was taken by his eight-year-old daughter. Those who, like myself, have the misfortune to possess a one-syllable surname will appreciate the problem; when Christopher returned home, he was told: 'Someone called *God* rang you up.' And so *God* I remained, for the next twenty-five years, though, once I had been elected to Balliol, I found it necessary to re-

17

establish a suitable sense of hierarchy by calling Christopher *Super-God*.

Of Christopher's carefully concealed benevolence—for he took a great deal of trouble to avoid being caught in being kind, it was part of his natural reserve—I have had many examples, both direct, and, more often, indirect, revealed by the indiscretion of others. At the interview for my first University appointment, I was at once put at my ease by the man sitting in the middle of a wide circle of interrogators (some, on the wings, in dog-collars) —and, as he was in the middle, he was clearly the most important —when, with an utterly winning smile, both with and around his startlingly blue eyes, he said: 'Mr Cobb, I think we have a mutual friend.' It was, of course, Christopher, far off in Oxford, going around mysteriously and doing good, in the middle of Cardiganshire. Several years later, when I was a candidate for Balliol, one of my referees—an important one—had referred, obliquely, but quite plainly, to my 'certain well-known weaknesses'. I do not really know what they were, or are; but Christopher obviously did (I have said he is wise; more, he has a sort of second sight) and at once took deflective action on my behalf by soliciting an unofficial moral reference from another, and, I would like to think, more *accurate* witness. Yes, Cobb did have certain weaknesses, but they were not incurable (he was wrong). I got the job.

In my first year at Balliol my natural enthusiasm, exuberance, and boisterousness caused me to get into some considerable trouble with higher authority. The Inner Circle was brought in to consider my case. The Inner Circle was, in fact, a half-circle, opened at one end, of large red-leather armchairs on which the *important* Fellows sat during College meetings. It was rather like the city plan of Amsterdam, with its concentric *grachts* and accompanying canals spreading, in ever-widening rings, outwards. There were the half-dozen occupants of the red chairs, including Christopher, then a further semicircle of uprights, and, right on the outside, the timid newcomers. While my case was being considered I received a note from Christopher, which I was actually able to *read* (I had been trained on Robespierre), or most of it. 'Do not fear,' it went, in mighty loops and wild squiggles, 'the Angels are watching over you.' And they did. Once more Christopher had stepped in, behind the scenes, where it mattered, to do good by stealth. I was spoken to severely, told it was time I grew up, and looked at with pained and paternal hopelessness, by the Dean and Chaplain, who, having known me as a schoolboy, also knew that I would not—and forgiven. Perhaps this is why—and I daresay others have the same reaction—when I see Christopher advancing towards me, *les yeux filtrants* in his Richard III *démarche* and more than usually orientally inscrutable, towards the Buttery, I feel full of vague guilt, wondering what I have done wrong now. Imagine then the relief of a benevolent smile and of a remark gently ironical.

Christopher is a master of irony. It seems to take the form of another series of concentric rings, *enceintes*, *glâcis*, ramparts, protecting the occupant of the inner fortress, the *donjon*, the dark Yorkshire baron, the Asiatic *khan*, from the gaze of the intruder, the inquisitive, and the brash. A great many people would describe Christopher as impenetrable, a man of few words and deep mystery, talking in elaborate riddles, vowed to secrecy, never giving a trick away. And these are certainly the airs that he likes to give himself, when confronted with the importunate, the silly, or the prying. But it is in fact only a cardboard set of earthworks and outworks. I have never been taken in by this elaborate and well-painted camouflage. There is no mystery there at all, but, in the middle, a great deal of natural shyness, a dislike of display and pretension, and a kindness that does its best to conceal itself, but which escapes every now and then from the ceaseless vigilance of its keeper, and a sense of humour that, in its measured and quiet delivery, can be quite devastating. There is, too, an impishness that would be revealed most effectively at our annual charades after History Schools Dinner—it was Christopher who assigned to a seriously committed undergraduate politician and putter-to-right-of-wrongs, the role of Miss Keeler, in a mock swimming bath at Cliveden, no. 22 staircase. There was a similar occasion that put an unusual demand on Christopher's oriental inscrutability, that would accept, as a sort of extra course, not on the menu, and reserved for him as senior History tutor, the presence, in his soup plate, of the head of his neighbour to the right, large, and covered in red curls, at one of these dinners, which began thus dramatically and ended disastrously. Christopher somehow managed to eat round the object.

But, when the occasion and the interests of Balliol demand, Christopher can completely overcome his shyness and his dislike of display. Many of us will remember—and treasure—the marvellous impromptu speech that he made on the occasion of the retirement of Theo Tyler, a tribute that contained the subtlest combination of affection, gentle observation, and sly humour. I have heard many more, not least, the most recent, at the Farewell Dinner given to Christopher and Bridget, when he struck exactly the right note with generous and delightful tributes to all those who had worked hard for Balliol and who had eased the way for him in the execution of his Mastership, and particularly to Lady Anna Keir and to Mrs Bridget Page. I think it is the measure of Christopher's attachment to Balliol that he should thus so successfully have overcome his natural reticence, his disinclination for public occasions, and should so completely have recaptured, in eloquent and affectionate public expression, what so many of us were thinking and what we wanted him to say, what Bert* too would have wanted him to say: surely the greatest quality in a public man, especially one so reluctant to be public. For what is quite an *open* secret about Christopher is the strength of his attachment to Balliol, an attachment that dates back to when, at the age of sixteen, he was spotted, while a schoolboy in York, by Vivian Galbraith. Christopher has always thought that Balliol was important. And, of course, it is; there is nowhere like it. Christopher is generally right, though he did let *me* into Balliol, and I am not sure if that was a wise thing to have done. I think he realized afterwards his mistake!

* My friend Bert Blaygrove, BEM, now aged eighty-two, porter still in the employment of the college. His portrait hangs in the Buttery.

David Williams

There is a particular stillness, an almost physical quietness, like the presence of something that is not there, that I shall always associate with an Aberystwyth Sunday morning, early enough for the cars from the Midlands not yet to have reached the coast. On this October Sunday the sea was a flat, even green, with straggling streaks of a bluish black, like dark veins, that moved sinuously, as in a slow oriental dance; the coloured sails, completely immobile, seemed to have been painted on, as if to emphasize the stillness by the perfection of their white, yellow, red and blue triangles. I had just rounded the Prince of Wales, green with salt and spray, looking blankly, perhaps boredly, to the motionless sea, when an apparently elderly gentleman—he can in fact have only been about fifty-five—very formally and soberly dressed: grey suit, grey burberry, hat, and umbrella, came alongside, and walking, rather solemnly and with a sort of deliberation, in my own slow, lazy Sunday step, introduced himself, with very distinct enunciation, saying: 'Shall we kick the bar?', whatever that meant, but I did not want to display my ignorance.

David, as deliberate in speech as in his steady walk, then having spoken of Mathiez, of his time in Dijon, of his first wife, a pupil of Mathiez, proceeded to go, in great detail, through my *curriculum vitae*, backwards, starting from my appointment to UCW, and working through, at an unhurried, even pace, to my birth in Frinton-on-Sea. Nothing much was left out, including quotes, naturally of great interest to me, from my referees; even addresses, in Tunbridge Wells and Paris, were duly noted, or at least a score of them, for even David could not have kept up with the hundreds of my parents' moves, my sister was identified, her husband's profession named. It was I who supplied their address. I think David was even a little disappointed that my family had not been more extensive. As we walked along the great curve of the bay, he spoke of mutual friends, adding little

21

details unknown to me; of Christopher Hill, he commented that, on coming to Cardiff, he had taken lodgings, in Gabalfa, opposite the cinema, and not in the Roath Park district, which would have been more suitable. Of another shared friend, he informed me that his great-uncle had been before the magistrates for drunken language. By the time we reached the Bar, he had completed, in the same inexorably steady tone, the Welsh place names lovingly modulated, the skeleton (often in both senses) biographies of twenty or so historians.

This was my first introduction to vintage David, a vintage of which I never tired, compounded as it was of minute, often intimate information, limitlessly prying curiosity, a great deal of kindness, and a beautifully contrived, often unexpected, and slow in coming, tiny gentle claw of malice. 'Confidential', for him, was an invitation to entrance and exploration, as it should be for any historian. His daily information about his pupils was astounding, and, to them, when displayed in slow, splendid detail, devastating: 'Yes, Miss Frances Hilary Jones (for there were always two names), so you have not finished your essay? I am not surprised. You have been spending a lot of your time this week in the company of Mr Hywel Ceri Jones.' On sunny days I could sometimes catch the glint of a pair of marine binoculars, as from behind a curtain, David viewed the Promenade, from his observatory, a top-floor flat right in the middle of the curve. Later, perhaps, he would put me into the secret, with his usual unblinking deliberation, of the exact state of the bank balance of the current High Sheriff of Cardiganshire, a figure, though a close colleague—none could have been closer—to whom he always referred, with suitable awe and emphasis, as 'the High Sheriff' or 'the Squire of Talybont'.

His curiosity about people, living, recently dead, or long since departed, was limitless. He seemed to have had access—and to have memorized, often in long, rolling phrases, like funeral epitaphs from the eighteenth century—the references and testimonials of every eminent man in Wales, and of a great many more less eminent. And he took an artistic joy in gentle iconoclasm, an apparent eulogy, indeed delivered as a eulogy, suddenly qualified, reduced to size, by a deflationary, treasured, and lovingly presented detail, little jewels from his well-stocked box.

'Richard . . . ah (pause) . . . *Duw, Duw* (pause) . . . the poor fellow . . . (pause) . . . a very sad business . . . (pause) . . . Cardiff gaol . . .' One would know when the good bits were coming from a slight flicker of his left eyelid, above his very blue, deceptively candid, eye. I considered perhaps as his masterpiece the formal lecture that he gave, before a most distinguished audience from all parts of the principality, on the occasion of the centenary of the birth of the second principal of UCW: *un bouquet de roses semé d'épines,* all the better for the fact that the roses were big and blooming, the thorns tiny, and very sharp. As we came out, a pupil of his and mine exclaimed, with admiration: 'David has surpassed himself.'

David was curious about people, because he was fascinated by them, loved talking about them, and loved hearing about them. His malice, always artistically presented, was directed mainly at pretence, conceit, and hypocrisy. It was a weapon in the service of egalitarianism. Yet he was a stickler for the proper formalities. What I admired most was his prodigious memory, his immense grasp of even the most distant family relationships, his love of truth, and his quiet, calculated joy in deflating blown-up vanity. He had the true historian's love of minute detail. His industrious inquisitiveness, and his gentle, yet devastating, side-steps of sudden malice, were disguises for his underlying compassion. He was a very caring man. He was also a wonderful historian, a discerning and exacting teacher—and what a boost to a student who, having walked all the way up that turning stone staircase to the top of the tower—David's Tower—came down with a carefully measured word of praise!—and a friend of whose company one never tired.

Pierre Loti*

Who now reads Loti? Few enough, no doubt, and that is a pity, for he is well worth reading, a miniaturist with a wonderfully visual gift, and a very acute observer of gesture, movement, and stillness. In his company we can hear the muffled sounds of a great oriental city and perceive its unexpected islands of silence and calm. He is a very good guide, and one still worth following, even if it means having to put up with so much breast-beating, sighs and tears.

I was surprised to have found *Fantôme d'Orient*, the only Loti I have to hand, such a good read, thanks to his alert eye for detail. The destination of his increasingly frantic journeys across the city and from one shore to another is of no great importance; it is in the getting there that the reader can find enjoyment.

Any pretext will do: the search for Aziyade's tomb is as good a one as the complicated plot of one of Ambler's novels (set in similar surroundings, but at a much later date). Let the author get on with his search for the grave and the gravestone, there is plenty of fun in following him on his funereal quest, and in a variety of forms of transport: boat, horseback, landau, on foot, or even in a sedan chair, in daylight, or at night, preceded by a runner holding up a lantern. His Stamboul, far from being contrived, is totally convincing, a wonderful period piece and an example of clear-eyed social observation.

If Loti deserves to be read, he is even better to read *about*, if only because his life was quite unbelievable and his egotism surely unmatched. And this is a very good book about that extravagant, often quite absurd, always impossible, yet engagingly childlike figure. There is a natural affinity between author and subject, both ardent Turcophiles, even to the point of a shared lushness and a common autumnal nostalgia.

* This essay first appeared as a review of Lesley Blanch, *Pierre Loti: Portrait of an Escapist* (Collins) in the *Guardian*, January 1984.

Un numéro, certainly yes, as Malraux observed of Loti, when the author told him of her intention to write a life of the naval officer, Protestant novelist. Malraux was one, too. And with Malraux, Loti shares supreme egotism and an unsparing self-preoccupation. Both passed their time surrounded by mirrors, and Loti, a rather improbable pseudo-Muslim, seems to have been obsessed with contemplating the human face, especially his own.

But, *unlike* Malraux, Loti seems quite often to have told the truth, if rather an inflated one; he was not a myth-maker, he *went* to all the places he wrote about, and bedded all the lovely, wild, exotic girls he put in his books. There was really no need for him to myth-make, there was at all times something quite outsize and outrageous about his daily life. There are times when one wants to shout 'Enough!' and then one is as suddenly disarmed by the sheer monstrosity of his behaviour.

And he had some very engaging features; he adored cats, he clung to every memory of childhood and to every object that recalled it, he delighted in boisterous practical jokes, he was an unrepentant provincial who abhorred literary circles, and when not indulging himself in thoughts on death or about his lost loves, he clearly loved a night out on the town in the rue de Lappe or Belleville or the low dives of Brest or Toulon, in the company of his own crewmen, especially if they were tall (he wore high heels to increase his own diminutive stature) and fair.

Once he had become a wealthy man, he proved wonderfully generous with his money. He was also an eloquent and impassioned opponent of all forms of colonialism, and for once got into serious trouble with his superiors by writing accounts of the savagery of the war in Tonkin. He wanted primitive peoples to be left to pursue their traditional ways, if only on aesthetic grounds.

Finally, he was rightly proud of the Huguenot roots of both sides of his mother's family; one could not imagine a more unlikely Protestant, both in his personal conduct and in his obsession with expiation and death. But his wife had to be a Protestant and he insisted that his son, Samuel, marry one.

But however did he get away with it all? Why was the French Navy, *la Royale*, generally so inflexible, so accommodating towards this extraordinary officer? How did he get so much shore leave? What can his shipmates have made out when they encountered their colleague, or officer, in some oriental port rigged out in full Turkish gear? Was it never pointed out to him that it was highly improper for an officer to dress up as an able-seaman and go around the night spots thus attired, with three or four of his own crewmen? Did no one object to his circus acts, in which he appeared, dressed in silver silk tights, in Toulon, of all places?

Of course, he was not the only serving officer, either then or since, to have enjoyed dressing up. At least he was not trying to play the prophet or to preach a crusade, and most of his fantasies were entirely personal: the pursuit of the exotic and the apparently unapproachable female, the delicious conquest of brown-skinned, illiterate, wild girls, the soft texture of a range of shades of *la peau mate*.

Did he *always* get away with it? Did no woman ever slap his face and call him *goujat*, which is what he was? We are not likely to know: seduction was his principal literary role; and he seems to have managed to convince himself of his irresistibility.

His domestic arrangements were more than odd: an outside lavatory, double-seated, at the end of the garden, no bathroom, no electricity, a diminutive kitchen; a mosque, a Chinese Room, a Japanese Room, a Renaissance Dining Hall, a whole enfilade of museums: to his mother, to his aunt, to his great-aunt, to his childhood, to his adolescence; a cabin-room, kept white and bare, in which he often worked and sometimes slept; but his real cabin at sea would be crammed with oriental knick-knacks, and hung with colourful carpets and silks and bright brocades—another indulgence allowed to this unconventional officer.

Perhaps all naval officers tend to become obsessive collectors of exotic curia, though how they manage to get the stuff back does remain something of a mystery. I had always thought that space, even on a battleship, was strictly limited. Yet here is Loti transporting back to Rochefort, for erection in the back garden of his suburban house, a whole mosque, in numbered bits.

From every point of view, it is a pretty amazing performance, and Loti's egotism is so outrageous that one feels like applauding, as an act that could not have been bettered. In his self-indulgence there could be no room for the awareness of other people, save in terms of their effects on himself. Yet he seems to have been a good officer, and a competent one, and to have enjoyed the respect and the camaraderie of the sailors under his command.

Certainly his books must have done wonders for recruitment: palm trees, coral reefs and welcoming, scantily dressed *vahinés* rowing out towards the great grey ships as they tossed in the gentle surf. The plots, however feeble, were such as would address themselves to any man, sailor or landbound. Most men must, at one time or another, have indulged in some dark-skinned oriental fantasy, and in this sense Loti has an almost universal masculine appeal that does not date. What *has* dated, without doubt, is his appeal to female readers. Most of them, sixty years on, would be likely to dismiss him as unreadable, ceaselessly lachrymose, rather repugnant, a period piece of late nineteenth-century satanism.

Yet can one be sure of even *that*? I know of at least one former Loti *vestale*, a worshipper at the Rochefort shrine, still very much alive and fervent. She too has set up her own private mosque in her ninth-floor apartment in a tower-block in the XIIIème, near the porte d'Italie. Now in her eighties, she moves with difficulty amidst the clutter of Moroccan brasswork hanging from the ceiling. She had met the Commandant as a girl of sixteen in Rochefort, had been shown the inside of the mosque by its owner, dressed in full Turkish gear, and had accompanied him on his daily walks down to the port: he had given her a gold ring inscribed on the inside in Arabic. She has been serving his cult ever since.

It is easy to laugh at Loti, as he postures before the camera in this disguise or that. He was a very little man who, as he grew older, dyed his moustache and painted his face. He was a sort of superior *Facteur* Cheval; he, too, managed to cram in a bit of ruined cloister in an unencumbered strip of the suburban back-garden, between the graves of La Suprématie, Moumoutte Ier, Moumoutte II, Kedi Bey, Eyoub, Tu-duc, Belkis, and Mahmoud, the deceased Cats-in-Residence. It was a matter of taking garden gnomery further than most. In spite of all the display of exoti-cism, Loti remains a provincial, engagingly and incurably so.

Raymond Queneau

Les actualités offraient en effet une cérémonie officielle à l'Université d'Oxford; le poulailler prenant les professeurs en toge pour des curés manifestait énergiquement ses convictions anticléricales sans d'ailleurs choquer le militaire anglais pour qui les sifflets n'avaient point cette valeur réprobative. Bref tout le monde était content sauf quelques bourgeois français qui comprenaient eux, grâce à leur instruction.

(Raymond Queneau, *Un Rude Hiver*, 1939)

Monsieur Vieillard was waiting for me at the barrier, as arranged. The station, being a terminus, had an elaborate glass roof. Monsieur Vieillard, who was President of the *Société havraise d'études diverses* (*fondée en 1830 par Bernardin de Saint-Pierre*), was a little man with a big, melon-shaped head and a very large umbrella. 'Madame Vieillard,' he said, 'nous attend pour le thé. Madame Vieillard est la sœur du général Koenig.' It also appeared that she lived within easy walking distance, though walking was not easy in face of the north-westerly gale. We started down the boulevard de Strasbourg, which, like all boulevards de Strasbourg in French provincial towns, was dead straight, sad, and pretentious, enclosed, on both sides, by five-storey apartments, their balconies sticking out like bulbous tummies. Leaning down to meet the gale, in an effort to pick up the items of information emerging, lower down, from my host, I gathered that the meeting was to take place at the Chamber of Commerce at 8.30 in the evening.

M. and Mme Vieillard lived half-way down the boulevard, on the right. The entrance to the *immeuble* was surmounted by an enormous and very *ventru* balcony, held up, without any apparent difficulty, by two stone figures, half-feminine, half-dolphin, wearing metal breastplates. M. Vieillard introduced me into the ground-floor apartment, furnished principally with *legénéralkoenig*, photographs of whom, starting from the hall, jostled one another on every available flat surface. As far as I could make out, in an initial circular glance, they seemed to be arranged in biographical order, beginning from the hall: a blond child with a large hoop, then the *communiant*, with white bow, and from there, into the *salon*, the beplumed *cyrard*, an assortment of uniforms, some of them white and colonial, an increasing foliage of *galon*, culminating in a sort of altar-piece over the marble fireplace: three busts, one in bronze, a portrait in oils, and four photographs with General de Gaulle, and bearing the latter's spidery signature. There were one or two more pieces that were, for some reason, out of chronological order, including a hobby-horse, with the paint coming off.

But I was unable to reflect further on the significance of this reversion in time, because my host was anxiously attempting to divert my attention to the tall, living figure standing like a statue in the centre of the room. 'Je vous présente Madame Vieillard.' 'Est-ce que vous avez connu mon frère à Londres?', she enquired. Once tea had been brought in, she continued with the family history. She and her 'little brother' (she herself appeared to be about six foot three) had been born in Caen, where their parents had settled, after the loss of Alsace. But she did not have much time for the Normans, either Lower or Upper, and even less for *les Havrais*, most of whom she declared to have been *gaullistes* of post-September conversion, though perhaps a little ahead of the inhabitants of the *chef-lieu*. Nor could she notice much difference between *Le Sémaphore du Havre*, the local newspaper of the Occupation years, which, whatever light it had shed, had not been that of *gaullisme*, and its successor, *Le Havre libre*, apparently very much the mixture as before, and with the same staff. Everything she said was instantly confirmed by M. Vieillard: 'N'est-ce pas, Robert, que mon petit frère adore le tabac anglais?' 'Oui, Adèle, en effet, le général Koenig adore le tabac anglais.' I said I was very glad to hear it. As I took my leave, 'Hélas,' said Mme Vieillard, 'je ne pourrai pas assister à votre communication, les femmes ne sont pas admises à la Société havraise d'études diverses.' As he accompanied me to the door, M. Vieillard reiterated: 'Les femmes ne sont pas admises à la Société havraise d'études diverses, même Madame Vieillard n'y est pas admise.'

The meeting took place in a room in the Chamber of Commerce, the door of which was marked, in white lettering, 'Société havraise d'études diverses'. It looked as if I had come to the right place. The room had the heavy, airless formality of Third Republican official *fastes*: heavy green velvet curtains, a dusty, triple chandelier, shedding a pale, yellowish light on to an oblong table covered in green baize. The marble fireplace bore a dying gladiator in bronze. A portrait of Félix Faure, wearing all the presidential republicalia, and looking very gloomy, faced, right across the table, a dusty, white marble bust of a heavy-faced man whom I took to be *le Fondateur*. There was a high-backed chair for the President, with a large inkstand and a bronze rearing horse in front of it.

Monsieur Vieillard introduced me to his neighbour to the right, an antique priest wearing old-fashioned black bands edged with a red stripe: *le chanoine* Lendormeur, onetime *curé* of Saint-François. I was then introduced, in strict rotation, to the other full members (I learnt on this occasion, that I had been elected *Membre Correspondant*); and having made the complete tour of the full membership, all nine of it, I was allowed to sit down.

Monsieur Vieillard announced the meeting open: 'Je donne la parole au Secrétaire pour la lecture de la correspondance.' There was one of this, the Secretary producing, apparently from under the table, the largest envelope I have ever seen, larger even than that delivered by one of the fish footmen in *Through the Looking-Glass*. The Secretary slit it open with an ivory paper-knife, unfolded a letter of the dimensions of a small towel, which he read out, in a quavering voice. It was from the President of the Republic, M. René Coty, the tenth full member, acknowledging most warmly the congratulations of his *co-sociétaires* and *co-havrais* on his election, the second Havrais in that office, to the Elysée. 'Versons aux Archives', said M. Vieillard; and the Secretary passed the vast document to my neighbour, the Archivist.

'Je donne la parole à notre Membre Correspondant' (it looked as if I might be the *only* one). I began reading my paper, soon to the accompaniment of the gentle rise and fall of the *chanoine* Lendormeur's breathing and of the rattling of the steel shutters outside. There was no discussion afterwards; and, after shaking hands with the full membership minus one, as the *chanoine* was still asleep, his ample chin covering his black and red jabot, I took my leave, bending down at the corner to meet the full force of the gale blowing off *la Porte Océane*.

Raymond Queneau

'Alors,' finit-elle par dire, 'vous ne haïssez plus les pauvres, ni les misérables, monsieur Lehameau?'

'Ni les Allemands même, madame Dutertre', répondit-il en souriant. 'Pas même eux. Pas même les Havrais', ajouta-t-il en riant . . .

(Un Rude Hiver)

Raymond Queneau is a novelist of le Havre, perhaps even *the* novelist of le Havre, *Quai des brumes* being very much a contrivance, fog and all, while, in Duhamel's *Le Notaire du Havre*, the town represents little more than a postmark on a letter. Queneau witnesses for his native town at a certain period—in this instance, the terrible winter of 1916–17, when he was coming up for fourteen—in the same gentle yet observant way as Marc Bernard witnesses for Nîmes and its many brands of Protestants, or Marcel Pagnol for the lost world of *le Vieux Port* and the *incendie de l'Hôtel de Noailles*. (Queneau, too, who was born in February 1903, on the day *les Grandes Galéries Normandes* were burnt to the ground, with considerable loss of life, seems particularly aware of the importance of such long-remembered local catastrophes as a means of locating a period in time.) As a novelist describing the impact of the First World War on the *arrière*, he is comparable both to Maxence van der Meersch, writing *Invasion 14*, and drawing likewise on his experience as a child—he was three years older than Queneau—of German-occupied Roubaix, and to Louis Guilloux, in his evocations of Saint-Brieuc in *Le Sang noir*.

Queneau is a great many other things besides: a tireless juggler with words, possessing a unique ear for popular speech, the poet of the *transports communs*, above and below ground, and of the humbler Paris streets, and the author of the immensely funny *Exercices de style*, which, apart from its brilliance both as parody and as conversation totally recaptured, might also be described as an essay on the relative value and interpretation of conflicting or overlapping historical evidence.

Nevertheless, he remains first and foremost a Havrais, spending there the first twenty years of his life, his visible world confined to the length of the boulevard Maritime and to the network of streets ending at right angles to this ultimate barrier, with occasional excursions across the estuary to Honfleur or to the split rock of Etretat. But his principal observatory is his mother's *mercerie*, in the fashionable end of the town. And there

31

are *merceries* in several other novels of his, quiet chapels-of-ease, small, old-fashioned, with a bell attached to the door, an *arrière-boutique*, and many little drawers for pins and needles, cotton, thread, and socks, the papers hanging on clothes-pegs by the entrance, the window displaying without conviction two or three maimed tin soldiers, dusty back numbers of childrens' weeklies, and liquorice all-sorts.

When he was twenty, his point of access to the capital was the Gare Saint-Lazare, reassuring in an insistently enveloping geography: rue du Havre, square du Havre, place du Havre, hôtel du Havre, café du Havre, Au rendez-vous des Havrais, au Tabac du Havre, au Salamandre, as if to comfort the Cauchois, 'monté à Paris'. Nor did he shake off le Havre even then. In *Loin de Rueil*, when things are going badly for his hero, he suggests: 'Si on allait au Havre', and then goes himself, encountering on the train, at the level of Sotteville, an old school-friend. Le Havre lingers on too in novels situated on the edge of Paris: Porte-Maillot and Luna-Park, Argenteuil, Rueil, Suresnes: *banlieue-ouest, banlieue-Saint-Lazare*, as though his characters could not bear to lose sight of the Seine, as it flowed greasily towards the estuary, and were still attempting to nestle on the Normandy-facing side of Paris: Paris-emprès-Pontoise, even Rueil-emprès-Pontoise. Pontoise is safely on the old *route haute* from Paris to Rouen, even if it is left out by the *ligne d'Etat*: Paris-Rouen-le Havre, which follows the old *route basse*, by the Right Bank of the Seine, and which was created, like the oldest football club in France, *le Racing Havrais*, now just a hundred years old, by the English. This insistence on le Havre is not merely sentimentalism on my part, though I must admit to a little of that: Queneau is an indefatigable explorer of private, fixed, familiar itineraries imposed by habit.

Seaside towns have a melancholy quite particular to them. This can be attributed to the obvious, and visible, fact that water occupies as much as a third, or even a half, of what elsewhere would be ordinary walking terrain. The resultant implacably predictable itineraries—basically only *two*: along the Front, or on the parallel street, to which the dustbins are confined, behind it—produce the boredom of imposed habit, and make any semblance of anonymity impossible. The *havrais* family will set out from the semaphore and the *Bassin du Commerce*, with a cursory

evaluation of the yachts (*les yôtes*, later *les yashtes*), proceed along
the boulevard Maritime to Sainte-Adresse, where several of the
large hotels on the seafront represented, during the First World
War, the provisional capital of Belgium, both *rue de la Loi* and
Palais Royal, ending at the lighthouse of the cap de la Hève. Then,
all one can do is to turn back and follow the same route, *de phare en
phare*, in the opposite direction. In Queneau's childhood the fixity
of such an itinerary would be further emphasized by the tram-
lines, and by the trams themselves that, in *Un Rude Hiver*,
provided the initial encounter between the embittered Bernard
Lehameau and the two children, Annette and Polo. No town
could offer a more convincing grid for the novelist of habit,
imposing on his sad hero a choice between the north-south axis of
the Front and the east-west axis of the interior.

Au lieu de remonter la rue Thiers, il descendit vers le boulevard de
Strasbourg et la Bourse. Les yôtes blancs cagnardaient dans une eau
lourde, à face d'huile, quelques-uns, allemands et séquestrés, pourris-
saient abandonnés . . . Sur le quai des Casernes, le lent flâneur croisa un
groupe de morveux à moitié ivres, de francs bandits de quatorze ans . . .
Il prit la rue des Drapiers et, après la pouillerie sordide et vibrante du
quartier Notre-Dame, se retrouva en pays civilisé, rue de Paris . . . une
foule autochtone, militaire ou belge, animait consciencieusement cette
voie principale. Sur la jetée il vit l'entrée de deux transports . . .

When, later, he begins to make a little progress with the
English nursing sister from the Base, Miss Helena Weeds, he
arranges to meet her: 'Demain—A quatre heures, au bout du
boulevard de Strasbourg, près de la digue?—Je vois, oui . . .'
—now the marvellously *optimistic* geography of the beginnings of
a timid relationship that can still say 'à demain' in 1916 and can
already name a place familiar to both. And, the next day, *promenade au bord de la mer*: 'Le vent ne se taisait pas . . . Ils étaient
arrivés à l'octroi de Sainte-Adresse.'

There is only one itinerary that might be described as quite
*un*predictable, because it is so unusual in terms of *havrais* habits,
as it is inland and uphill, rather than seawards and level. This is
when Annette suggests that they go for a walk in the wintry forêt
de Montgeon, a distant, desolate place, beyond Graville, next to
the cemetery. And the last we see of a considerably humanized
Lehameau, no longer going on about the Jews and freemasons, is

waiting at a tram-stop, on a snowy day, to be taken to the
unfashionable heights of Sanvic: 'Il attendit longtemps un tram-
way. Qui le traîna péniblement vers la hauteur. Autour du fort de
Tourneville le vent galopait comme un chien fou qui essaie de
mordre sa queue. La neige dansait. Enfin Bernard arriva devant la
villa aux animaux de faïence . . .'

And it is absolutely appropriate that the villa in which
Madeleine, 'nott' grand' sœur', receives her many officer friends
from the British, Canadian, and Australian forces should have a
china dog on the doorstep and a china cat on its red-tiled roof.
Queneau is a provincial, with the provincial's genius for discovering reassurance in the small, enclosed dimensions of habit, as the
bourgeoisie havraise, over all these years, still makes its slow,
purposeful way, up and down, down and up, the boulevard
Maritime, decked out in *le grand pavois de dimanche*, and vaguely
taking in the ships and sailing boats, Bassin du Commerce, or
climbs steeply, puffing, towards the black-and-white lighthouse,
a *coup de chapeau*, here and there, *en cours de route*, as other family
unities, sporting the same flag, struggling against the wind, and
floundering under the weight of the same cargoes, are encountered in the busy shipping lanes, marked out by coloured electric
lights, between the two lighthouses.

Not that he is under any illusions about his compatriots,
especially the comfortable customers of his mother's shop, placing in the mouth of Madame Dutertre, the *bouquiniste*, something
of his own observation: 'elle avait toujours pris le Havrais pour
une buse, un obtus . . . elle ne régorgeait pas d'intellectuels, la
bonne ville franciscopolitaine, ça non, et le feu de sa salamandre
n'en avait pas fait éclore beaucoup . . .' At Lehameau's brother's,
Sénateur, the conversation alternates between food and the
progress of the war. Sénateur is enthusiastic about the former,
optimistic about the latter:

J'ai ouvert une boîte de sardines pour les hors-d'œuvres et voilà du
beurre qui vient en ligne droite d'Isigny. C'est Shigot qui me l'envoie.
. . . Et ce poulet, qu'est-ce que tu en penses? . . . Ah, on en mangera un
fameux poulet le jour où mon Charles entrera à Berlin pour y pendre
Guillaume . . . goûte-moi de ce camembert, il est épatant . . . tiens, tu
vois ces oranges? Elles viennent en droite ligne d'Espagne . . .

But soon even food, the war, the fact that the dockworkers are overpaid, the moratorium on debts, the enthusiasm shown by much of the female population for the Allied Cause, as represented by English officers, are abandoned in favour of the old old theme of the wickedness of Rouen and its inhabitants:

Les hommes menaient grand train autour d'absinthes. On parlait de l'avenir du port du Havre, du chemin-de-fer de la Seine-Maritime et de la perfidie des Rouennais qui faisaient tout pour empêcher le dit chemin-de-fer d'être construit. . . . Ce n'était d'ailleurs pas une discussion, car tout le monde s'accordait sur le bien fondé des revendications havraises, mais plutôt une série d'invectives contre l'oppression du chef-lieu du département.

a topic that has scarcely changed, either in tone, or in content, in the sixty years that have followed *Un Rude Hiver*: Rouen strangling the direct access of le Havre to Paris, the denial of credit for a line to connect up with Pont-l'Évêque, and so on.

The English, however, are also very much present, both linguistically and physically; the children, Annette and Polo, collect cap badges, and the little boy lets out: 'Chez nous . . . on entend parler anglais toute la journée. C'est à cause de nott' grand'sœur. Elle a beaucoup d'amis anglais . . .' Indeed, the Big Sister is doing so well out of the war that she is able to offer Annette and Polo an education socially more suited to the improved position of this orphaned working-class family: 'Lui, dit la petite fille, je le conduis à l'école Saint-Magloire, et moi, je vais au Collège Sainte-Berthe. Avant la guerre, on allait à la communale, mais maintenant notre grande sœur nous paye l'école religieuse. C'est plus chic qu'elle dit . . .'

The English had always been familiar to the *havrais* notion of the world. But the needs of the Base had brought further contingents of manual workers: Algerians and Indochinese, provoking, on the part of the inhabitants, including Madeleine, *la grand' sœur*, who repeatedly refers to *les bicots*, hostile reactions. But *Un Rude Hiver* has above all an endearing quality of childlike innocence, even when the children are as knowing as Annette and little Polo, an innocence that gives equal freshness to *Pierrot mon ami* and *Loin de Rueil*, but which somehow runs out before reaching the all too knowing *Zazie*.

Queneau retains, in his later novels, the visible and mental dimensions of a provincial world still easily discoverable on the edge of Paris, or nestling close to it: *petit* café, *petit* restaurant, *petite* rue, *petite* boutique, it is the adjective that matters, in a diminutive territory inhabited by *petites gens*. For all his novels are closely related to the large-scale grid of the *Planisphère*: Plan de Rueil-Malmaison, Plan de Suresnes, on its concrete base, outside the yellow stations of the *banlieue-ouest*: 'Eh bien moi, dit Thérèse, je connais bien des gens à Rueil qui n'ont jamais vu Notre-Dame . . . T'as le cinéma le dimanche. Et si tu veux danser tu peux descendre à Suresnes où l'on mange des moules et où les frites sont bonnes.' And the poet, des Cigales: 'à Rueil il est très connu, à Nanterre et à Suresnes, un peu moins . . .' And here is a quiet street, still in Rueil of course: 'la porte . . . qui donne rue de la Pierre-de-Morts. Personne ne passe par là. Il n'y a pas de voisin en face. C'est le mur de la distillerie Sabatier. J'ai examiné le coin . . .'

It is the same dimension in *Pierrot mon ami*, with its suggestion of *la campagne à Paris*, of rural quiet and one-storeyed simplicity:

Depuis deux ans, Pierrot habitait le même hôtel, *l'hôtel de l'Aveyron*, une bâtisse d'un matériau léger et à un seul étage, avec un balcon extérieur qui faisait communiquer entre elles les différentes chambres. La cour était une ancienne cour de ferme, une lucarne donnait vue sur un jardin de couvent.

Assured of such a base, Pierrot likes above all to make for the Seine, pont d'Argenteuil, to sit on the bank, and watch the fishermen, immobile in the green boats: 'les chauffeurs de camions qui, malgré leur strict horaire, s'arrêtaient au coin du pont pour boire le dernier verre de vin rouge avant d'entrer ou de sortir de Paris', for Queneau's characters find a particular peace in watching, from their own immobility, the regular comings and goings of others. This time, Pierrot falls asleep on the bank. When he wakes up, nothing has moved on the river: 'Dans les barques vertes, des fanatiques étaient rivés . . . il rouvrit les yeux . . . les pailles immobiles surveillaient leurs lignes stériles', a weekday scene of complete stillness, so still it might be Seurat. Always just the right, reassuringly small dimensions that shelter the relatively humble ambitions of his characters: 'Vous souvenez-vous de nos promenades au bois de Saint-Cucufa et au Mont-Valérien et plus tard nos baignades au Club Clodoaldien et nos parties de tennis chez vos amis de Suresnes et tant d'autres charmants souvenirs . . .?' Slightly grotesque, even a bit comical, but also touching.

But the other dimension, utterly bizarre, of *Pierrot mon ami*, is the old Luna Park, before it was burnt down, suitably a little before the outbreak of the Second World War; the dotty geography of *le Palace de la Rigolade, l'Alpinic Railway, l'Admirable's Gallery*, and *La Rivière Enchantée* ('depuis hier soir elle a un nouvel amant. Elle s'est donnée à lui dans une des petites barques qui promènent les amoureux dans une Venise de carton ignifuge . . .'); the clanging, screaming, sweaty, smoky cardboard world of the permanent pleasure gardens, the smell of the dodgems: 'Des parfums variés qui se pressaient dans ses narines, caoutchouc, tôle, vernis, poussière et autres, Pierrot ne retenait que le voluptueux houbigant dont s'imprégnait sa mignonne', and the continuous din of the fairground: 'Le bonisseur . . . fit donc fonctionner le piqueupe qui se mit à débagouler Travadja la moukère et le Boléro de Ravel . . .'

The contrast between the sulphurous extravagance of l'Uni-Park and the modest proportions of the semi-provinical world outside the cardboard portals, a little beyond the Porte-Maillot, is provided by the rue des Larmes, and the tiny triangle of territory jutting out into the fairground, containing the tomb of the *prince poldève*, as well as between the cacophony of the roaring, screaming fair and the alarming silence of the night, in an area still very much on the edge of Paris, at a period when the old *Zone* had not yet been entirely destroyed:

Là-bas, entre l'Alpinic Railway et le Dancing, près de la porte à l'angle de l'avenue de Chaillot et de la rue des Larmes . . . il n'y avait autour de nous que terrains vagues, petits ateliers, remises ou écuries, baraques zonières, entreprises insalubres, équarrisseurs, fermes et prés même. Le quartier était mal fréquenté; on y trouvait parfois des femmes en morceaux ou des mouchards exécutés . . . plusieurs fois j'entendis hurler dans la nuit, la nuit tout cela retombait dans une détresse taciturne, et les appels des assassinés venaient seuls distraire une attention captivée par l'intensité du silence . . . mon père [adds the narrator] . . . était le dernier représentant d'une vieille famille d'Argenteuil, qui, un moment, se trouvait posséder la plupart des terrains situés entre les fortifications et la Seine, de ce côté-ci de Paris . . .

I quote this at length, for it represents the semi-secret geography of Queneauvin inquiry and exploration: 'un terrain vague où quelques années auparavant on avait mis des fragments déshérités d'une exposition internationale . . . des ateliers de réparation d'automobiles et quelques bistrots occupaient la rive gauche, ainsi qu'une villa qui devait dater du temps de Louis-Philippe . . .'

The characters of *Pierrot mon ami*, human and animal, both employees of l'Uni-Park, hide reassuringly suburban origins, *banlieue Saint-Lazare,* under exotic names:

Je parie, dit Léonie, que vous avez connu He'lem Bey—He'lem Bey, c'est un fakir célèbre, natif de Rueil et prénommé *Victor*. Il est bien connu sur la place de Paris.

 . . . De quel bled vous êtes, monsieur Crouïa-Bey? demanda Léonie.
—De Tataouine, dans le Sud-Tunisien, répondit le fakir en tranchant avec décision dans un falaise de roquefort. Ah! Tataouine, Tataouine! *agi, mena, fiça, l'arbrya, chouia chouia barka*, excusez-moi, c'est le mal du pays . . . la nostalgie du désert. . . .—Blague dans le coin, dit-elle, je parie que vous êtes de Houilles ou de Bezons, peut-être même de Sartrouville, je reconnais ça à votre accent.

Queneau's military service in the 1920s had been spent in Algeria, where he had acquired at least the elements of the language of *Cagayous*, the people's philosopher of the *pied-noir* quarter of Bab'l-Oued. But there are philosophers more avowedly Parisian than the ill-disguised Crouïa Bey, as one of the profession expresses himself, while wiping the *zinc* of his bar with a damp cloth: 'Tout change vite sur cette terre. Rien ne dure . . . on ne se lave jamais deux fois les pieds dans la même flotte. Si on dit qu'il fait jour, quelques heures après il fait nuit.'

In *Pierrot* and *Loin de Rueil*, Queneau, after having experimented with Franco-English in his le Havre novel, now tackles Parisian *grasseyement* and its north-western variations. 'Je fais mon éduc*aaa*tion', observes a lady, in a café, and there is a reference to the early career of Léonie: 'une Léonie qui gambillait dans un bastringue'. And there is a strictly Parisian rendering of Dr Jekyll and Mr Hyde: 'Il s'agissait d'un docteur, médecin de jour et hideux la nuit. Le jour il se conduisait très bien, mais la nuit, il hantait les bouges, fréquentait les vilaines filles et zigouillait les pantes.'

But perhaps the most marked progress in fantasy since *Un Rude Hiver* is to be discovered both in the speed and the melancholy of the projection of imaginary careers, backwards in time, but all in direct and chaotic contrast to the forward march of *legénéralkoenig* in the wax-floored family museum of the boulevard de Strasbourg, for Queneau's characters move forward only to slide backwards, or they embark on a zig-zag course. Here is Pierrot, about to illustrate a suburban Rake's Progress, with the help of a moralizing pointer, at the fair:

. . . en tableaux avec des titres: les parents, la communale, l'apprentissage, le service militaire, l'agence privée AZ (enquêtes en tous genres, spécialité de divorces)—[Queneau, a persistent and wondrous traveller underground, keeps his eyes about him in the Métro]—première indélicatesse, première escroquerie, premier chantage, mariage, autres indélicatesses, autres escroqueries, face à face avec la police (la vraie), l'expiation, la rédemption, les *tout* petits emplois.

The next time round, the tone is more plaintive, the parabola more abrupt, *style PTT* ('Visitez Ancenis, Centre Gastronomique et Artistique, Son Abbaye, Ses Eglises, Son Château, Son Parc Municipal, Sa Piscine Chauffée'):

'Son enfance heureuse, ses folles ambitions, ses amères déceptions, sa carrière de bureaucrate, son expulsion pour négligence, son mariage avec une peau, finalement après maints métiers de moins en moins reluisants, celui de concierge, une vieille vérole achevant cette triste vie, pouah!'

Then in the first person: 'Je suis un fils de bonne famille, mon père possédait même une écurie de course mais voilà—les mauvaises fréquentations—Clairvaux—Foum-Tatahouine . . . ah mais!'

Much of the charm is due to the fact that Queneau is never cruel at the expense of his *marginaux*; and, even if the *dégringolade* is inevitable, can be seen approaching with steeple-chase rapidity, he allows his characters to depart in peace, as befits their innate modesty—and their author's—*sans fanfares ni trompettes*: 'Fermez cette fenêtre simplement, et revenez demain ou après-demain voir si je suis mort. J'aime autant être seul pour procéder à cette transformation. Adieu, mon jeune ami, et merci . . .'—a manner of death as discreet as Châteaubriand's description of the assassination of the unfortunate duc d'Enghien on the orders of Bonaparte. 'le dépêchement du Prince'.

The characters of Queneau's novels are so constantly attractive because they are so ordinary, attempting to find reassurance whether in a fixed itinerary, or in a regular routine of leisure (rather than work) which will allow for the *apéritif* and a visit to the PMU (for they are mostly *hippophiles*, and animalophils generally), entirely predictable exchanges about the weather ('"Oui, mais le fond de l'air est frais", réplique Jacques'), somewhere to stay like Pierrot's room in the Hôtel de l'Aveyron, *la toute petite vie, les tout petits emplois*, out of reach of conventional ambition, and content merely to survive. Of course, it is an illusion, an attempt to make time stand still; but, for a moment at least, he has indeed succeeded in stopping the clock, in immobilizing us in an extremely talkative, marvellously banal *Paris et son pourtour* of the 1930s, just as Pierrot seeks daily reassurance in the perpetual ballet of the little metal balls, *roulements à billes SKF*, in their show-window, avenue de la Grande Armée: as long as they do their daily and nightly dance, nothing much can happen, life will go on.

It is such a comforting world, because it is both private and limited in space: a couple of streets, a *terrain vague*, a quarter, a *terrasse de café* on a corner, facing two ways, enabling the customers to enjoy a double vision of movement and colour, as the steel tricolour of a *lavoir municipal* creaks in the light wind, their conversation of the utmost banality, employing a vocabulary a thousand times overheard: free people, going their own uncertain, timid, and modest way, their ambitions distant mirages at unattainable heights and as changeable as cardboard scenery, familiar, unpretentious, provincial places, one-storeyed, or two or three, on the edge of the city:

Foutaises . . . Foutaises que tout cela! La politique, les guerres, les sports: aucun intérêt. Ce qui me botte, moi, c'est le fait divers et les procès. . . . L'erreur, le crime, et l'adultère: voilà ce qui rend les hommes intéressants . . . 3 colonnes pour une guerre . . . une pour une élection à l'Académie—Tout ça, c'est du collectif, du galeux, de l'épidémique.

Here is an author who has got his priorities right. That is why I like Raymond Queneau; that is why I am a historian, concerned with Queneau's sort of people, and who would echo Zazie, when she exclaims, with her vigorous irreverence: '—Napoléon, mon cul. Il m'intéresse pas du tout, cet enflé, avec son chapeau à la con.'

Lefebvre the Historian

Georges Lefebvre, who died in 1960 and was born in 1874, was an extraordinarily distinguished and varied French historian. He stands in a class quite of his own—or perhaps 'class' is the wrong word, because he was very much of an individualist. He was a man who from start to finish had to make his own way. He really only started his career as a modern French historian very late, in 1913 or 1914, at which stage, of course, it was interrupted by the First World War. This also accounts for the fact that he only became *docteur-ès-lettres* at the age of fifty. It took him this amount of time to complete the work that made his reputation, his thesis on the peasantry of the North of France, *Les Paysans du Nord*, covering the whole revolutionary period from 1787 right up to the Restoration.

Until round about 1909, he thought of himself primarily as a geographer and a medievalist—rather an ironical preparation for the career of undoubtedly the most distinguished French historian of the French Revolution. Up to 1914, he never moved from his native Département du Nord. About 1909, he started working directly on the local records of the revolutionary period, which, he discovered, were exceptionally rich, partly owing to the fact that, during at least some of the period of the French Revolution, there existed institutions—*comités de surveillance, sociétés populaires*—which produced a type of documentation that has really never existed, as far as French history is concerned, before or since, and which witnessed for low levels of society that, in the normal course of historical documentation, would not be represented at all.

Part of the explanation of this switch was the experience of the Dreyfus affair. He often told us that not only he himself, but others of that generation, like Marc Bloch and Lucien Febvre, first became politically aware of themselves as republicans as a result of this experience.

Before Lefebvre, most of the debate on the history of the French

Revolution had been between protagonists of the Revolution and committed royalists. This debate had taken place almost entirely on the political level. Lefebvre was the first historian to get away from this and ask more fundamental questions: how did the general mass of peasantry in French Flanders fare, as a result of what was a social and an economic and an agrarian revolution, as well as a political revolution? How much land changed hands, who acquired the land? How did the revolutionary period affect the living standards of the general mass of your rural population, how would the disappearance of the seigneurial communities, the sale of communal land, *les biens communaux*—how would all this affect the majority of the population of a given region? In his case, it was his own region, in which he had grown up.

This, it seems to me, is his fundamental originality; and when, in about 1924, he presented his thesis on *Les Paysans du Nord* for the degree of *docteur-ès-lettres* in the Sorbonne, some of the members of the *jury d'examen* objected that this thesis was not history at all. It is very, very interesting, it is most important, it is a sort of dig down below any level we would ever have thought of: but is this really history? The other thing about his thesis is that it made him aware of a level of popular mentality that had previously resisted historical illustration. After all, he worked primarily on an area in France which had gone through the traumatic experience of the Counter-Revolution. This was one of the very rare areas of France which were occupied by the Duke of Brunswick and by the Duke of York, and in which those who had collaborated with the Revolution were given very, very dire punishment. Also, being a frontier area, it was perhaps more exposed than areas of the interior to every sort of panic rumour. Lefebvre himself was a frontiersman: he was always very fond of saying that his great-great-uncle had fought in the Bataillon de Lille of the Garde Nationale against the Duke of York.

His work made him almost uniquely aware of the strength of completely irrational—but often very ancient—fears and prejudices within a local community. His book, *La Grande Peur*, is about the waves of rumours, myths, prejudices, the politics of violence, the politics of vengeance and counter-vengeance, and so on. It is an almost clock-like, chronological account of a society, which is a walking or riding society, in which news, rumour, panic, travels at least slowly enough for the plodding historian more or less to be able to keep up with it, so that he can say: 'Well, look, you see, in Lons-le-Saulnier the news of the arrival of a group of strangers dressed in black, with their faces blackened, arrived on market day at four o'clock and in Château-Salins at 5.30. Well, there you are in Lons-le-Saulnier, now where does one go from there, where do the roads go? This is a Thursday, this is a market day in Lons-le-Saulnier, villagers will have come in from this, that and the other areas, and so the mail coach will have come in'—he's looked it up in the Almanach Royal. 'Well, surely the next place to look is Dôle, and the place after that is Dijon and the place after Dijon is Nuits-Saint-Georges, and the place after that is Chalon-sur-Saône, and so on and so forth.' It is partly based on simple commonsense knowledge of the normal channels of communication, partly on very intelligent use of the Almanach Royal, which gives you the time of departure and the time of arrival of stage coaches, water coaches, *coches d'eau*, partly on reconstruction of where people, at a given time, would be likely to be.

The other thing that is unique about *La Grande Peur*, and that can be accounted to some extent to his own very wide previous historical knowledge, not only of France but of Europe, is the ancientness of popular memory. Jeanne d'Arc is very much alive in Lorraine in 1789, and Charles the Bold of Burgundy is very much alive, because the people in Franche-Comté and Burgundy, when they hear of rumours of armed strangers descending upon their villages, naturally assume that they are Swiss.

Lefebvre was a very remarkable historian of the crowd when it was a matter simply of attempting to reconstruct the facts of the diffusion of a panic, let us say. But when he attempted to explore the hidden sources of some sudden act of extreme violence, he tended to have rather a Carlyle-like approach, as you can see in his article *Les Foules Révolutionnaires*. These *foules révolutionnaires* are concepts, they are Daleks, they do not even have faces. He is very much back with a sort of Comtiste neo-positivism of the nineteenth century—and indeed, as he thought about humanity as a whole, he did not have a great deal of time for humanity; it was something that had got to be somehow disciplined into rational behaviour. My objection to articles like *Les Foules Révolu-*

tionnaires, or what he writes about the September Massacres, or even some of the things he writes about in *La Grande Peur,* is that he is attempting to impose some sort of intellectual discipline, a sort of logic, on to people and on to events which have no logic, or very little. There was lacking in him a certain spark of, as it were, individual imagination which would prevent him from seeing why, on this particular occasion, let us say, a laundrywoman would feel particularly enraged.

It is probably characteristic that Georges Lefebvre's favourite novelist was Balzac. He understood Balzac, because Balzac tended to make judgments about the various levels of society in terms of money. What interested Lefebvre most, and what he investigated with the greatest patience, was all the possible transmutations and commutations of money, as a result of a social revolution such as the first French Revolution—although I know many people have said it did not change all that much. However, as Lefebvre himself, as a result of enormously laborious individual work, was able to prove, it did change an awful lot in terms of individual possessions: the dispossession of this landowner, the dividing up of his estate. There is something absolutely admirable about Lefebvre's patience and diligence in following up every imaginable source of fiscal archives, tax rolls, contributions, the various land taxes imposed by successive regimes; and I very much doubt whether nowadays one would find any single individual historian who would have the courage to impose this formidable task upon himself without any help at all, no computers, no *travaux d'équipe.*

Lefebvre looked forward with great eagerness to a time after his death, when every imaginable historical problem would be able to be solved scientifically. I remember him talking with enormous enthusiasm about some article he had read in one of those popularizing scientific reviews that you have in France, on brain cells; and he said: 'You know, *mon petit Cobb,* you are lucky, you will probably live long enough to see the day when every form of individual human conduct will be predictable.'

Albert-Marius Soboul. A Tribute

There was the enormous statue of Marshal Gouvion-Saint-Cyr coming up high on our left, amidst contrived rocks, broken columns, a grotto and abundant natural foliage. It must have been for the fifth time, as if the wretched thing were shadowing us and were determined not to let us go. It became obvious that for the last hour and a half we had been walking round and round in a vast circle in this silent metropolis, its greyness combined with greens enlivened by the bright October sunshine. We had taken a plan of the place at the main entrance, but so far it had not proved of much help. Pausing every now and then at one of the numerous *rondspoints*, we would sit on a stone bench and look out the plan, and then head down one of the dead-straight *allées* that intersected, like huge spokes, the series of circles. But each time we were brought back to the neighbourhood of the Marshal and his contemporaries, as we turned yet again around the implacable Outer Inner Circle.

Professor Deng, my companion, was hobbling more and more, making our circular progress slower and slower. I had gathered, through the clumsy filter of his barely recognizable French ('g's and 'f's eluded him totally, 'j's got dreadfully mauled), that a large pig had broken his right leg during the Cultural Revolution, and that it had not been properly set. As we got more and more tired, our tempers became frayed, and, on several occasions, I abandoned my fellow-traveller, striking out ahead in an increasingly desperate search for a new landscape of tombs and monuments. In fact, by the time of our fifth encounter with the wretched Marshal, I was by now in favour of abandoning the search altogether and of attempting to escape from this enveloping map of the dead, in an effort to reach the more reassuring terrain of the living. But Professor Deng, who no doubt had stored up a considerable fund of patience and tenacity during his years on the pig farm—or on several pig farms (I gathered that it had always been pigs)—was quite determined not to give up. He had an old, frayed, dog-eared black notebook that, like his formal, rather crumpled, blue suit, looked as if it had dated from long before the Pig Era, which he kept on consulting. Lot No. 223 was our destination; but it continued to elude us. We had long since lost any sense of direction, all the circular avenues looked much the same, all the straight ones seemed to be running steeply downhill as if the whole silent city were about to topple over into whatever lay beyond and below.

Finally, in desperation, we took one of the downhill *allées*; at the bottom, surely, we would run into a wall and find a way out. At least it was a change from the Outer Inner Circle. We were in much more recent territory by now, having at last shed both Empires, the July Monarchy, 1848, and the massively monumental middle years of the Third Republic. We had even walked out of the Fourth, and it looked as if we were now well on into the Fifth, for my attention was soon caught by a very new tomb in black marble and marked in gold lettering, with a photograph encrusted in the top of a hairy man with a black moustache and huge dark eyes, aged about thirty, and dressed in what looked like vulgar wedding clothes: a Croat Nationalist who had been assassinated in Paris in 1980. There was a poem, also in gold lettering, in Serbo-Croat, with a French translation alongside: *O ma Croatie, Ma Patrie Chérie*, it went on, uninspiringly and predictably. It did not seem a very original poem. There were a lot of fresh flowers on the grave, which was covered in silvery stone chippings. But at least it now looked as if by keeping straight, we might be heading further into the 1980s. By now we were advancing into territory where the tombs not only looked new, but often had fresh flowers and fresh chippings. There was one to a Lebanese Christian, with a small crowd of people around it, including three dark children, as if the man had only recently been buried, perhaps that very week: perhaps this one might be another, much more recent *assassiné*, perhaps there might be a special corner set aside to accommodate the latest victims of political murders, provided, of course, that they were Christian: the Croat had revived my flagging appetite and there had been quite a number of political murders in Paris in the previous five years. Deng had shown no interest in the Croat; and I left him sitting rather sadly on an elaborate tomb, his back leaning against

47

a broken column. From a short distance it looked as if even he might be ready to abandon the quest.

The Lebanese had not been assassinated, the golden letters carried no such message, there was no accompanying poem in two languages, he was no Martyr to the Cause. He had merely died. I could not make out what all the fuss was about, why there was such a crowd round this disappointing shrine. His tomb was halfway up a steep alley, so that it overlooked a small cluster that nestled further down. I don't suppose that, in that situation, it would much matter any more about being overlooked. There was even a wall in sight, so we must have been near the edge. I had had fears of being trapped in the place over the whole of the weekend (they locked the gates at 5 p.m.); the wall at least meant that we were now within easy reach of the land of the living, and, indeed, of a restaurant, drinks and lunch. The cold and the long, mostly circular, walk, had given me an appetite. And then, looking down, I saw it, at only two or three graves' distance: a very large, flat-topped affair, a double-bed at least (the width seemed appropriate, though I don't suppose it had been deliberate, for he had seldom slept alone), in shining black marble, the letters indented in gold on the middle of the top in bold lettering: ALBERT SOBOUL, 1914–1982. It was certainly a very grand affair. I wondered whether the Party had contributed towards it. The Party went in for really big tombs to cover the faithful (who were of course immune from Resurrection so that it would not matter how much weight was on top). Perched on the flat-topped tomb, balanced on a wire stand, was an open book in white marble, a bit vulgar and provincial, but at the same time softening the solemn pomp proclaimed by the tomb itself in its massive shining black width. I found the marble book rather touching, there was something both modest, rural, ordinary, and rather childlike about it. I got closer and read: A. M. SOBOUL, HISTORIEN DE LA GRANDE REVOLUTION FRANÇAISE. He would have liked that, for him there had been only ONE Revolution, and that a French one, the adjective would have especially appealed to him. On top of the smooth black surface of the tomb were half-a-dozen little brick pots containing flowers and evergreens, each pot surrounded by a tricolore ribbon tied in a neat bow and suggestive of a caring and indeed recent feminine presence, that perhaps of his daughter, or of his *compagne*, certainly not of both together. Perhaps they had come to an arrangement to visit at different times. He would have liked the tricolore ribbons as much as the adjective GRANDE. It really did seem that the tomb spoke with two different voices: the one, solemn, pompous and in marble, that of the Party, that of orthodoxy; the other, warm, familiar, romantic, with more than a hint of a southern accent, with recollections of a stern childhood in Nîmes, of the aromatic smells of the *garrigue*, of caressing velvety eyes, of an unashamed simplicity. The tomb spoke with the voice of Albert, the open book and the pots and the ribbons spoke with that of Marius. The two names had never quite made a pair.

I felt strangely moved after all. I had found my old friend, though I had not expected to discover him in quite such a grandiose setting. The grandeur seemed a bit outsize, commenting perhaps more on the importance of the function, HISTORIEN DE LA GRANDE REVOLUTION FRANÇAISE, a monument partly to the Chair, partly to the succession to the austere Georges Lefebvre (no marble tomb for *him*, merely a niche in the columbarium), *le Vieux Maître*, than on the warm and affectionate personality who had occupied the Chair ever since the death of Marcel Reinhard (buried, as it turned out, with the whole of his family, at no very great distance, though in a less uniformly political territory). I called to Professor Deng, still sitting against the broken column, in his frayed bourgeois suit and overcoat, saying that I had found it. He got up carefully, leaning on his stick, and climbed up the steep path. He read the two inscriptions carefully, took out the battered black notebook, wrote something in it, and then, laying his stick beside the tomb, and putting his arms straight against his sides, he bowed deeply from the waist. I suppose he had come all the way from Peking thus to pay his respects.

We hung about in silence for a few minutes, then left, still without exchanging a word. Lower down, in a long straight row of enormous tombs, were all the leading figures of the PCF: Thorez, Duclos, Waldeck-Rochet, Cachin, Croizat, Paul, Casanova, Vaillant-Couturier. From where they were, they could not have seen Soboul, higher up on the slope; but Soboul could have seen them. He was right among his own people; and this too seemed right. He had always been faithful, both to the Party, to *les copains* (that is, members of it), to his Aunt (the incarnation of the Party) and to that generation of young southerners who had come up with him to Paris in the early-thirties or whom he had met subsequently at the *Cité Universitaire*. The tombs of the Party leaders faced on to a yellowing lowish wall, with clusters of red roses planted in front of it in regimented lines. I pointed the wall out to Professor Deng, explaining that it was *le Mur des Fédérés*. He made another deep bow, this time in the direction of the Wall, but holding his stick. After he had straightened out, the black note-book re-appeared in his hand. He had shown no interest at all in the massive, rather garish tombs of the leaders, though I had pointed them out to him. He had not come all this way to see them, he had come to look for Soboul. But no doubt *le Mur* had been an unscheduled bonus too. Again, I thought that Soboul had been doubly fortunate in his location after death. He had always been sentimental on the subject of the Commune; and in Brighton, in 1971, he had concluded an impassioned lecture by singing, the tears running down his cheeks, Potier's song of hope: *La Commune n'est pas morte*. For a man who had no religious beliefs, he had shown a curious attachment to immortality. For him the Great French Revolution had also remained very much alive; and, in 1968, he had denied the infantile *événements* even the title of a *small* revolution; it would have been a sort of blasphemy to have allowed them even that.

But was Soboul actually *in* the grand tomb? I had been told, by someone who had been at the ceremony in the Père Lachaise and who had been quite close to the family, that his body had been brought up by train from Nîmes for the ceremony, and that it had been sent back by train, the following night, to be buried in the cemetery of La Croisette, the village of his ancestors at the southern tip of the Ardèche. He had always told me that he wished to lie there *parmi mes aïeux paysans*. He had even asked me, should I be around at the time, that I was to ensure that such wishes were to be carried out, specifying that he was to be buried beside his uncle, a patriarchal bearded figure, a retired carpenter, whom I had once met, should he survive his sister. Like most southerners, he had attached a great deal of importance to this sort of thing. His father, back in the Nineties, had gone out from La Croisette to Algeria; but his father had ended up in a war cemetery somewhere in the North-East of France. So it was *his* turn to go back home to the ancestral village. So it looked as if he might have had it both ways, have enjoyed a grand public ceremony and a simple private one. But I did not mention this to Professor Deng; I felt it was a small secret between Soboul and myself.

We walked out of the cemetery into a small street of low houses that led on to the long rue de Bagnolet. I left the Professor at a bus stop, after we had shaken hands. It was a beautiful October day—so often the best month in Paris—and I had not been in this faraway quarter for a great many years. I set off down a wide, sunny avenue in search of somewhere to eat. I wanted to stay a bit longer in the neighbourhood, whether my friend—he had been in the habit of addressing me, in his letters, *vieux frère*, and, by name, *Ricardo*, both terms of extreme affection—was actually in the grand tomb or not. I eventually found an unassuming-looking restaurant down a quiet side street; it had a long green front, with the words RESTAURANT YOUGOSLAVE written across the top in white letters. The *patronne*, a good-looking dark woman with a classical profile and who was very pregnant, was talking animatedly in a strange language to a man in blue overalls; a girl of about thirteen came across to hand me the menu. I wondered whether the murdered Croat had ever eaten there. He certainly could have afforded to do so, for it was very cheap. His grand tomb must have been set up by public subscription; judging from his rather *Belle Jardinière*-looking suit in the photograph, he would not have been able to afford a thing of such size and ostentation himself. I had quite enjoyed the outing after all, though it had been very tiring trying to pull myself back all the time to Professor Deng's halting pace. It was a relief to be sitting down at last. I ate with enjoyment, listening to the conversations that must have been in Serbo-Croat, and ordering more wine. I was quite content to be on my own, as if I had wished to share only with myself the encounter with my old friend, or at least with his official tomb, just over a year after his death.

Albert-Marius Soboul was born in Tizi-Ouzou, *chef-lieu* of the Department of the same name, Algeria, a fortnight after his father had been killed on the third day of the First World War. His first name no doubt owed something to the events of the July Crisis. A great many children, in France, England, Belgium, and no doubt in Canada, Australia and New Zealand, born in the second half of that momentous year, were given the name of Albert. His second name, Marius, was a predictable reminder of his southern origins. Albert must have been the personal choice of his mother, after his father had crossed the Mediterranean. Marius had no doubt previously been agreed upon by both parents. Throughout his life, he would remain Albert to his sister Gisèle, to his aunt, and to the other members of his family. Marius was reserved for his many friends.

Soboul could have been described as a *pied noir* (and one that had had the foresight to sell out at the right time in the early Fifties) though the designation would have been more appropriate when applied to his parents. His father, a carpenter from La Croisette, had emigrated to Algeria in the 1890s, taking advantage, like many artisans, small farmers and *journaliers* from the poorer southern Departments of Metropolitan France, of the offer of free land, under fairly severe conditions of clearance completed within a specified time limit, in the Algerian Departments. By the summer of 1914, after twenty years of slogging effort, his parents, with the help of two Algerian farm hands, had succeeded in clearing some two hundred hectares of scrub which they had converted into a mixed holding of cereals (mostly maize), pasture, and vineyards. His father had been confirmed in full ownership in 1912 or 1913. It had been a considerable achievement, a lesson above all in the virtues and rewards of sheer hard work and determination.

After the death of his father on one of the earliest battlefields, Soboul, as a war orphan, became a ward of State, a *Pupille de la Nation*, which ensured him a free education right through the State system, from primary school to University till he had obtained the *agrégation d'histoire*, which would guarantee him an advantageous place in the same system. All his life, he was to take considerable pride in his status as a *Pupille de la Nation*. As such, he could later insist, with reason, that he had enjoyed very few advantages and that none the less he had achieved considerable academic success. But also for him the word Nation, far from being an abstraction, took the almost physical form of an adoptive father. It was typical of his pride that he should have positively rejoiced in this rather bleak paternity of the State. I think much of his attachment to the austere and seemingly egalitarian First Republic must have owed something to this early intervention of a somewhat faceless and impenetrable *Marianne* on his behalf. Like his semi-hero Robespierre, Soboul remained all his life something of a scholarship boy. There was no fiercer advocate of the privileges due to *agrégés*, no more active member of the *Société des Agrégés*, no more eloquent defender of the importance of that terrifying scholastic hurdle. He had been through it all and come out the other side. Let others go through the mill the way he had. Had he been a *normalien*, he would no doubt have been almost a professional one. Later he was to become a zealous upholder of the conventional university hierarchy and of the deference due to holders of Chairs.

The facts about his father's death—I think in the *Tirailleurs Algériens*—as a war hero right at the beginning of the conflict are incontrovertible. His adoption as a *Pupille* is convincing proof, if any proof were needed. In the course of the thirty-three years of our friendship, which was always close—we had no secrets from one another—I never heard him suggest anything to the contrary. It was the same with the other members of his family. They would say how hard it must have been for him never to have known his father, how hard too on his father never to have known that his second child had been a boy. Nor would I have raised the matter here, were it not for the fact that, since my friend's death, I have been assured, from two different sources, both of them entirely reliable, that, in the late-Thirties at the *Cité*, and throughout the Forties, in Montpellier and in Paris, Soboul seems at least to have allowed it to be believed, especially in Communist circles (he had few contacts outside them) that his father had been shot in 1917, after having taken a leading part in the mutiny of the French Black Sea Fleet. Both my informants told me quite independently (they have never met) that, apart from his southern good looks, his ability to chat up the other sex, his charm and his cheek, what had greatly contributed to the success of *le beau Marius* with the no doubt deeply romantic and single-minded female would-be revolutionaries of the PCF, was the belief, widely held and no doubt transmitted from one to another as an item of blindly accepted Party truth, that he was the son of a *fusillé de la Mer du Nord,* and thus a sort of honorary godson of the Russian Revolution itself. Such spurious parentage—there could be no contesting the fact that he was indeed a son of the French State—seems greatly to have helped many of these true believers into his always inviting and readily available bed. It would have no doubt been like sleeping with that Other Great Revolution at one remove. Of course, if they had wanted to believe such myths, one could hardly blame the subject of them for not having attempted to disillusion them. Or perhaps he merely allowed them to go on believing what they so clearly *wanted* to believe. They were after all members of a sect. Did any of them ever ask him outright? What would he have answered? The improved (from the point of view of the *sectaires*) version would have raised his unfortunate father from the dead, given him the dubious bonus of three extra years of life, a transfer to a different service, perhaps even an opportunity actually to see the son he had never known about, and a dishonourable death as a mutineer.

It all does seem a bit unfair on his poor father, no doubt a simple patriot, in blue jacket and red trousers, of the unquestioning August 1914 vintage. And it is very bad history, or not history at all. I suppose one should not sit in judgement. But at the time—and I met my two informants in the same week—I felt both amazed and rather distressed, as if I had inadvertently discovered something vaguely shabby about a dead friend, a grubby little secret revealed by a letter lying hidden under a lot of papers at the bottom of a drawer, a missing section of his biography that I would have preferred not to have known about. In retrospect, it all seemed so pointless. He could have bedded any number of girls, French and foreign, without needing to allow what was a complete fabrication to run its steady course over at least a decade unchallenged. But then it would not always be easy to reject honours so eagerly thrust upon one, especially when they contributed so powerfully to one's own sex-appeal. *Militantes* can often be incurably romantic, and members of a Party so ready to tamper with the record of public history can perhaps be forgiven for taking similar liberties with the private, or semi-private (for a *fils de fusillé de la Mer Noire* belongs by right to the official chronicle of ultra-orthodox revolutionary history) truth. As it was, I felt stained myself and considerably deflated, as if I had been in-

directly associated with something disreputable. It did not fit at
all with my own cherished portrait of a warm-hearted, affectionate, generous and impulsive friend, quick to burst into flame in
brief anger and quicker still to forgive and forget. And it also
seemed quite out of keeping with his own very strongly-felt sense
of family loyalties. Worst of all, my friend had been a historian,
and a pretty distinguished one at that. I think that is what upset
me most. It was as if he had helped betray a vocation.

At the time, under the impact of what my two friends had quite
inadvertently let out (the one, a man of simple integrity, had
simply commented that he had felt no desire to get to know *un
beau jeune homme* – I think in fact he called him something even
less complimentary and as better suited to the young man's
southern origins—my informant had been born in Caen—
rastaquère perhaps—who had appeared to have given currency to
myths about his dead father in order to make himself more
attractive to a lot of doting Party girls; after all, he added, one did
at least possess the minor luxury of being able to choose one's
friends), I felt so discouraged that I decided there and then that I
could not go ahead and write anything at *all* about Soboul; it was
as if he had betrayed me—or perhaps that is to put it too
grandiloquently—anyhow, had held back on me—from beyond
the grave; and that seemed a cruel trick to have laid in store for an
old friend.

This was very much to over-react to something that may have
been quite trivial. More recently, with the benefit of time, I have
taken the whole episode as a much-needed reminder that people
are more complicated than they would like us to think. Indeed the
whole thing has become for me yet another problem of the
interpretation of historical evidence. After all, in his recollection
his father can have been little more than an emblematic figure; he
would often have heard about him (but no doubt only the good
and glorious things about him: *Albert, sois digne de ton pauvre papa,
modèle-toi sur lui, souviens-toi de son sacrifice*, and that sort of thing,
a cult figure assigned the posthumous role of ensuring good
behaviour in the son whom he had never seen) from his mother,
his uncles, his aunts (the one in Nîmes would have at once
erected the poor man into a sort of Moral Principle in stone),
though presumably his sister, four at the time of her father's

tragic death, might have filled him out and given him recognizable human proportions. Even so, he would still have been
somewhat lacking in reality as far as the boy and the adolescent
were concerned. At the best, he might have survived as the
fading photograph of a man with a heavy moustache, very dark
eyes and a starch collar—the sort of photograph that one sometimes sees on graves in French provincial cemeteries, men and
women apparently permanently fixed in their forties (I don't
know how old Soboul's father was when he was killed), or as that
of a soldier in uniform, tight tunic, baggy trousers, his head
topped by a *chéchia*. Or there might not have been even that much
to give the pious memory some more solid consistency. His father
might in the end have been little more than a figure on the top of a
village war memorial: a Soldier, *any* soldier, with all the usual
gear slung around him, rifle and very long bayonet, standing
above two dates: *mort pour la Patrie, mort pour la France*, or
whatever the official formula might be, anyhow, something as
exemplary, as impersonal, as coldly monumental as all those
uplifting sayings that *La Tante*, the educationalist who was later to
bring up the orphaned girl and her little brother, constantly
employed as a form of pedagogic monologue: *n'est-ce pas, mon
petit Albert, l'argent ne fait pas le bonheur, souviens-toi, Gisèle, que
l'Instruction fait la Grandeur des Nations,* as if all her conversation
had consisted of writing on the wall, more especially painted
writing on the walls of schoolrooms. There would never be any
shortage of the Examples thus offered to the dutiful niece and the
dutiful nephew. I think if the Aunt had had her way, Soboul
would have been called Emile. And the Aunt lived to a very
considerable age. Anyhow, in all the years I knew Soboul, I
hardly ever heard him mention his father, save that he had been a
carpenter, had worked hard in Algeria, and had been killed so
early on in the war, no doubt among the first hundred of the
millions to come. I am not suggesting that he ever believed in the
mythical father of later vintage that, at some stage—I think it
must have been at the *Cité Universitaire* round about the time of
the Popular Front—the female and southern *militantes* had
provided him with, but that there was little enough reality to the
real one. Which one would have the greater sales value: the
tirailleur of August 1914, or the revolutionary sailor of 1917? It

would be a matter of taste. What is certain is that both must have been pretty misty figures. Perhaps it does not matter very much either way. What is one to make of a father that one has never seen? But here is enough of such speculation. It is time to return to the narrative of Soboul's childhood, adolescence, and student days.

After her husband's death, Soboul's mother, with two small children on her hands, soon found herself unable to carry on the running of the farm single-handed, the two Algerian farm workers having been called up early in the War. She had never been strong and the effort to carry on soon proved too much for her. In the end she had to put the estate into the hands of a manager (who turned out to be anything but, and such was the extent of his *mis*management that what had once been a prosperous farm went for almost nothing when, in the early 1950s, Soboul and his sister—both of them active members of the French Communist Party—apparently they did not see any incompatability between such political commitment and ownership of land in what was in fact a colonial economy—decided to put it on the market while there might still be a few Europeans prepared to risk such an investment). Having, as she thought, left the estate in good hands, she moved to Algiers with the two children, taking a flat in one of the poorer white downtown quarters: Belcour or Babl-Oued. Although she had a pension as a war widow, she was driven to seek some form of employment, if only to keep the two adequately clothed and fed. I think that, unlike her sister-in-law in Nîmes (who had taken her educational diploma), she had very few formal qualifications beyond the *certificat primaire*, so that teaching, the post office or secretarial work would not have been available to her. And she was no doubt too proud to throw herself on what would have been the rather exiguous charity of her brothers and sisters in the Ardèche. So she went into domestic service as a cleaner, as well as taking in washing; a form of employment that must have been particularly humiliating in a society in which nearly all the servant labour force would have been provided by non-Europeans, who were prepared to work for a pittance. I don't know how long she was able to carry on in that double capacity: perhaps only five or six years, for her health was failing rapidly. At the beginning of 1922, she had to be taken into hospital in the last stages of tuberculosis. I am not sure what happened to Soboul and his sister while their mother was away. Perhaps they were looked after by a neighbour, perhaps Gisèle managed to cope in the role of a little mother, or they may have been sent to France (a place that they had never seen). Their mother never came back. She died in hospital after a few weeks, the same year, 1922. Gisèle was by then twelve, Albert-Marius was only eight. And now they really were orphans.

I think it must have been at this stage—or it might have been a little earlier, possibly at the time that their mother was first taken into hospital—that the two children were taken on by their father's unmarried sister, Mlle Soboul, who, in 1922, was already *Directrice* of the *Ecole Normale de Jeunes Filles* of the Gard in Nîmes. In the strict hierarchy of French State education, it was an important post, involving considerable responsibility, much social prestige, and a great deal of power, so that Mlle Soboul was a respected, even feared, figure in the vigorously anti-clerical circles of the educational élite of this southern town that not only included a proud Protestant population, but also aspired to the title (self-awarded) of *l'Athènes du Nord* (and there were few more ardent, more convinced Northern Athenians than Mlle Soboul herself, who, though a convert—she too was from the Ardèche —or perhaps *because* she was a convert, in conversation, hardly ever referred to Nîmes as such; *Vous ne savez sans doute pas, Monsieur Cobb, qu'on appelle notre cité*—*ville* would not have been good enough for a town which had on its coat-of-arms a large green crocodile, the emblem of a Roman legion once stationed there—*l'Athènes du Nord*? And I would dutifully acknowledge my ignorance of this important fact, renewing my ignorance each time I met *La Tante*, which must have been fifteen times at least). Mlle Soboul liked imparting information on the most varied subjects, and it was as well to accept such information with a carefully balanced mixture of interest and surprise. Indeed, so keen was she on the Athenian identity of the town that, once a year, mercifully in the summer, a little before 14 July—for the winters could be bitterly cold and icily windy in this southern town—she would have all her girls—future teachers like herself —dress up in vaporous white robes, which, if the hot wind were blowing from the *garrigue*, would, so Soboul would tell me with keen interest, reveal delectable areas of the well-formed, though occasionally hairy, brown legs of the young female Athenians from the upland villages of the north of the Department—and act out ancient Greek dances as *vestales* shod in golden sandals. Soboul would also comment that, such was his aunt's concentration on the grace of the movements of the white-clad young virgins and her almost total innocence, that she would express gratified surprise, following one of these performances, at the enthusiasm with which the undulations of the dancers had been received by the male members of the audience. She took it as further evidence of the Hellenization of the *chef-lieu du Gard* in which she occupied such a central position. Civilization was indeed flourishing in the dry and stony soil of the *garrigue*. Like the republicans of the Year II, like the Stalinists of the 1940s, like no doubt a great many people exercising the same profession as herself, Mlle Soboul had as great an appetite for euphemisms as she had for moral statements. Nîmes was not the only case in point; Marseille, in her vocabulary, was given similar treatment as: *la cité phocéenne*. Soboul, who adored and respected his aunt, was also given to imitating her, on all occasions referring to the capital of France as *la Babylone Moderne*.

From the age of eight to that of sixteen, when he went up to Paris as a boarder in the *lycée* Louis-le-Grand, Soboul grew up in the austere and parsimonious surroundings of a French educational establishment, an environment so convincingly described by Marcel Pagnol (the pungent smell of the *urinoirs*, the smell of chalk) when writing about the school in central Marseille (*la cité des Phocéens*, or *la cité phocéenne* to his father, too) of which his father was the immensely proud headmaster: long, echoing stone corridors painted a dullish green below a rancid cream, stern and bare dormitories, class-rooms with inky desks and maps depicting all the Departments, the *chefs-lieux* marked with a big black dot, the *sous-préfectures* marked with a smaller one, a concrete courtyard shaded by a few sad-looking stunted trees, the regular, imperative sound of electric bells, the stone staircases echoing the running feet of children and adolescents in black smocks (the everyday envelope even of Mlle Soboul's once-yearly female Athenians). It was an environment which few would ever be likely to regard as home. Yet it was so regarded by Soboul, who would return there from the *lycée* further down in the town, and by his sister, who not only lived there, but was later a pupil there, going out from there to become in her turn a headmistress, but only of *l'école communale* of the small port of Le Grau-du-Roi, set among the salt pyramids on the edge of the Camargue.

Of course the place would not appear quite as bleak to the niece and the nephew of the Headmistress, once they were on the other side of the French equivalent of the green baize door that separates the House Master from the boys over whom he rules, as to the inmates of the dormitories. The spacious flat assigned to the *Directrice* might contain a few timid and tentative luxuries denied to the class-rooms and to the public areas of the establishment. For one thing, the floors would not be stone, but parquet, well-waxed (there would be no rugs or carpets, and Soboul and his sister would have to put on cloth slippers over their shoes in order not to mark the perfect shining lustre of the polished floor). There would be a few plants (*useful* plants, medicinal, herbal, anyhow, *instructive*) in green wooden boxes on the window-ledges. I think there would have been more similarly instructive plants and acorns and potato seeds and that sort of thing showing their roots in long glass bottles in order to illustrate the various slow stages of natural growth. Sea shells from the beaches of Le Grau-du-Roi or Palavas-les-Flots would be displayed, not as objects of natural beauty, but for instructional purposes; and there would be an abundance of fossils, collected from the rocky valleys of the *garrigue*. Instruction would indeed speak from many walls and even shelves, and there would be some suitably edifying message in coloured wool in a prominent place above where the mantel-piece might have been if there had been one; but there would not have been one, as the flat, like the rest of the place, was centrally heated.

But instruction did not preach, by example or allusion, from *every* wall, from *every* shelf. There were areas of silence, there were even a few timid concessions to a neat and easily washable comfort. The long administrative windows, completely bare and stern and unrelenting, whether looked through from the inside on to the bleak courtyard, or staring darkly out onto the street, in the public areas, would be surrounded by cotton curtains in red and white checks, to match the table-cloth and the tiny, rather lumpy cushions on the wicker chairs, the latter because they made you sit up straight, and there could be no question of Gisèle and Albert ever being allowed to *lounge*, which was something as bad as being idle. She also belonged to a Wicker Period; wicker had been very much in evidence, along with mimosa, pampus grass in vases, and little bobbled mats, the bobbles made of beads, when she had been a young woman fresh from the training college. And, like my mother, she belonged too to a Water-Colour Period; the general impression of controlled austerity could be softened by the presence, on the washable walls, of some of Mlle Soboul's delicate water-colours, most of them dating back to her early years as a teacher, long before she had put her hair up in a severe headmistressy bun, when perhaps she herself had been nervous, uncertain, and rather shy, even not entirely convinced about the nobility of her vocation, some time long before the First World War, and when the French Communist Party had never even been thought of. (Her hair was already greying when I first met her in her nephew's flat, rue de Gergovie, in the XIVème *arrondissement*: Mlle Soboul seemed out of place and rather apprehensive when in Paris; I think *la Babylone Moderne*, a mild joke at her expense in Albert's mouth, represented the reality. There could be no doubt that, in her Moral Geography, Virtue lay to the south, Vice, and, worse, Frivolity, lay to the north—a case of turning the map upside down, for the inhabitants of the Département du Nord, including the PCF militants from that area, would have had no doubts at all that Virtue lay to the north, was in fact home-grown, Vice, Idleness and Frivolity, to the south. But each would have at least agreed that Paris was a sink of iniquity.) The water-colours might even have been painted as a discreet appeal to the eyes of a man, possibly some young teacher and fellow-labourer in the educational vineyard. She must have been proud of the water-colours, because, when she retired from the school, she took them with her to the rambling villa, set in an aromatic garden, and almost hidden by the tall-growing plants, to the north of Nîmes, beyond the little chapel of the Pentecostals. Soboul showed them to me with a wistful reverence. They were pretty landscapes of the Pont du Gard, the bluish rocks and the very dark greens of the *garrigue*, but all far removed from the harsh glare of the implacable southern sun and under pale blue and white skies that might have been those of Normandy and the Ile-de-France (like all true southerners, native-born inhabitants of Provence or Languedoc, Mlle Soboul was no sun-worshipper, the garden of her villa was designed for shade, each path running through a *tonnelle* of over-hanging foliage, and in the spring and summer, she always had her head covered in a wide-brimmed straw hat). I was glad at the time to have seen the water-colours, in their frames of pale wood, for they hinted at the existence—partly, but not entirely, buried under the many years of educational effort and eminence —of a more private woman who had a measured, rather hesitant sense of beauty, and who could find a few spare moments for private enjoyment, away from the insistent burden of public duty and political commitment. There were several layers to *La Tante*, and the public image, so relentlessly didactic, so insistently rousseau-ite, so utterly humourless, did not offer the complete picture.

Soboul, who reserved for his aunt a great deal of tenderness, as well as a considerable degree of awe and reverence, was well aware of the fact that, beneath that formidable and strongly armoured public exterior, there still subsisted several little pockets of rather cramped femininity and a surviving, semi-secret attachment to objects and to pets that were pretty and that served no useful purpose. What, for instance, could have been the educational value of the little yellow canary in its golden cage? Or of the huge tabby cat with a red collar—the very picture of enjoyed and well-rewarded sloth—as he stretched out full length in the dappled shade among the nasturtiums in the large vege-table garden that went with the flat provided for *Madame la Directrice*? Both canary and cat—kept well apart—were quite outrageously indulged by their mistress. But what useful Lesson in Life could either illustrate? I don't think *La Tante* had ever heard of Dick Whittington's cat; and the idle tabby was so well fed, so pampered, that he soon became an indifferent mouser. Both cat and canary showed a total incapacity to *learn*.

So there was a milder side to the childhood and adolescence of the two orphans. There were sunny moments far removed from the driving force of Instruction, there were even visits to the seaside, though, of course, these could be justified as opportunities to learn to swim. The aunt's garden was full of flowers, as well as of carrots, peas, and runner beans; many of the flowers were later pressed into books, not so much to illustrate lessons in botany for the benefit of the two children, as to satisfy their aunt's craving for collecting. A place could even be found for objects, if not of luxury—for luxury was corrupting (like the wicked Paris that had done so much to Albert as a sixteen-year-old, for it was there that he had first developed his passionate and insatiable pursuit of girls, an activity to which he devoted a great deal of time and effort for the rest of his life)—at least of proved uselessness. There were even times off from the patiently conducted Lessons of Life. It was possible to have a walk that did *not* have an educational purpose, though most walks did. *La Tante*, an economical person by nature and no doubt originally by necessity, much favoured the accumulation of values through example, and walking could double up as an opportunity for careful observation and as a healthy exercise. And, after all, Jean-Jacques had once walked from Geneva to Turin. I even think that, in later years, Soboul may have exaggerated the bleak austerity of his childhood, perhaps in order the better to enlarge on the humbleness of his origins, just as much as he was prone to go on about his peasant ancestry. Of course he was not a peasant, had never been anywhere near the land, including his own in Tizi-Ouzou, which he only visited once as a grown man, and then with the purpose of selling it. And his aunt had managed to escape from that unhappy state by sheer diligence and determination. Being the only one of her brothers and sisters who had done so, she was regarded by the rest of the family with some awe and considerable deference as the only one of the Sobouls who had succeeded in removing herself from the trap of rural poverty in a desperately poor agricultural area of France. *La Tante* was indeed the jewel of her family, the very embodiment of republican rectitude. Her life could be seen as the perfect illustration of one of her own moral samplers.

So, in many ways, once in Nîmes, Soboul had in fact enjoyed a rather privileged childhood; and he had certainly not lacked educational stimulus and opportunity. He had the Aunt constantly at his side to remind him of the importance of getting on, through application and practical example. It may well have been that he had never been allowed toys, nor Gisèle dolls (Rousseau had, of course, once more pointed the way: a piece of wood would do, it would stimulate a child's imagination, an argument employed, without much success, by Soboul, in his role as parent, when confronted, in the matter of expensive and well-dressed dolls, by his seven-year-old daughter, Lucie, for whom a piece of wood just would *not* do. Soboul had certainly managed to suck in quite a few of the Aunt's Lessons, especially when they could be applied to someone else, whether his wife or his daughter), but I do not have the impression that they had felt any strong sense of deprivation, or that they had envied other children for what they themselves had not been allowed to have.

The constant homilies must have been pretty burdensome but the likelihood is that they went in by one ear and came out by the other, at least as far as Soboul was concerned, for, later in life, his sister seems to have modelled herself on her rather redoubtable foster-mother, even to the extent of echoing her careful and very precise manner of speech, as if conversation had taken the form of a *dictée*, and its subject-matter, that of the *Dictionnaire des Idées Reçues*. Much of Mlle Soboul's stern puritanism seems to have rubbed off on her niece, certainly a more docile pupil than her brother. When I knew Soboul during his fairly brief period of marriage—I was one of his witnesses at the *mairie* of the XIVème *arrondissement* on that very inauspicious occasion—I used to marvel at his capacity totally to switch off when his wife, a remarkably humourless and exceedingly fanatical Romanian, a worthy compatriot of Anna Pauker, to whom he referred, in such moments, in her presence, as *Le Gouvernement* (*Le Gouvernement est de bien mauvais poil aujourd'hui*, he would observe amiably for the benefit of their lunch guests, as if the object of the remark had either been absent or was some sort of abstraction, with the result that, throughout the ensuing meal, his wife would maintain a heavy silence that could be *felt*, like a menacing presence, right across the room) was in one of her frequent nagging moods, moods that she tended to reserve for such occasions, as if she had needed the presence of witnesses to the infelicity of matrimony.

Yes, certainly, his aunt was a pedant and a pedagogue, she could be immensely boring, but she was also warm, affectionate, and, in certain matters, unexpectedly indulgent. She did not even seem to mind all that much about all those girls. What she *did* mind was that Albert seemed incapable of ever fixing on *one*. She certainly did not approve of his marriage to a Romanian Jewess; and Gisèle was equally disapproving. International communism apparently would not stretch that far, although Nuşa—for that was the name of the unwelcome interloper—was herself a militant communist of the fiercest and most intolerant kind—I can recall one occasion when she turned on her husband, accusing him of being only a lukewarm Party member and of having failed in the primary duty of vigilance, because he had not denounced to the appropriate authorities various Romanian intellectuals who had confided in him because he was French and had expressed reserves on the subject of the régime, on the occasion of one of his regular visits to Bucarest; and he had defended himself by arguing that he was not prepared to publicize what had been said to him in private: certainly a very non-Communist morality—and was quite as humourless as Mlle Soboul (she had written her medical thesis on the subject of *les gauchers non-contrariés*, using myself as a model for her wonderfully ponderous investigation; it appeared that I had shown *all* the ideal symptoms of that happy state, including an ability to draw), with whom she shared a taste for primitive forms of pedagoguery. In matters of direct concern to the family, his aunt, and her pupil, Gisèle, appeared to reject internationalism. I think that they would have liked Albert to have married a local girl, perhaps one of the former pupils of the Nîmes *Ecole Normale*. So their commitment to World Revolution managed to co-exist quite happily with a comfortable provincialism. Nuşa indeed never gained full acceptance from any of the extensive Soboul clan, who, whatever their faults, did not count among them the Romanian girl's single-minded joylessness. In short, the Aunt could be tiresome and was generally rather boring; but she was anything but a monster. According to her own very demanding lights, she had done very well by her niece and her nephew, and they were duly and quite genuinely grateful. They were well-brought-up children.

There would be little more to say about a woman who could best be described as the female version of Monsieur Prudhomme and whose company was always stiflingly boring—fortunately I was never exposed to more than an evening of it at a time, coming away feeling desperately in need of frivolity and flippancy; and I think even Soboul found it a bit of a strain being on his best behaviour throughout the evening, for I noticed that the aftermath of one of her visits to *la Babylone Moderne* would always be marked by the rendering, in his loudest and most vigorous voice, of one or other of his favourite songs: *la Pompe à Merde*, or *l'Infanterie de Marine*, neither at all suited to the hearing of Mlle Soboul, as if to exorcize her recent cleansing presence—were it not for the fact that she was much the most important and lasting single influence in the life of my friend. Indeed, her influence on him survived her at least twenty years. *La Tante* was constantly evoked, in such openings, again reminiscent of *Les Grandes Verités* of her original masculine model, as *La Tante prétend que . . ., La Tante a toujours cru que . . ., La Tante n'aurait pas approuvé . . .*, in his conversation with myself, in a mixture of deference and mild humour. He would readily acknowledge that she had her blind spots, her foibles, that she believed home-made jam was much better than anything that you could buy in shops, though he had found that *her* home-made jam was always so bitter as to be almost uneatable (but he would loyally go through the agonies of eating it); and he evoked, with horror, a period, fortunately brief, in which she had attempted to make her own *wine*, in order to economize, but this had soon been abandoned, as much in her own interest as in that of the young people (wine was a *necessity*, not a luxury, and she was not willing to deny herself a bottle of Tavel, taken of course in moderation); but these very foibles would make her all the more appealing. Of course he wanted to look up to her, made it something of a duty to do so, as if to convince himself; but he was also well aware that never for a moment could she forget the call of duty and abandon her role as a perpetual round-the-clock Headmistress (even sleep must have been instructive). And she went on being a Headmistress, especially in her relationship to her two wards, long after she had retired and gone up the hill to her quiet villa. To her Soboul owed two things that were to be very important to him throughout adult life: his commitment to the French Communist Party, a commitment based on fidelity to *La Tante* rather than on any clear understanding of the Iron Laws of Marxism—I don't think he was ever a true Marxist, if only because he had not read the works of the Master; he was much more of a neo-Jacobin nationalist, and was indeed denounced as such by some Party ideological stalwarts in the last years of Stalinism—and his intense attachment to the hierarchical values of the French state educational system. A Headship was something to be accorded respect. So, by the same token, was a Chair, and none more so than that of the History of the French Revolution at the old Sorbonne. Late in life, Soboul even came to regard himself as a sort of official roving Ambassador of the French Revolution, carrying the sacred flame —it was always the same one and did not need to be relit—to Latin America, North America, Australia and New Zealand, China, Japan, the Soviet Union, the Popular Democracies, the countries of the West, including Eire, Wales, and Scotland. Indeed, I do not know where he did *not* carry the precious torch; but he may have omitted the Republic of South Africa.

He often told me, long after his aunt had died, that he could never contemplate leaving the Party, for to do so would have been a betrayal of *La Tante*. He also felt that to leave the Party would have been to let down *les copains*, young southerners like himself, men and girls from the Gard, the Ardèche, the Aveyron, the Cantal, the Bouches-du-Rhône, the Creuse, who, because they were second-raters, looked up to Marius, hung on his every word, who always deferred to his judgement and who, in consequence, were not very good for him, his quite devoted friends —how well I got to know them a decade or so later, and how deadly earnest and boring I found them!—from Deutsche-de-la Meurthe days at the *Cité* in the second half of the Thirties (Soboul's binding sense of fidelity was as much generational as parental: it was also no doubt a fidelity to a certain image of *himself*, *le beau Marius*, of the velvet caress and southern good looks, of his utterly self-confident mid-twenties; Soboul was a romantic, and the first in a line of his romantic heroes was the young man from Tizi-Ouzou and Nîmes; there was something quite refreshingly juvenile about his conceit, and I think it is significant that the very first book that he published, under a pseudonym, in 1938, should have been a short study of Saint-Just). But it was the cult of his *aunt* that above all kept him on the somewhat shaky level of an uneven orthodoxy (for he was a rather undisciplined Party mem-

ber, he resented being told off, he was given to answering back
and to losing his temper, in the knowledge that he could get away
with a good deal more than would be allowed the more humble
faithful, if only because he was the *only* decent historian that they
had) and prevented him from ever thinking of leaving the Party.
There was something touching and even admirable about such
tenacious loyalty. To me it seemed a better reason for being a
Communist, and remaining so, than most; and I used to tell him
so. He had little time for those who failed to stay the course,
especially those younger than himself. He wrote them off as
ambitious young *arrivistes*, and I think he found it easy to dismiss
them in such terms, especially when, previously, they had denounced *him* as entertaining unorthodox opinions about the
significance of the French Revolution. There was something
old-fashioned, and perhaps very southern, in his touchy sense of
honour.

Of course there were other reasons too. The Party people
—especially those abroad—made a great fuss of him, flattered
him, helped boost his sales in a score or more of languages,
including Japanese and Polish, Czech and Slovak, Romanian,
and Serbo-Croat (all the translations were lined up in neat rows
on the bookshelves of his study, itself a small museum of revolu-
tionalia, contemporary prints of Robespierre and Saint-Just and
of a standard *sans-culotte* smoking a clay pipe and holding a long
pike—the sign of office—and, like a museum, kept immaculately
clean, the parquet floor freshly waxed and polished, though,
unlike his aunt's flat in Nîmes, covered in brightly-coloured
Algerian and Romanian rugs, every article in its place, rows of
pencils on the desk; it was a museum in more senses than one, for
he had clearly long ceased to do any serious writing in it, merely
working over the same book again and again—the bookshelves
as a sort of invisible, but felt international presence in his back,
when he was seated at his desk, in an *attitude* of writing, or as if
about to do so, 119, rue Notre-Dame-des-Champs). They entertained and fêted him, and assured him an eager and admiring
international audience, in fact always the *same* audience, though
in different places and speaking different languages. Soboul
liked, and deserved, applause, because he was a first-class per-
former with a very good delivery; but the Party people supplied

him with a *claque*, as well as with an enlarging mirror to reflect his world-wide reputation as he moved from country to country, giving the same lecture (it was generally Robespierre and the Popular Movement). Historical orthodoxy could purchase easy fame. And fidelity brought its own material and no doubt physical rewards. (Soboul did not like being alone, either as a historian, or in bed; as a historian, he was assured of a tame readership, a responsive audience, and the company of the faithful and the like-minded; and I noticed that, in later years, East German girls, no doubt more disciplined Party members than most, succeeded one another, in the wake of the previous French occupants of his bed.) But I don't think any of this had very much to do with it. It was just that he could not contemplate letting down his aunt. There was something religious about his attachment to the carefully cultivated pure memory of his Aunt, by now herself transformed into a sort of Ancestral Monument in southern basalt. And it was *La Tante* who, long beyond the grave, could be said to have had the last word. Soboul died, for once alone, in her villa (left to his sister, his brother-in-law and their children, and to himself) among her pale water-colours and fading nick-knacks, in Nîmes, in mid-September, 1982. And he died in the Party. His body was given a splendid send-off in Paris, with speeches from all the Party high-ups, and massive wreaths of red roses, his daughter Lucie heading the procession behind the coffin carrying a single red rose. But if, as I suppose he did, he had left instructions that he be brought back and buried at La Croisette, it would have been to be near what remained of *La Tante*. He was never going to allow himself to forget all that he owed her, and a great deal more, too. And this would be a sort of extra, posthumous testimonial to that unexciting but undoubtedly worthy lady.

It is time, more than time, to leave the wearisome company of Mlle Soboul and the guiding strings that attached Albert to her physical and moral presence and to her revered, unsullied memory, in order to follow the adolescent's and the young man's more than conventional climb up the steep and laborious French educational ladder. For his career was almost entirely predictable, it could have written itself in advance, and it contained

nothing remotely unusual. It was indeed a copy-book career of
steady educational achievement: *lycée de Nîmes,* boarder at *lycée
Louis-le-Grand, hipokhagne, bachot, Cité Universitaire, Sorbonne, li-
cence, agrégation d'histoire,* something indeed so exemplary that it
could have come out of a primer: How to Succeed in Life by
Working Hard. (Soboul, in all matters concerning education and
educational values, was strikingly conventional, displaying an
orthodoxy even more impeccable than in politics. Having been
appointed in the spring of 1948 to an assistantship in French at the
University of Glasgow, and having signed a contract, when the
time came for me to leave Paris in October of that year, I simply
could not bear to do so. October was my favourite month, the
oysters were out in their baskets, there was all the excitement and
promise of *la Rentrée.* So I simply stayed put, without informing
the University of my intentions; they would soon find out about
these when I failed to turn up. When I told him, quite casually,
about my decision, he was horrified, as if I had done something
indecent. Such conduct, he claimed, would ruin my prospects of
a University career, one just did not *do* that sort of thing. It
seemed no use arguing with him about the impossibility of
leaving Paris in October.) One can imagine the reports proudly
sent back to the Aunt, as each successive hurdle was triumphantly negotiated. He had made all the right moves at the right
time; and there were only one or two minor setbacks; he did not
make the rue d'Ulm. This must have rankled, for, from the time
when I first met him, at the beginning of 1947, till the end of his
life, he professed an abiding dislike of *normaliens;* they were, he
claimed, élitist and exclusive, they formed an educational *mafia*
designed to look after one another's careers. All this was undoubtedly true. But *agrégés* too were élitist and exclusive, and so
was Soboul among the *agrégés.* I was to note that he did not seem
to have any *normaliens* among his very wide circle of friends and
admirers. Yet there were a number of them in the Party. I think he
must have avoided them deliberately, perhaps for the same
reason that he tolerated, even encouraged, the company of a
great many ponderous bores, of both sexes, because they had
always looked up to him ever since *Cité* days and deferred to his
superior judgement in all things. One had, of course, to be true to
les copains; but it must have helped if *les copains* were not very

clever. They seemed to me to be uniformly mediocre and dull. He certainly liked to sit at the top of his personal pyramid. So *normaliens* could not be readily accommodated. None was ever seen either at the rue de Gergovie or at the rue Notre-Dame-des-Champs. It was different with foreigners, especially if they were readers of, or contributors to, the *Annales historiques de la Revolution française*—and he had any number of foreign friends—but they were not engaged in the French educational Grand National, so they were not competitors. Indeed, throughout the period I was living in Paris, his main criticism of myself was that I was not competitive *enough*, that I was not getting on with my career, but was indulging myself by dawdling through the boxes and bundles of French national and provincial archives out of sheer enjoyment. That, he would point out, in a friendly, but stern, manner, was *not* the way forward. But *some* foreigners, like *all normaliens*, would not do.

Later in life, in fact, once he had completed his *doctorat-ès-lettres* at the relatively early age of forty-two, and had been appointed to a University chair, first in Clermont-Ferrand, then, the crowning of his career, in Paris, he would always display a similar and openly expressed hostility to the institution that more and more was becoming the principal rival to the old, traditional *Université: l'Ecole pratique des Hautes Etudes*, and, more especially, to its redoubtable *Sixième Section*. There was no bitterer opponent of what he always referred to as *la chapelle braudélienne*; and he had no time at all for those—both French and foreign (Italians mostly)—who worshipped in that exclusive temple. His criticisms were entirely justified: a great deal of money, both French and foreign, was being diverted in the direction of an institution that was parallel to the normal University structure. I fully shared Soboul's personal dislike of the *mafiosi*; they were a uniformly unpleasant lot. There was something quite sickening about the sycophancy of Braudel's Renaissance Court. And his indignation was altogether genuine. He had climbed up the official way, and it had been a hard climb; but now a great many people younger than himself were getting up by the backstairs. Many of them —French and foreign—had managed to insinuate themselves in research institutions, without ever having been through the normal teaching mill. Others were being admitted into University

teaching without having completed their State Doctorates. He
had been over that steepest hurdle of all. Let others do the same.
But some were managing to avoid it altogether. I sometimes
thought that it might have been different if, at an earlier stage, he
had been admitted into the Braudelian Presence. Still, he was
quite right to be indignant.

I have jumped ahead of my narrative. At some time in the
mid-Thirties, Soboul did his military service in the artillery (*l'artil-
lerie hippomobile*, with a mocking emphasis on the adjective, which
does indeed have a comical sound about it, so that one would not
like to think of the existence of any artillery that was *not hippomobile*). He liked too to recall the parrot-like delivery of a *sergent-
chef* as he conducted a lesson in weapon-training and maintenance
and who was in the habit of accompanying each component of a
rifle or a machine-gun, as it was lifted up and displayed, with the
expression *ad hoc*, pronounced, and perhaps in his own mind,
identified—as *haddock*. I think it must have been during his time
in the Army that he had acquired his marked taste for the sort of
chansons de garde on the model of *l'Infanterie de Marine* with which
he would enliven the late evening company in his flat in the
presence of many opened bottles. He trained in a southern
regiment. He was called up again in September 1939; but his
service during the 'phoney war' seems to have been quite un-
eventful. His regiment—horses and all—ended up, at the time of
l'Exode, somewhere well down in the South-West, where it was
dissolved, or dissolved itself.

On his discharge, he was appointed to a teaching post in
History in one of the *lycées* in Montpellier. But he was summarily
dismissed from this late in 1940 or some time in 1941, by one of the
Vichy Ministers of Education, as part of the systematic purge of
teachers and other civil servants who were known Communists
or Freemasons. His name was presumably on a list supplied by
the *sûreté*, or he may have been denounced by a neighbour or a
colleague. I know little about his life during the next three or four
years, and what little I do know did not come from Soboul
himself, who seldom talked, at least to me, about his time in
Montpellier, as if he had not wanted to evoke a period that cannot
have been a very happy one, but from one of his many female
admirers, Suzon, the daughter of a railwayman of Polish origin,

but who had been naturalized, from the small railway town of Saint-Germain-des-Fossés, who was in Montpellier for much of these difficult and presumably dangerous years. Suzon may not have been a very reliable witness, for she nursed an abiding dislike for Nuşa, the Romanian girl friend, for whom, as a Jewess and the holder of a Romanian passport, these years must indeed have been extremely dangerous. Nuşa's rival—Nuşa had in fact replaced her, at some recent stage, in Soboul's affections—would later argue, in her rather bitter account laid on for my benefit, as if to fill me in on this, to me, unknown period of contemporary French history, that the very presence of Nuşa, especially after the occupation of the southern zone, had greatly endangered Soboul himself, as well as the local Communists or sympathizers whom the two frequented. This seemed to be rather unfair, for where was the poor girl to go? To have returned to Paris would have meant for her the certainty of Drancy and deportation. Had she returned to Romania, her fate would have been much the same. I could not help thinking that it was greatly to Soboul's credit to have stood by her during this difficult time. It may well have been the case, however, that the presence of Mlle Friedman, if not at his side, then at least in close proximity, may have greatly added to Soboul's already considerable difficulties as a *révoqué*, deprived of a salary and whose name had been on a number of Vichy lists of Party militants. But what seems certain is that the local Party network—a powerful, close-knit and effective one, especially in conditions of clandestinity—must have had a hand in looking after the two of them, providing them with a string of safe addresses, and warning them of impending moves against them. They were both given false papers and plausible new identities, though little could be done to remedy Nuşa's accent in French—it must be said that it was not *quite* so bad as the uncharitable Suzon (who had been educated entirely in France) would have it—save to warn her to keep her mouth shut in the presence of strangers, and this would not have been difficult, silence always being one of her most effective weapons, especially when in company.

Soboul himself, on the rare occasions when he talked to me about these years, often referred to the semi-complicity of a *commissaire de police*, who, whether out of ideological motivations (and this seems very unlikely in prevailing conditions, when the police, like all branches of the civil service, were being subjected to a series of purges), or simply because he was a decent chap, was in the habit of telling him if he or his girl friend had been spotted, and advising them to lose no time in moving on. On three occasions, the flats that they had just vacated were raided by the much-feared *Police aux Questions Juives* (PQJ), only a few hours after they had responded to the urgent tip-off from the friendly *commissaire* (who, because he was in the ordinary police, may have taken a certain satisfaction in thus putting a spoke in the wheel of the much pampered PQJ). I am pretty sure that neither of them ever went very far out of the town throughout the Occupation. Nor was either ever directly involved in any positive act of Resistance or clandestine activity. They seem to have kept their heads well down, in an altogether understandable effort to survive. And for Nuşa it had been very much a matter of just that.

The Liberation in Montpellier was particularly violent. But Soboul does not seem to have taken any part in *l'épuration*, which, in this south-western town, claimed a record number of victims, at least in proportion to the size of the population. Violent and immoderate in speech when angry—he was always very much *soupe au lait*—he was not a naturally violent man, being much too forgiving and indulgent ever to have made a good revolutionary. And, like a great many French Communists, he was a great believer in discipline and order, hating anarchy, whether public or private, though he could be remarkably tolerant of the anarchical tendencies displayed by my own manner of life in Paris. I think he was even a bit envious of the considerable measure of freedom that I allowed myself, though he approved of my decision to 'do the right thing' by my French girlfriend, when I decided to marry her. I think that in my very much indulged capacity as *le vieux frère, l'ami Ricardo*, I may have offered him a tempting, if elusive, and altogether resistable image of total irresponsibility, of living for the day, something that he had to deny himself. My manner of life was a constant subject of disapproval on the part of *les copains*, who saw in me the personification of anarchy and criminal *manque de sérieux*. I laughed much too much, and I laughed about things that were not to be laughed about. Some went even further, taking Soboul aside and warning him that I must be a paid-up agent of *l'Intelligence Service*. What was I doing all these years hanging about in Paris? Research was nothing but a cover. Soboul's comment on this was that, if I were indeed a full-time agent of the IS, they must have paid their agents very little. On all such occasions, he would always stand up for me; sometimes, when they were being particularly critical, he would give me one of his wonderfully eloquent winks. (I have never known anyone who could wink with such emphasis.) Anyhow, such was the measure of his influence over these dull and plodding people, that, whatever their misgivings about me, they went on tolerating me and even feeding me, however reluctantly. Soboul was his own hard task-master; but he did have dreams of *évasion*. (They mostly took the corporeal form of shapely girls.) And *l'ami Ricardo* was certainly a change from the utterly predictable and sadly limited horizons of most of *les copains*, with their fenced-in minds and their fenced-in villas (a number of them actually lived in neat *pavillons de banlieue*, protected by large dogs and elaborate burglar alarms, in order to ensure *double* protection from the forces of anarchy coming from outside, in such places as Sucy-en-Brie, Montreuil-sous-Bois and Combes-la-Ville). However I am jumping far ahead of my narrative again; I have not even *met* Soboul yet, and so this is perhaps not yet the place further to enlarge on the complexities and the mutually recognized frontiers of our always affectionate relationship as it developed over the years. It is time to return to the fairly predictable course of his career after the Liberation.

Soon after that event, he left Montpellier for Paris, to resume research in the *Archives Nationales* and to take up a teaching post in one of the most fashionable *lycées* of the capital, that of Janson-de-Sailly, rue de la Pompe, in the XVIème *arrondissement*. It was a prestigious, if not entirely appropriate appointment that must have represented a well-merited compensation for the years spent in the educational desert during his *révocation*. (He would, of course, also be entitled to financial compensation to cover the loss of salary.) Certainly, after the way in which he had been treated, he had more than earned the longed-for posting to Paris. But Henri IV or Louis-le-Grand would have seemed a more suitable choice, for Janson drew on probably the most right-wing, and certainly the wealthiest, elements of the schoolboy population of Paris. Soboul was to teach there for a little over ten years; and it is without question a striking tribute to his ability as a teacher that he was able to hold the interest of classes mostly composed of boys from the most reactionary backgrounds and whose parents would not have regarded the French Revolution, as Soboul regarded it, as a sort of National Monument. My friend, who never made any attempt to disguise his political views—that would have been most unlike him—was entirely successful in maintaining discipline in class. He also seems to have earned the respect, even the affection, of his pupils, though I very much doubt if he managed to secure the conversion of more than a very few of them.

On his return to Paris, Soboul managed to find himself a small flat, on a short lease, on the seventh floor of one of those very tall houses that used to characterize the XXème *arrondissement*, almost at the top of the steep rue de Ménilmontant. The flat, which was very light, seemed to hang in space. There were only three rooms, two of which overlooked, within touching distance from the little balconies, the very top of a gigantic plane tree that gave to the flat an agreeable feeling of provincial calm which contrasted with the noise of the climbing street and of the constantly changing gears of the green buses as they struggled their way up to the top. It was always a surprise to emerge from the long, dark climb of the staircase, to come out on to the brilliant greenish luminosity of the two little rooms, the white ceilings of which seemed to ripple and move gently to the shadows thrown by the broad leaves as they swayed gently in the light breeze. After so many moves, Soboul must have been pleased to have at last come down to rest in a place that seemed to be of his own. But there were difficulties over his tenure. The flat had been in the possession of a Jewish couple at the outbreak of the war, so it had been expropriated following the introduction by Vichy of its anti-Jewish legislation. The original owners, who had managed to leave France, were now proposing to return and were seeking to reassert possession. When I first met Soboul at the beginning of 1947, he was still managing, as a result of a series of delaying actions, to hold on to the place; but his days there were numbered, and soon after he was made the object of an expulsion order delivered to him by the *gendarmerie*. Of the three flats in which he was to live, from 1944-5 up to the time of his death, the two rooms perched high above the huge gulf of the courtyard in Ménilmontant were much the nicest.

Soboul had come up to Paris on his own. He was soon followed there—but I don't think at his suggestion or invitation—by Nuşa, who could now come out into the open street, lead a more normal life, and resume the medical studies that she had had to interrupt in 1940, though, as a foreigner, she would still not be able to put up her plate, even when once qualified. She did not follow him directly to Ménilmontant, she was far too prudent for that, far too skilled in the arts of hanging on and biding her time; there was always something crablike about her movements, which were never made in a single, bold jump. On this occasion, she took a room in the flat of a medical colleague who lived in Le Perreux, not in Paris itself, but near enough to enable her to keep a discreet eye on Soboul and on his current domestic arrangements as transmitted to her by the more loyal of *les copains*, well trained in this sort of surveillance. For some time there was no indication from that suburban observatory of what might be the next move in what looked like a long waiting game of attrition. The silence, as it was designed to do, must have seemed a bit ominous. Or Soboul may even have been led to think that he was at last out in the clear following his long stint in Montpellier. Then a single suitcase, rather forlorn, had made an unannounced appearance on the landing where Soboul had discovered it one evening, on returning from the Archives. This was only the opening shot. The suitcase had been followed by two others that arrived together after an interval of ten days. Then there was a pause of almost a month, enough to give Soboul fresh hope. Then, and then only, had come the more powerful stuff, the heavy artillery: a tin trunk bearing the labels of Bucharest hotels, a huge leather hold-all, six wooden cases of thick medical books, a box containing the heavy Friedman family silver, a complete dinner service, delivered by a van.

Gradually, inexorably—and it was the calculated slowness of the operation that was so frightening—Soboul's little bedroom was being crowded out, the bed itself only reachable over a mountain of silently reproachful luggage—and Nuşa, who came from a wealthy upper-middle class family from Bucharest, had a

77

great deal of it—the presence of which was designed to address itself in no uncertain terms: 'Get out, get out, while there is still time, do not tarry, on your way!' to anyone who shared with Soboul the besieged piece of furniture. In my experience over a period of more than ten years, Nuşa had gradually perfected the technique thus of following on as a rearguard, having sent her voluminous luggage ahead of her as a sort of silent and vaguely menacing declaration of intent, designed as much to frighten whatever girl—and he would take them one at a time, there would be a Monday one, a Thursday one, and perhaps a week-ender—was sharing his bed. There would generally be an interval of three or four weeks between the arrival of the trunks, suitcases and packing cases, and that, travelling light, her hands free, of their owner. The strategy had first been worked out in the steady build-up to the final occupation of the Ménilmontant flat. The expulsion order had at least enabled Soboul to get away altogether for a period of six months, during which he stayed in the flat of the historian Edith Thomas, at that time still in the Party. Soboul, now safe from Nuşa, was soon exposed to a different sort of danger, for Edith had designs on him, and, in order to reach his own bedroom in her flat, which was near the *Ecole des Sourds-Muets*, he had to pass her door which, as soon as he came level with it, and even when he was holding his shoes in his hands in an effort to creep past the danger spot undetected, would invariably open, in silent invitation, from the inside. On one occasion, he felt so embattled by this silent siege that he asked me to share his bed. We went past the perilous door together. It still opened. He went through a difficult six months before eventually finding a flat of his own, rue de Gergovie, in the XIVème.

The two of us inaugurated the new flat together. It seemed a case for celebration, for Soboul had managed to repulse the insistent advances of the ardent Edith, and Nuşa had gone off to one of her suburban observatories, surrounded by her luggage. Soboul was not even certain where the Romanian caravanserai had actually landed up; but he thought it was in one of the eastern suburbs: Nuşa, for some reason, favoured that side of Paris. So we had a little supper party on a Tuesday night; and, subsequently, I would go there every Tuesday, to eat horse steak (*hippophage* seemed to belong to the same category of verbal badinage as *hippomobile*, and there was a horse butcher, his shop bearing seven golden horses' heads, right next-door) and chips, cooked by my friend (Soboul was an excellent cook). Tuesday was one of his nights off from girls. The move had cheered him up considerably, and, on this and subsequent occasions, there would be regular Tuesday night renderings of *L'Infanterie de Marine*, the battle hymn of Liberty Recovered, celebrated in the company of *l'ami Ricardo*. It really did look this time as if he had indeed at last got clear away. Then, one Tuesday, after about two months—it was spring, I remember, always a time of danger, like the advent of the campaigning season, for the caravanserai was liable to be on the move once more about then—as soon as I had come through the door, I remember commenting on the changed appearance of the spare room to the left, thus converted, in between two visits—and I think Nuşa must have known about my Tuesdays: she would have been tickled, in her rather perverse way, at the thought of confronting an extra witness—into a left luggage office. There seemed to be more of it than ever, it was piled up almost to the ceiling, completely blocking the long window. I did not need to ask: whose luggage? Besides, there was a certain amount of medical equipment, including a thing with a rubber horn on its end used for taking blood pressure which lay prominently on the top of one of the piles, as if asserting its right to be there. My friend pulled one of his inimitable faces—something only southern Frenchmen and Italians are able to do with full dramatic effect—raising his eyes and revealing their whites, in an eloquent expression of agony, even crucifixion—when I had commented on the changed appearance of the room. Better make the most of it, *mon pauvre Ricardo*, the days of liberty are numbered. Soboul was a fatalist, Nuşa was something that would recur, like summer asthma, there was nothing one could do about it, there was no prevention and no cure. Perhaps he did not even *want* to be cured? Anyhow, to celebrate what looked like being our last Tuesday evening *en garçons*, there was an unusually spirited rendering of *L'Infanterie de Marine*, with *la Pompe à Merde* thrown in as a bonus. The *concierge* came up at about midnight to complain about the noise. And, sure enough, the Tuesday following, Nuşa herself was there, having at last followed up her luggage. She sat in silence, looking at me in an amusedly quizzical way, as if challenging me to take in the full measure of her triumph. I could not help thinking that, with all the gear now tidily in place, it would not be very easy to get her out again. She seemed to be able to give a new, even *more* threatening, meaning to the word, so recently in everyday use, 'occupation'. There was something massive about it, though she herself was quite slight. Of course Soboul retained his Monday girl and his Thursday girl; it must have been much more complicated with the weekend girl. But he had to see them somewhere else. As far as I was concerned, Tuesday had lost the savour of a shared, if unspoken complicity. My friend had always needed an independent witness to his amorous exploits; and I had been assigned that role from some time back in the late Forties. I don't know why I had been chosen for this rather questionable honour, it might have been because I had nothing to do with the Party, and that these were matters best concealed from the surrounding circle of zealots. Anyhow, he had always made a point of introducing me to the current mistress, generally at lunch somewhere near the *Archives*, before the two of them eagerly made off to an afternoon hotel somewhere in the Latin quarter. They were generally very attractive, and, not being able at the time even to afford offering a girl a cup of coffee, I envied my friend his apparently endless good fortune, though I sometimes wondered why he could not stick to a single relationship. Now, on my Tuesday visits, I had to make do with an elaborately coded language of winks and glances, a form of communication in which, as I have said, Soboul excelled. His favourite stance would be to take up a standing position behind Nuşa and send out his messages from behind her back. He always seemed particularly keen that they should be intercepted, which would have been easy enough, Nuşa had only to study *my* face, as it registered each emphatic and repeated phrase of Soboul's wonderful clowning.

They were still living in the rue de Gergovie when, on one of my Tuesday visits—Nuşa was absent on this occasion on some psychiatric congress—Soboul suddenly asked me if I would be his witness on the following Saturday morning. He suggested that we meet outside the *mairie* of the XIVème *arrondissement* at eleven o'clock; his brother-in-law, who was sure to be late, had agreed to be the other witness. He was vaguely apologetic about the whole business, pointing out that it was a purely administrative step that he was about to take, in order to enable Nuşa to obtain French naturalization. She had apparently managed to persuade him that she was in imminent danger of being expelled from France and sent back to Romania; and this may well have been the case, as the French authorities in the early Fifties were expelling large numbers of citizens from the Iron Curtain countries. It seemed likely that, as a known Communist, her name would have been on one of the current Ministry of the Interior lists of persons destined for what was euphemistically described, in administrative language, as *refoulement*. Actually, I could not see why, as an ardent Communist, she should not have welcomed the opportunity to return to Romania—it is true that her parents, her uncles and aunts had all been liquidated in the death camps; but she still had a brother who, favoured by the regime, occupied an important teaching post in the University of Bucharest. However, I did not make any comment on his sudden and entirely unexpected decision, merely concluding that, despite everything, Nuşa had probably meant more to him than he was prepared to admit, even to himself, and that he could not bear the prospect of her definitive departure (he admitted as much to me a few years later, when he was trying to make up his mind what to do about Marie-Louise, a very attractive Corsican girl who was deeply in love with him and who remained so for the best part of ten years). I said that I would be outside the huge *mairie* at eleven on the Saturday. And, on the day, getting there a little early, I bought a small bunch of spring flowers from one of the florists facing the little park opposite the elaborate building; and when first Soboul, then Nuşa turned up separately, and from different directions, I gave the bunch to her. It seemed the right thing to have done, it was after all an occasion. She was both surprised and, I think, rather touched, for years afterwards she would remind me, with one of her sad smiles, and looking at me through her glasses with her rather fishy grey eyes, of the little bunch. It had, she would comment, been a *thought*, adding that *others* had not even had a *thought*. Soboul, responding at once to his cue, would raise his eyes in mock agony. Soboul's brother-in-law turned up a quarter of an hour late, out of breath, his bearded face redder than ever, and flowerless. Soboul and Nuşa were then married by the *adjoint* of the *maire*. I think the four of us had a few drinks on a café terrace. Then each went his or her different way. Shortly after this, Dr Irène Soboul put up her plate in one of the eastern districts of Paris: *ancien interne des hôpitaux de Paris*, it said, in gold letters on a black background.

After a few years, Soboul left the rue de Gergovie for a much larger flat in the rue Notre-Dame-des-Champs, within easy walking distance of the old Sorbonne. During the move, and for some weeks after it, Nuşa once more went east, her luggage following her. Both were soon back, the familiar and much battered luggage now augmented by a number of brightly coloured Romanian rugs and Carpathian dolls in national costume. Now that she had a French passport, she could make regular trips to Bucharest. Soon a whole room was given over to all sorts of articles of Romanian folklore: table mats, table cloths embroidered in bright floral designs, plates, jugs, coffee trays, china horses. I suppose they were genuine, though they did not *smell*, Nuşa would not have tolerated anything that smelt, she was as strict on hygiene, as on tidiness, diet, and the Party Line. Perhaps she had had these Balkanic nick-knacks cleaned up and rendered *inodore* through some process in a medical or pharmaceutical laboratory. The room, with even the heavily embroidered cushions each in its assigned place on various low couches and coloured leather *poufs*, soon took on the aspect of a small museum of Popular Democratic Culture. Soboul avoided the room as much as possible, working, and receiving his visitors, in the room next-door, his study (which was also a museum) and which lead to his bedroom. Later the Romanian Room would provide the usual terrain for his more barbed comments, accompanied by eye-rolling, on the current moods of *le Gouvernement*. It did not seem a room much lived in, it seemed to be rather frigid and unloved; and the walls, the shelves, the floor, the cushions, the glass corner-cupboards, and the heavy round brass trays standing on their little wooden legs all seemed to be proclaiming something, I am not sure what, but whatever it was, it was unwelcoming, chilly, and orthodox.

The Romanian room remained untouched, immobilized, and regularly dusted and waxed, long after Nuşa and all her luggage had abandoned the terrain, setting up, first in Montreal, then in a tower block in Maine-Montparnasse. For, in the end, it was Nuşa who moved out, leaving Soboul in sole occupation. I even think that at times he may have missed *le Gouvernement*, her unnerving silences, her sustained sulks, and her acid or mocking references to *les sans-culottes*, the inhabitants and cherished toys of the rival museum in the room beyond (Nuşa expressed no interest whatever in these worthy people, and she regarded historical research as a monumental waste of time). Of course, for a long time, they had lived mentally poles apart; even the Party would not provide them with a shared terrain, for Soboul tended to be lazy about his orthodoxy, over-indulgent about heresy, and unwilling to devote any of his leisure to promoting the collective activities of the faithful, he certainly had never been seen selling *l'Huma-Dimanche*; and these frailties would arouse in her an increase in fanaticism and vigilance. They had always worked apart, Nuşa in a series of *cabinets*, as well as in Ville-Evrard and other psychiatric hospitals, Soboul in the *Archives*, and above all, in the Institute of the History of the French Revolution in the old Sorbonne. They had ceased ever taking holidays together, the breaking-point had come through Nuşa's insistence on encumbering the two of them with local nick-knacks, Greek or Moroccan, Italian or Portuguese, as well as Romanian. The only thing that they had produced between them, and that seems to have been something of an accident, was a daughter, Lucie. But Lucie, far from bringing them closer together, seems to have accentuated the gulf between them. Her upbringing and education were the subject of endless disputes, Soboul quoting the example of Rousseau and *La Tante*, and accusing his wife of spoiling the child by giving her expensive toys and pretty dresses and indulging in her an unhealthy attachment to material objects (Soboul himself liked his little luxuries and tended to be fussy about the standard of hotel rooms; I suppose he had every reason to be, for he must have spent almost an eighth of his life in these chillily anonymous sleeping places). He complained that she was bringing up the child to respect bourgeois standards. Nuşa, on her side, used Lucie as a further weapon in her armoury; in the end, she took her off with her to Montreal, where the two of them remained for three years. When Lucie was twelve or thirteen, she brought her back to Paris and established her in the no doubt immaculate flat in the awful tower block. The little girl, then the adolescent would come and have lunch with her father, accompanied by a cook, once a week, on Thursdays, then still the school half-holiday. Soboul petted her, showed her off admiringly to his other guests; but there was a formality about these occasions, one had the impression that they were both glad of the company, and that they would not have had very much to say to one another if they had been left just the two of them; but there was always someone else. I don't think Lucie ever became a Party member, though she was—and is—regularly seen at *les manifs*. I don't know what she made of all the girlfriends—some of the later ones no older than herself—but she must have known about them. I think in later years father and daughter became much closer. She now lives in the flat at no. 119. I don't know what she has done to the Romanian Room, but I am prepared to bet that there is not an object out of place in her father's study.

I had abandoned Soboul somewhere between Janson-de-Sailly and his first University appointment, already launched on research, but his research still uncompleted. His academic career had then followed a conventional and already rather old-fashioned pattern, not taking any short cuts and owing nothing to personal favour, following, on the contrary, a course of rigour that must have pleased *La Tante*. After nine or ten years' research, he had completed and sustained his doctoral thesis, taking rather less time than most in that arduous uphill climb from *secondaire* to the heights of *universitaire*. It had been a hard slog all the way. In 1957, he had been appointed to a chair in Clermont-Ferrand, staying there two nights a week in a hotel, and cramming all his teaching there into three days. (His conversion to Parisian attitudes had been remarkably complete.) In 1960, on the death of Georges Lefebvre, he had succeeded to the editorship of the *Annales historiques de la Révolution française*. Eight years later, on the retirement of Marcel Reinhard, he had been appointed to the Chair of the History of the French Revolution, a post that, with his almost religious reverence for the principle of heredity, he had long regarded as his *right*. Was he not the pupil of Lefebvre? He was indeed. But he tended to forget, on occasions, that there had been *others*, assigning to himself the role at least of favourite disciple and only authorized guardian of the tomb. Still, one should not be too hard on such touching and exemplary fidelity. I don't know what Lefebvre himself would have made of it, for he had always had his reservations about Soboul (and about all his other pupils, he was not in the habit of readily awarding prizes), and, being a man both austere and simple, he would not have much appreciated having become the object of what amounted to a posthumous cult of *le Vieux Maître*. Or he might have been amused by such an improbable turn of events, accompanying his amusement with his dry laugh. Soboul's appointment, however, was undoubtedly the right one, there was no one at the time better qualified; and the publication of his thesis on the *sans-culotte* movement was a major historical event. I would not say that, in his new post, he contributed in any way to the *renewal* of French revolutionary studies, it was rather the opposite, his general effect was somewhat to mummify them, as if *Notre Mère à Nous Tous* (she was certainly never *mine*) had been put in a glass case: *Ne pas se pencher sur le verre*. But it is not my intention to attempt to assess his value as a historian of the period of *La Grande Terreur*, nor his influence as the editor of a review and as the director—sometimes rather a prickly one, very prone to stand on his dignity—of a research institute. That has been done with devastating thoroughness and analytical skill in a long historio-graphical study, the work of Dr Geoffrey Ellis, published in *The English Historical Review* a little before Soboul's death. At least, dying when he did, in September 1982, he died in harness. I don't think he would have much enjoyed the prospect of retirement, even if it had been to the favourite retreat at Nîmes.

I have suggested that Soboul generally surrounded himself with mediocrities; and this was as true of the foreign Party comrades who used to be seen regularly, rue de Gergovie (not, mercifully, on Tuesday evenings, I think even Soboul felt the need occa-sionally to have time off from them), as of the French ones, including his irretrievably petit-bourgeois cousins, a pale fair couple who spent most winter evenings planning their summer holidays. There was a young Dutch blond giant, Joost, a sort of Communist Panurge, dutiful and quite strappingly stupid. A

Dane, Christian Jensen, was almost equally literal, but he greatly improved when drunk, which he would be most nights. I remember a sinister Czech called Jilek, a sanctimonious, creepy-crawly propagandist, who edited some Czech monthly in French translation, and who was suddenly recalled to Prague. He never returned to Paris. In 1947, the Ménilmontant flat was still the evening rendezvous of a crowd of rather jolly Yugoslavs who would get through vast quantities of red wine. But these all disappeared from the Soboul circuit when it was discovered that they were all paid-up agents of the *vipère lubrique,* the Party name for the now infamous Tito. By 1948, many of the French members of the entourage recalled having had misgivings about them from the start, there had been this or that had made them suspicious, blaming themselves for having been lacking in vigilance; it would not happen again (I, too, was pretty sure of that). But somehow one of the heretics, a fair girl from the Banat called Vera, got left behind, washed up on the beach, after the Yugoslav tide had receded. The poor thing became the object of whispered conversations and was, I believe, denounced anonymously to the police. She became extremely unhappy, confiding in me. What had she *done,* now that they all shunned her, when, only a few weeks earlier, she had been warmly welcomed everywhere. I told her that I did not think she had *done* anything, it was her nationality that was the matter, and there was nothing that she could do about that. She lingered on a few more wretched weeks, then disappeared. I was told that she had been expelled from France, and quite right too, as she had been a notorious Titoist agent. They were a boring lot, and when they were not boring, they were sinister. Jilek was both boring and sinister. Joost and Christian were merely stupid, and irredeemably good-natured.

But it would be an utterly misleading portrait of my friend were I to suggest that he never moved outside the Party circuit (I think most of the girls, Monday, Thursday, weekenders, were Party members, it must have helped them into bed). Within his own family circle, there was a self-avowed heretic who was openly and devastatingly cynical about politics. This was Gisèle's improbable husband, Jean-Charles Lallemant, a former student of the *Ecole des Beaux Arts* (*premier prix de sculpture*), and, indeed, a sculptor of an international reputation that went right round the

Mediterranean. He had, at one stage, worked with Picasso on a statue ordered by the municipality of Marseille; but the two had quarrelled over money. His nickname of *Bacchus* was perfectly suited to his very blue, forget-me-not eyes, his wide rubicund face, closely surrounded by a curling very blond beard, his enormous round head, and his thickset frame, *bas sur pattes*. *Bacchus* was a Champenois, an adopted child from a village somewhere near Troyes, a man of the north and who looked it. He was totally indifferent to politics. I remember him sitting, like a vast schoolboy (and he had a naughty schoolboy face), at one of the tiny desks in his wife's school in Le Grau-du-Roi, and, like a schoolboy, thoughtfully licking his dip-in pen, before writing, in a large sprawling hand and in violet ink, on squared maths paper. He spent the whole of a sunny afternoon writing to a score of *maires* of southern or south-central *communes*, reading sections of the letters out loud for my benefit, and asking me to check up on the spelling (which was rather erratic). 'This one', he would say, 'is MRP, so let's lay on the Catholic line.' 'This one is PCF, so we'll pull the Party stuff. Listen to this. Am I overdoing it?' 'Here is an SFIO, so we'd better make it strongly anti-Communist.' He was writing around to propose himself as the sculptor of the local *Monument de la Résistance* (it would have to be in capitals). It generally worked, he must have done thirty or forty of them all over the South of France, including the enormous *La Pyramide* in Nîmes, and massive bits of marble statuary in La Grande-Combe, Port-Vendres, Alès, Banyuls, and all over the place. He had chosen his terrain well, because the Resistance had been strong in this area, or it was discovered to have been strong retrospectively. If there were a *large* monument to the Resistance, there MUST have been Resistance; and *Bacchus* liked large monuments, he got paid for the kilos of marble that went into them. This was the line that *Bacchus* pulled with impudent cynicism. That afternoon, he looked innocence itself, as, laboriously, he wrote out letter after letter; if he had been wearing a black blouse with long sleeves over his stocky frame, the schoolboy image would have been complete. He did not care either about politics or about the Resistance (he was himself a man of extreme and commendable prudence who, in 1939, had deliberately got himself mobilized in a southern regiment because, as a Champenois, he believed a southern regiment would be more likely to run away, whereas his own people would probably stand and get themselves killed to the last man). All he wanted was contracts. He got plenty of these. Soboul would roll his eyes at his brother-in-law's more heretical asides, but I think he was vastly amused by them. Gisèle merely looked shocked. *Bacchus* was very good for both of them. And he was very good for me. He gave me the opportunity to take part in the wonderful anarchy of the annual *Bal des Quatz'Arts*, at the end of which I ended up nude, in the company of a dozen similarly unattired males and females, at 6 a.m., in the fountains of the Place de la Concorde; and he introduced me to one of his former models in his studio off the rue Losserand, *la Grande Hélène*, a big-limbed blonde girl who at the time was plying her trade on the pavement of the rue Sauvageot, and who, because I was a friend of *Bacchus*, gave me a special rate. I got rather fond of *la Grande Hélène*, who laughed a lot and had a marvellous sense of humour. Years later, at the level of the statue of Etienne Marcel, she came up to me, soberly dressed, and looking almost dowdy, but still very attractive. *Je ne fais plus le métier*, she explained, a priest (she was a Bretonne) had pointed out the errors of her ways, now she had become a night telephonist, commenting, with her young laugh: *après tout, je suis habitué au travail de nuit*. I burst out laughing too. We had a drink together on the terrace of a large café at the bottom of the rue des Archives. She was a wonderfully good-natured girl.

Bacchus was immensely energetic. He worked in marble for days on end in his workshop by the canal, just outside Aigues-Mortes, had an immense appetite, especially for fish, and would disappear, for weeks at a time, working in a monumental mason's yard at the other end of the coast. There were girls awaiting him in every place a monument was to go up. He was one of the freest people I have ever met, an embodiment of *la bohême*, of the old, wild, feckless life of the nineteenth-century *étudiant des Beaux Arts*. Yet he had his head screwed on the right way, was quite ruthless in bargaining, and made a great deal of money, which he spent like water. Soboul was devoted to him and to his niece and nephew, Françoise and Jean-Marie, the latter, an exact replica, in miniature, of his stocky, massive father. *Bacchus* had a large car, which he drove too fast. One day, returning from his workshop along the narrow causeway that ran beside the canal, he ran head on into a lorry coming from Le Grau, and was killed instantly. With his death, most of the laughter went out of the family. Soboul himself never fully recovered from the loss; and it was from this time that he became constantly preoccupied with the imminence and the finality of death. The ebullient presence of *Bacchus* had prevented Soboul and his rather melancholy sister from giving all their thoughts to the interests of the Party. There had always been a frivolous side to Albert-Marius, and this his brother-in-law had succeeded in bringing out. He had kept a tiny spark of total anarchy, impudence, and comedy alive in that stony and unfertile terrain. Soboul had been particularly glad that *Bacchus* and I should have got on so well together from the very moment we had first met, rue de Gergovie, when *Bacchus* was up for one of his regular visits to his former teacher at the *Beaux-Arts*. I think we were both excuses for him to take off time from the serious business of militancy. And *les copains*—always so censorious—one of them, now very highly placed in the hierarchy of the PCF, even took me aside: Soboul's sex life was damaging to the Party, there was this business of Marie-Louise, it would be so much better if he were to give her up, people were talking, could I not point this out to him, he might take a hint from me?—could hardly complain, *Bacchus* was his own brother-in-law, even if *I* was a fully (under-) paid up agent of the ubiquitous Intelligence Service. Even *La Tante* seems to have been won over by the stocky man's sheer vitality and infectious good humour; and I have even seen the solemn Gisèle laughing rather timidly at one of *Bacchus*'s appalling commercial traveller jokes.

Bacchus is more than an affectionate and cherished memory. His massive monuments witness, over much of the Midi, South-East, South-West, Massif Central, to his driving energy and to his immense creativity. But his son, Jean-Marie, who runs a fish restaurant in Le Grau-du-Roi, is the best monument to his father. He has *Bacchus*'s slightly rolling gait—both father and son looked like seamen, in their thick blue jerseys that accentuated their massive torsos, and, though *Bacchus* had never been to sea, Jean-Marie had served, for a number of years, as a wireless-operator in the French merchant navy. He moves, on his short

legs, like his father; and he talks like his father, greeting people
from afar in an accent that has no trace of mediterranean. He has
his father's high colour and small, very blue eyes, the same curly
blond beard, the same capacity for immediate repartee, and quite
as vast a capacity for drink. He is likewise an extremely good
cook. This younger Champenois is totally accepted by the local
community of fishermen: no small achievement in a society of
deeply suspicious Mediterraneans. Jean-Marie is his father's
most consummate monument. After his brother-in-law's tragic
and futile death, it became much more difficult to put Soboul in
the mood to strike up *L'Infanterie de Marine*. A sort of Mediterranean sadness had taken over. Tears would quickly fill his eyes
every time I mentioned his very lovable brother-in-law. It was
something that we had in common. I think that much of the warm
affection that he always displayed towards me, despite my
numerous historical heresies (I don't think he counted them for
very much, he was too forgiving, and he put more value on
friendship than on historical interpretation; and he was quite
right), was because I had fallen in such a big way for that irresistible roly-poly man.

I first met Soboul at the beginning of 1947. Lefebvre had given me
the Ménilmontant address, suggesting that we work out our
mutual research subjects together; it was typical of him that he
should have been unwilling to intervene. I went to see him, there
was a great deal of wine, and the Yugoslavs finished the evening
singing, I thought rather dolefully. Then, for the next two years,
we worked opposite one another in the *Archives Nationales*, on the
400-odd boxes of the Committee of General Security, Soboul
starting at the letter A, I starting at the letter M. His shameless
ability at chatting up young female researchers left me staggered
by his impudence, very envious, too. At this time, we used to
have lunch in a small restaurant behind the Palais Soubise, and
opposite a big telephone exchange. The restaurant had two
storeys, connected by a corkscrew iron staircase. We used to go
there on the stroke of one; and Soboul always chose a table as near
as possible to the foot of the staircase. Just after one, the *standardistes* began to appear, legs first, down the staircase. As each pair

of shapely legs would emerge, Soboul would address himself, in a voice in which there was a trace of southern velvety caress, to their owner: *Mademoiselle, vous avez de bien jolies jambes.* In most cases, the girls would take it well, they did not seem to mind, some would even smile. I was enormously impressed by the sheer cheek. I think my presence encouraged Soboul to push further and further ahead in effrontery.

Later, we moved from there, despite the legs. Perhaps the place closed. We went to a restaurant rue Vieille du Temple, near the Hôtel de Rohan. Soboul's Thursday lady, the wife of an engineer, with huge dark eyes, would join us there. The husband was generally away, inspecting coal-mines. Then we moved to Madame Alice, the owner of a tiny restaurant called *Chez Madame Alice* (Soboul composed, in her honour, the jingle: *Chez Madame Alice, tout est délice*, which wasn't quite true: the food was very cheap and not very good). Madame Alice was a massive Auvergnate who was very short-sighted and who wore enormously thick glasses. Like many very fat people, she was extremely affable to all her regular customers, and always addressed the two of us: *Eh bien, jeunes hommes, qu'y-a-t'il pour vous aujourd'hui?* and would then tell us what she had. And I suppose we *were* still pretty young then, and certainly fairly silly.

Later, we did a great deal together, going on holiday together, but always with a sprinkling of *les copains* in tow, including, during a tour of Upper Normandy, a ponderously boring *inspecteur primaire* from the Pyrenees and who had been posted to Forges-les-Eaux. He was indeed very *primaire*; and he complained endlessly about the selfishness of the Normans. I *liked* the Normans. I visited Nîmes and Le-Grau-du-Roi several times; and Soboul came over to Oxford four or five times. He liked Oxford, and much appreciated High Table and dessert. One of his most cherished evenings there was a Sunday guest night at Keble. Both of us came away, full of port—it had gone round about ten times—and with the memory of a room in black, gold and silver, full of Chinese screens, and the table lined, at head level, with a row of purple faces, above white dog collars. Soboul commented with enthusiasm, on the way back to Jesus, where we were staying, that *MM les pasteurs* seemed to do themselves pretty well. He thought Oxford did the right thing by its *universitaires*. It was a pity there was nothing similar in France. He was a strong advocate of privilege.

My friend had an engaging habit, southern maybe, of using diminutives. He always referred to my children, in his letters, as *la famillette*. The diminutive, like his habit of caressing parts of the female anatomy, was an expression of his warm and very affectionate nature. In later years, I did not visit him as much as I should have done. I knew that if I called at the flat, No. 119, I would not see him alone, there would be some plump East German girl there, whom he would show off as if she had been some sort of thoroughbred. And they were generally rather boring. I wrote to him on hearing of the death of our mutual friend, Kohachiro Takahachi, whom I had met on his very first visit, rue de Gergovie. One of his pupils had sent me a long letter from Tokyo. Soboul wrote back to me, from Nîmes, on 26 July 1982, on his official notepaper headed: *Institut d'Histoire de la Revolution Française*, a proud letter-press:

Mon vieux Ricardo, vieux frère,
J'ai été très sensible à ta lettre qui me parvient à Nîmes.

Oui, notre Taka est mort, et ainsi s'en vont, au fil des ans, ceux que nous avons aimés, qui ont donné du sel à notre existence. Je n'oublie pas les soirées de la rue de Gergovie,—trente ans déjà. Ce sont de bons souvenirs de notre existence. Mon cher Ricardo, soyons fidèles à nos années de jeunesse. Toi, mon vieux Cobb, tu es toujours vivant dans mon coeur.

Mes félicitations pour ce petit William qui te comble de joie, sois heureux, et habitue-toi à ton nouveau dentier!

Je t'embrasse, AM.

In mid-September of the same year I got the telegram from Nîmes, sent by the family. I could not get away for the funeral, but I wrote a short obituary for *The Times* and rang up the *Morning Star*. At my first lecture of the Michaelmas Term, I thought I would say something about my friend; but I had to break off after a few sentences, my voice was going and I found myself choked with tears. So I turned back to the Revolutionary Government. I still find it hard to evoke the memory of my affectionate and generous friend without the tears coming into my eyes.

Simenon at Eighty

The first time I met Georges Simenon—it was in November 1979—I was struck by how much he looked like the photograph that had been on the back of all his books for the previous twenty years or so. Although he was seventy-six, he did not look much over sixty; his hair was dark, without a trace of grey. Within minutes, he was puffing at one of his many pipes; there were about thirty of these, including a gold one, on the window-ledge within reach of his armchair. He was wearing yellow trousers, slippers and an open-necked shirt. As I had always thought of Maigret as a big, bulky man, I had expected his creator and *alter ego* to be big and bulky too. But he was quite small, short, though thickset. His eyes, slightly hooded, blue-grey, very bright and sharp, but with a hint of benevolence and good humour, kept me under close scrutiny through his heavy spectacles. They were the eyes of an observer who did not miss very much, the eyes of a man who, as a writer, was above all a visual artist, a man supremely able to put seeing—and, indeed, smelling, touching and listening—into writing, lending his readers his own wonderfully acute sense of place and his ability rapidly to take in the appearance and oddities of someone seen only fleetingly.

It was his eyes that I remembered most on this occasion. Apart from that, he not only looked just like his own photographs, minus the trilby and the heavily belted mac; he looked like a great many other people, French, Belgian, Dutch or Swiss. I could see that he would pass in a crowd, and that people would not notice him. He had no trace of a Belgian accent, though I could believe him when he told me that he could put one on when he wanted to capture the confidence of Walloon or Flemish bargees and rivermen, at the time he was working on his canal-and-lock novels.

His manner was bluff, matter-of-fact, without a trace of pomposity. For one so famous, he struck me as modest, even shy. I had gone into the sitting-room preceded by a veritable barrage of

93

flattery in my most elaborate French—'*Maître*' and that sort of thing, walking behind my flow of words—but he told me just to call him Simenon. We talked for three hours—he did most of the talking—and then Teresa said that it was time for me to go, as he would be having his supper.

I saw him a second time in June 1982. I noticed that he had aged quite a bit since my previous visit. Now he was rather bent and seemed to have shrunk. One could still see the traces of the famous photograph, but at some distance away. He was seventy-nine, and beginning to look it. He was dressed entirely in white, with a white hat; and when he sat under the big cedar in his little garden, he looked exactly like the new photograph, the one on the cover of the French edition of his memoirs, his latest work. The one piece of bravado was a red cowboy tie. This time we talked mostly in English; and, once he had got into his stride, his English became more fluent, especially when telling a story, which he did quite vividly and with gusto, sometimes to the accompaniment of sound effects—the noise, for instance, of Vlaminck's big motorbike, which he did extremely well.

Again I was struck by his simplicity, as well as by his compassion. He might go on a bit about Man (and, of course, Woman), striking now and then a philosophical note. But he seemed a simple, uncomplicated man, with a tremendous appetite for life, and an ability to understand and to sympathize with ordinary people, humble people, *les petites gens*. I have often thought how strange it was that a man who had made such a success of his life—at least in material terms, and, I think, ultimately, though very late, in human ones—should have made so much of people, characters both in his Maigrets and in his straight novels, who had been failures or semi-failures, or were in the process of becoming failures.

I had heard it said that, in interviews, he was given to boasting, to holding forth about this or that, but, on my two visits, I could not detect a trace of either. He was direct, earthy, enthusiastic and, at times, sentimental. I came away from my second visit even more pleased than the first time; and both he and Teresa, who this time took much more part in the conversation, seemed pleased too. They both came out into the quiet cul-de-sac to see us off in the taxi. Simenon's observant eyes were smiling, and he and Teresa waved as the taxi turned into the main road.

Simenon lives in a small pink house, two storeys only—it looks like a converted stables and has a roof of rural red tiles—in a quiet street at the western end of Lausanne, not far from the main motor-road to Geneva. The house is just below one cemetery, just above another (which prompted him to say that he would have the choice of going up or going down). The house is quite bare and sparse, there are no books, no gadgets, and few visible comforts. Simenon, who has travelled so much in his enormously vigorous life, never leaves Lausanne and hardly ever goes into the town, limiting his walks to the nearby lakeside. From the garden he can see the whole line of the French Alps.

The house gives a strong, comforting impression of repose and serenity. A man who has travelled so frenetically, always on the move, as if constantly trying to escape from something or always trying to find something—perhaps love, affection, understand-ing—by moving on to a new place, has now come to rest. The search is over, he has found what he had been looking for. I had the impression that it was a happy house, and that Simenon, at eighty, is a happy man: a happiness, however, tinged with a huge amount of sadness at the loss of his adored daugher, Marie-Jo.

His secretary lives in Lausanne and acts as a filter between Simenon and the outer world. Each morning, she reads out his mail over the telephone, arranges for visits and interviews. All his books, in their hundreds of translations, are kept in the Lausanne flat, which also contains all the gadgets that formed so much part of the Simenon image when he was at Epalinges. It is as if he were now living at one remove both from his immense volume of work and from his international fame. There was something childish about this self-made man in his enjoyment of expensive toys. Now he seems to have outgrown the toys, and the toys have been put away. He has also outgrown success and the enjoyment of wealth. In short, he is as near as he is ever likely to be to being happy and contented. The street is quiet and tranquil, quite safe for children to play in, riding their bicycles, or kicking balls. It is a cul-de-sac that takes some finding. It seems secret and forgotten, though I have no doubt that the *police cantonale* keep a discreet eye on their illustrious resident. From what he told me, he gets on very well with their senior officials.

Part of the charm of Simenon's books is that they satisfy an enormous range of readers in quite different ways. Enthusiasts for detective stories will settle on Maigret when he comes to terms with a problem and ends up, as much by intuition (*au pifomètre*, to use Simenon's own words to me) as by systematic elimination, by finding a solution. Furthermore, each reader will construct his own Maigret. I have always seen him as very large and burly, wearing a rather battered bowler, a hard white collar, the front stud showing above the carelessly knotted tie, black boots, a black overcoat with velvet collar: a man with a red face, dark eyes, shaggy eyebrows and greying curly hair. Others will picture him in mac and trilby. My own forty-year-long appreciation of Simenon comes above all from what I regard as his unique sense of place, of ambience, his slow, apparently haphazard exploration of topography, his ability to look at the backs of houses, as seen from canals or railway cuttings—his perspectives are always unusual—his genius in giving, in a few brief brushstrokes, the feeling of a town, a village, a landscape, the smell of the wind, of the sea, a moving sky.

No wonder Vlaminck was such a close friend. Often, they share subjects, and Simenon writes as Vlaminck paints. They are both northerners, both at their best when describing wet, flat places in Flanders or la Campine, or the flat countryside inland from La Rochelle. To read Simenon is to travel with him from place to place, and to go to the places which he has described in his books is to discover, again and again, with a sense of excitement and pleasure, that he has got it exactly *right*: a rainy day under the arcades in La Rochelle, the long, dreary main street of Fontenay-le-Comte, a Belgian tram-train (*vicinal*) as it passes by waterlogged fields of sugar-beet, the rue Mouffetard, the Marais, the Ternes, the Batignolles, the XIIème, the slow-moving carpeted lifts of the rich blocks of the XVIème, the little brick houses in Charleroi, the low, crouching white farmhouses of East Flanders.

I suppose everyone has his own favourite Simenon topography. I feel he is at his best, his surest, in his native Belgium, Northern France, canal-country, the coast of the Charentes, Lower Normandy (Port-en-Bessin, for instance), and, of course,

Paris, *all* of Paris, in its immense variety, smallness, in its once-identifiable quarters and villages, in the colour of its walls. But he can manage *Alphaville* equally well.

Although Simenon himself fell in love with Porquerolles, I don't think that he writes as well about the Midi, about the Mediterranean, as he does about, let us say, Moulins, Nevers, Meung-sur-Loire, Vichy or, for that matter, Alsace. There is something stagey about his Midi, the south as seen and appreciated by a northerner. My own view is that he does not get London right, that he is rather out of his depth with England and the English. I enjoy the seedy, steamy exoticism of his accounts of the Canal Zone, West Africa and Tahiti—the stories of white men going native and taking to drink; I enjoy his gleeful descriptions of the sordid, mean-minded tensions of long journeys by sea; and I have no doubt that, once again, he has got the atmosphere just right.

He never sits in judgement on people, he tries to understand us. I find him compassionate, as well as intuitive and imaginative. He would describe himself as a collector of souls; and I think he is; but they are not disembodied souls, nor do they languish in some dramatic Hell. Hell is where they are, like the couple each of whom has his or her own key to the two separate larders.

Simenon was eighty in February 1983. His achievement has been stupendous. Having found his form at about twenty-six, he has been writing steadily for over fifty years: 400 books, 200 of them novels, of which, perhaps, a score or more first-rate. *Au bout du rouleau, Lettre à mon juge, La maison du canal, Le train, L'aîné des Fercheaux, La tante, Le déménagement, Les anneaux de Bicêtre* would come at the top of my list. I prefer the straight novels to the Maigrets. But this is a matter of taste.

Part of the attraction is derived no doubt from the fact that so many of his characters are in a much worse mess than we are, that they have often reached the end of the line and that there is no way out for them. But there are also little timid shafts of sunlight, sometimes quite literally, for Simenon is a very sensitive painter of the seasons, and I know few writers who can write so well about rain, about the wind.

He is a novelist of the weekend (particularly on the banks of the Marne). Many of his characters all at once try to escape, to go on

97

the run; few succeed. However much he may write about women who wear no knickers, he is in fact a moralist, even a Catholic one. He believes in the virtues of the family, of obedience and respect; and so many of his young provincials, in his books, come to grief because they leave home, and come to Paris. Without the jargon of sociology, entirely self-taught, and expressing himself in the simplest language, he is a marvellous social historian, with an eye to every tell-tale detail, a window-watcher, a reader in secret signs and private semaphores. He knows where people are likely to be and when, all his itineraries are wholly convincing.

It is an unparalleled achievement both in terms of vigour, of volume and of quality. One remains astonished at his industry, at the way he has driven himself on, at his single-mindedness, his devotion to his craft, his marvellous and ruthless ability to exclude any disturbing element. Perhaps what I admire most is his ability to shut out such passing inconveniences as war and Occupation. Some of his best books were written between 1940 and 1944. Quite right too. He was a writer, so he went on writing. Why should he have agonized over the fate of France? What good would it have done? He was not French anyway, he was Belgian. He got his priorities right.

If the true quality of French is concision—it used to be—then Simenon writes very good French. Sometimes the dialogue seems a bit stiff, and a French critic has pointed out that he makes peasants from Western France speak like Belgians. His style is so concise that it must be very difficult to translate, leaving as it does only a very narrow choice of possible renderings. Yet he must have had excellent translators, as he has been read with equal pleasure in so many languages.

Simenon is not a man of the Right, nor of the Left. He is apolitical. During his long career as a journalist, he worked for magazines and papers of the Left such as *Vendredi* and *Marianne*, and for those of the Right, such as *Paris-Soir* and *Match*. His first French employer was a provincial nobleman, M. Destut de Tracy—a direct descendant of Descartes, as Simenon was to tell me; and his time as his secretary, as well as introducing the young Belgian to the somewhat casual attitude of his noble employer to bills sent in by tradesmen, gave him the background to Maigret's childhood as a son of a gamekeeper on an estate in the Nièvre. His next employer, M. Bunau-Varilla, was a newspaper tycoon of the Right; the young Simenon much enjoyed working for him as a sort of super errand-boy, because the work took him, in the course of the day, to pretty well every newspaper office in Paris, reinforcing in him his delight in the smell of printer's ink and in the noise of printing machines; it also took him to pretty well every quarter of the city. His approach to the Stavisky Affair was what would now be called 'investigative'; and he found out a great deal, too much indeed for some of the French authorities.

Simenon was given a rough time by the French Communist and Resistance writers who, as self-appointed members of the *Comité National des Ecrivains*, had set themselves up as censors of their fellow writers, because they had had books published—as had Sartre and Camus, and nearly everyone else—during the Occupation. There was not much that they could do about him, as he was not French; but I think this experience accounted for his decision to leave France for Canada and the United States after the Liberation. During the Occupation, he had a visit from the *Police aux Questions Juives*, a member of which attempted to argue that the name Simenon was derived from Simon; and he and his mother were put to a great deal of trouble to produce evidence that he was not of Jewish descent.

His boasts about his sexual prowess have been much publicized. I don't think they should be taken literally. A man who has written about 400 books could not have spent half his time in bed. Both his marriages turned out very badly, though he has maintained friendly relations with his first wife. He seems to have spent much of his life, from adolescence onwards, in search of an idealized woman, of love and affection. He got very little of either from his mother, who did not disguise from him her preference for his younger brother, Christian, who was killed while serving in the Foreign Legion in Vietnam. He went to bed with a great many women (unfortunately, we get a blow-by-blow account in his recently published *Memoirs*)—the number is unimportant—and, every time he finished a book, he celebrated the occasion by a night out in a brothel. His quest seems to have been as tragic and as unrewarding as that of that other tireless traveller, Don Giovanni.

But now he seems to have found in Teresa the ideal companion whom he had been seeking for so long. Certainly, in his novels, women are not given very attractive roles; if they are not shrews, or avaricious yellow-faced writers of anonymous letters, they are adventuresses. Only Mme Maigret is motherly; but she is somehow unconvincing. She seems to spend all her time either making coffee or cooking. As one French critic has commented, Maigret sleeps beside Mme Maigret, but not with her. Maigret certainly does not share his creator's appetite for sex.

Like many self-made men, Simenon used to display plenty of signs both of vulgarity and social unease. (Maigret, too, is uneasy in polite company, even more so when confronted with what he takes to be *le Tout Paris*.) He has never shown any interest in the past; cathedrals, colleges and art galleries seem to have passed him by; and his friendship with Vlaminck seems to have been derived from a common simplicity and for the painter's enjoyment in going flat out on his big motorbike. At the time of his earlier successes, he greatly enjoyed meeting the wealthy, and at Epalinges he had close relations with the Chaplin family. For him, the height of luxury and the recognition of material success was to stay in the Savoy, or in the Trianon-Palace in Versailles; he also took to the experience of travelling first class on transatlantic liners.

I think he felt more at home with Americans than with Europeans. He was convinced that Jamie Hamilton, his English publisher, must be an Etonian, because he had the appearance of an English gentleman, and all English gentlemen went to the *Collège d'Eton*.

John, his son, has a wonderful description of him, deep in one of his roles, as a sea-captain, the man at the helm, during a storm off the Dutch coast. There was a time when he clearly liked dressing up; and he displayed the same enjoyment at playing the cowboy as a string of American Presidents. When he was living in Porquerolles, a French submarine put in at the island. He threw a monster party, inviting the whole crew. But he was also genuinely hospitable, and as he so much enjoyed good food and drink, he liked to see other people enjoying them too. He had come up the hard way, had experienced the very worst sort of poverty—genteel poverty, what he described to me as white-collar poverty—throughout his childhood, when he had few toys, just a paintbox, and often not enough to eat. So he had to make up for it later. I found the little red cowboy-style tie both incongruous and rather touching. He remains still something of an eighty-year-old child.

Simenon's Mother*

The walloon city of Liège, astride the Meuse and the Ourthe, lies a little to the west and the south-west of one of the most bizarre frontier areas of Western Europe, bordering on the pan-handle of Dutch Limburg and the approaches to the ancient town of Aachen.

Within tram distance of the city, the language changes from French to Flemish at Tongres; and even the suburban *commune* of Herstal lies almost on the linguistic border, while a very little to the east there exists an important German-speaking enclave. In the middle of the nineteenth century, with the establishment of heavy industry in Liège, the city drew heavily on migrant labour from the poorer rural areas of Dutch Limburg, as well as from the Belgian Ardennes. For centuries, it had developed its own peculiar *patois* of Walloon, as expressed the most eloquently by the salesmen and saleswomen of the *marché de la Batte*, on the quays of the Meuse. But a peculiar mixture of Flemish, Dutch, and German had also penetrated the eastern outworks of the town by the middle of the last century.

Georges Simenon's mother, Henriette Brüll, who died in 1971, aged ninety-one, when the author was himself seventy-one, was the thirteenth and last child in a family that had originated from Dutch Limburg, and that had moved across the frontier, first to Herstal, then to the poor quarter of *Outremeuse*, in Liège itself, some time in the 1870s.

Henriette's father, Simenon's maternal grandfather, was a German, married to a Dutch woman, who, before emigrating, had been manager of an estate in Dutch Limburg, as well as occupying the socially prestigious office of *dykemeister*, master of the waters. And, even after moving over the border, he remained in the river trade, owning at one time five barges and estab-

---

* This essay first appeared as a review of Georges Simenon, *Letter to my Mother*, trans. Ralph Manheim (Hamish Hamilton) in the *Guardian*, March 1976.

lished as a relatively successful lumber merchant. However, one of his creditors having defaulted, he was totally ruined when Henriette was still a child, dying an alcoholic when she was only five.

For a time, Henriette was taken in by one of her many sisters, who exploited her as a servant, treating her often abominably, but with sudden accesses of generosity when she was in her cups, which, fortunately, was quite often. At nineteen, still only speaking, like the other members of her enormous family, an odd mixture of Dutch and German—her son says that she never really managed French and that her language often caused laughter among her neighbours—she went into service as a shop assistant at the Liège branch of the big chain store, *l'Innovation*.

While at *l'Innovation*, she acquired her principal Walloon friend, and met her future husband, Désiré Simenon, a clerk in a large insurance company. Characteristically her son speculates on how his parents first met. Did he see her through the shop window? But then he must have gone out of his way, for *l'Innovation* did not lie in his direct route from home to work: a problem that, regretfully, Simenon has to leave unsolved.

Désiré Simenon belonged to a Walloon clan that was almost as extensive as that of the Brülls, and that congregated, every Sunday, around the patriarchal table of the blind grandfather, rue du Puits-en-Stock, in the parish of Saint-Nicolas, in the old city. Simenon's mother, barely speaking French, a foreigner, seems to have been hardly welcome in this closed and proud milieu of skilled artisans and comfortable tradesmen, and the Simenon estimate of their in-laws was certainly not raised by the daily spectacle of one of Henriette's brothers, an alcoholic semi-tramp, as he weaved his way across the city's bridges.

Désiré died of a heart disease in his middle forties, a few years after his wife, greatly to his inconvenience—for he was a quiet man who liked his corner chair and his newspaper—had started to take in lodgers, mostly students from the University, in an effort to put money by for the time when she would be a widow. Some time after his death she remarried; her second husband was a pensioner who had been employed on the Belgian railways, and who owned a small house and a plot of land, on the hills overlooking the city.

By her second marriage, Henriette finally attained the economic security that she had always sought, and was able to buy the house in which the couple lived and which was cluttered by two lots of identical *faux-Henri II* furniture, so identical that, in old age, she had become unable to distinguish which lot had come from which side of the family, much to her son's evident distress.

Identity of furniture—even down to portraits of Albert and Elisabeth in each ground floor room—did not, however, induce identity of views. The marriage was a disaster, Henriette and her husband, André, remaining, for years, *face à face*, without speaking, exchanging only scribbled notes, each with his or her own locked larder, and taking it in turns in the kitchen, each for fear, surmises Simenon, of being poisoned.

Once, by the 1930s, Georges Simenon had become a wealthy man, he made regular efforts both to help his mother financially, and to persuade her to abandon her tiny house in Liège, and come to live with him, in the Charentes, in the USA, or in Switzerland. She did stay briefly in all three, always returning to her home, which she repainted herself, inside and out, when in her eighties, and finally giving Georges back all the money that he had sent her over the years.

On her last visit to Epalinges, near Lausanne, she had also brought bags of gold coins that she had set aside for her grandchildren. Many years before her death, her second son, her favourite Christian, was killed in Indo-China; and, from the age of nineteen, when he had gone off to Paris, to that of seventy, Georges had always been very much a stranger to his mother, who seems only to have had one worry on his account: that he was not financially solvent. Her relations with his second, French-Canadian wife, seem to have been more than indifferent, indeed bad.

These are the bare bones of Simenon's own account of spending a week by his mother's bedside, Hôpital de Bavière, in Liège, and of the reflections that her death raised in him.

We can perhaps best leave the psychology to Simenon himself; but what must be of great interest to all his readers is the revelation, far beyond that of *Pedigree*, of the extent to which the novelist drew on his family as a source for his plots, as well of his constant awareness of topography, channels of movement within a city, and specializations by quarter. Perhaps unconsciously, he has thus added yet another layer to his already immense reputation as a social historian, though his intention was undoubtedly quite different; the filial desire to render a tribute to a brave, tough, and very good little woman.

Robert Lageat*

A long, dreary avenue, its width emphasized by the low line of grey, peeling houses on each side, bordered by sad, regimented trees. Down the avenue march the men in blue, without a word, without music, to the weary sound of regular *ran! ran!* Robert, aged six, holds the hand of his elder brother, Roger. For a time they run, following the blue men, till, tired, they stop, as the men disappear, leaving the avenue empty, quiet, and restored to its infinite hopelessness: no *voie triomphale*, rather the *chemin de l'abattoir*, as the men—from Chartres or farther still—tramp northwards, to be swallowed up by the Gare de l'Est and the Gare du Nord in 1917. The men are there, then they are there no more, as if by some trick of early cinema. The children, frightened, Robert clinging more tightly to his brother's hand, turn off the avenue, towards home, rue du Docteur Henouille, in Cachan, on the southern rim of Paris: picture-postcard country, the terminus of a tram, two *pissotières* facing one another, the *monument aux morts* is still to come.

It might be Dabit country. It is in fact the first distinct memory of Robert Lageat, nicknamed 'Robert des Halles', no *banlieusard*, but a true Parisian, conceived in the rue des Lombards, spending the most active part of his life within a topography bordered by the rue Beaubourg, the rue Quincampoix (la Quincampe), the rue Rambuteau (la Rambute), the boulevard Sébastopol (le Topol) and the sinister *commissariat* of the rue des Prouvaires, the favourite abode of the Parisian *gaspard* (rat). Lageat is now in his late sixties and the co-owner, with his son Jacquy, of a *bal-musette*, 9, rue de Lappe, in the XIème.

Robert's mother, at the opening of the spoken film, is a laundress (*blanchecaille*) who does all her laundry by hand and then delivers it all over Paris in a handcart. The father, Jules

---

* This essay first appeared as a review of Robert Lageat, *Robert des Halles*, avec la collaboration de Claude Dubois (Lattès) in the *Times Literary Supplement*, July 1980.

Amadieu, a hard-drinking fighter, working intermittently, when not whoring or eating, on the uncertain frontiers of les Halles, had been killed somewhere on the Marne in 1915. Roger helps his mother in the house. Shortly after the Cachan scene, the three move back into Paris—the laundry work must have been merely a temporary, desperate stop-gap—passage Pecquay, off the rue Quincampoix. Most of the relatives on the mother's side—the Magdeleines—had been connected with the fruit and vegetable trade in the Halles ever since the Second Empire.

The close connection between trade specialities and family relationships is once more emphasized when the mother remarries. Lageat, the stepfather, is a fruit and vegetable *marchand de quat' saisons*, trading from a barrow off the rue Quincampoix. The rough, boisterous Halles dominate the lives of the whole family, dragging them from bed at two in the morning, and releasing them, for some secondary employment, after midday. Robert, for a time, spends the afternoons and early evenings working for an Auvergnat *bougnat*, hauling sacks of coal all over northern Paris, even to the very foot of the Sacré Coeur, an area which, he says, seemed to be 'aux daches' (in the antipodes) as seen from central Paris. Save for the old Vélodrome-d'Hiver, in Grenelle, there is hardly a mention of the Left Bank in the whole book.

In the immobility of their work and leisure topography—the daily itinerary is rue des Blancs-Manteaux, rue Simon-le-Franc, rue Beaubourg, rue Saint-Merri, rue Saint-Martin, rue Quincampoix—as well as in the recruitment to their trade of provincial relatives of the stepfather, from Decazeville, the Lageats, working, at a killing pace, in the 1920s and 30s, conform, perhaps even consciously, to an eighteenth-century pattern, rough and brutal, but also fraternal, gossipy, honourable, relying entirely on the spoken word—Robert's employers, the midget couple, the Lourds, vegetable wholesalers, are illiterate—and dominated by physical effort, by immense meals and by immense libations.

Lageat describes les Halles as a village—alas, a lost village—in which, in the summer, the inhabitants of la Quincampe bring their chairs out on the pavement, in which no one ever goes away on holiday, and in which, on Sundays, the men withdraw to a small café, kept by an Auvergnat, *pour taper le carton, belote*, etc. It

is a world peopled by ingenious and eloquent nicknames, referring either to provincial origin or to physical characteristics. Later
we encounter an all-in wrestler who has a stutter and who is
called *Qué-qué*.

But for Robert, before the grinding work, yet the relative
freedom, of the anarchic Halles, there is an abominable interlude
as a border in a clerical school at Vaujours north-west of Paris, the
Collège Fénelon, a dreadful place, the children, most of them war
orphans, subjected to the brutality of *pions*, who compensate for
their own wretched condition by taking it out on their small
victims and by an archaic attachment to bonapartist or royalist
convictions. It is a classic account of six years of misery that might
have been written by Vallès. Black years made even more sombre
by the death of Roger in 1919 and by the perhaps calculated
hardness of a mother apparently incapable of a word of affection:
'mon trésor', 'mon petit chéri' were not expressions of tenderness
ever heard passage Pecquay. His half-sister, likewise confined to
the feminine equivalent of the awful Fénelon—called, rather
appropriately la Pension Jeanne-d'Arc, 'la bonne Lorraine' having so often given her name to the rancid and sparse institutions
of French ecclesiastical charity—also died, shortly after leaving
the cheerless Pension. Such early deaths are a reminder of the
realities of working-class life in central Paris in the 1920s. Later,
we learn of the death of Raoul, Robert's brother-in-law, a miner
from the Decazeville coal *bassin* at thirty-three, from silicosis.

At sixteen, Robert is fully engaged in helping his mother and
his stepfather in the back-breaking work of their stall. Lageat's
account, as recollected in talking to Claude Dubois, a journalist
and a native of the same quarter, is dominated by the nostalgia for
a marvellously living world, now nothing more than a memory,
and even that soon to be lost. Why, he asks derisively, call the
métro station Pierre Lescot, 'les Halles' when the old population
has been swept away, the markets exiled to Rungis, the *gaspards*
too in search of a new home, and the whole area museumified
and devitalized? His *récit* has the sad charm of what is already a
piece of Parisian social history.

The young Lageat, with more and more of his relatives engaged in the night work of the markets—after his marriage to a
girl from Decazeville, she too is incorporated in the brilliantly lit

night of *fruits et légumes* (the bloody territory of butchery and carcass is a little to the south)—develops in pugnacity as well as in muscle. Compact and low on the ground, by eighteen he has established himself as a respected fighter, his cauliflower ears attesting to his expertise.

The Halles and its extraordinary mixed and transitory population, as it changes through the night—only the garish prostitutes operate right round the clock—are the principal heroes and villains of Lageat's book. But he moves on from the Halles, first to accomplish military service in the Chasseurs Alpins, something that he greatly enjoys, including the discovery of the Mediterranean and the Alps. Then he takes to the boxing gymnasiums of the faubourg Montmartre, switching at the time of the Front populaire (to which he is a whole-hearted adherent) to acrobatics and wrestling. After brilliant war service in the *corps francs*, he returns to the lurid blue nights of the Occupation, in various team acts, appearing, in the great cinemas, before a mixed audience of Germans, black marketeers, collaborationists, and specialists in torture from the rue Lauriston.

The description of the febrile night life of the capital in 1940 and in 1941 has seldom been bettered, save in films. The Paris of *Les Enfants du Paradis*, itself filmed in 1943, is relived with intensity, and with the same bizarre encounters, the same *équivoques*, the same intermingling of villains and heroes, of torturers and *résistants*, in the darkness of immense *salles*—the Rex, the Normandie —the audience riveted to Robert and Andréa, as they evoke, in acrobatic dance, to the tune of a *java*, the swift and sinister movements of the bad boys *à gueules de raie*, a beautiful phrase, and the bad girls, rue de Lappe, offering the audience a *frisson* of violence, while the red-and-black proclamations of executions go up outside.

All at once disgust ensues. Lageat contacts a French officer in Madrid, who points out that his place is in France. He takes a leading part in the Resistance in the Lot, is severely wounded, and nearly dies. At 33, his career as a wrestler and as an acrobat is at an end. At one stage he lives perilously on the rim of organized crime. There is a very visual evocation of Marcel Delrue, at one time a Lille hairdresser, on the run from the Germans, after his escape from Loos, and soon engaged in vast operations suited to his origins, involving Belgian tobacco. Delrue, blue-eyed, fearless, always dressed in black, with a black trilby, is involved in a shoot-up in which a gendarme is killed, is reconverted to Catholicism in prison, and is guillotined in 1952. One of his former officers manages to persuade Lageat to keep on the right side of the law.

The family move to the rue Beaubourg and, after the war, Lageat and his son Jacquy acquire the Balajo in the rue de Lappe. The last section of the book describes that remarkable street and its surrounding quarter—la Bastoche and the rue de Charonne, in the XIème that Lageat, a refugee from the Halles, believes, perhaps trustingly, will hold out, at least for a few years, as one of the last enclaves of 'l'esprit parisien', of Parisian speech, and of a night life that has managed to survive the hopeless darkness of the old centre and in which the coloured neon signs still spell out excitement, violence, and impudent fraternity.

Lageat's life is exceptional. Few people of his background could ever have managed to escape from the iron time-table of les Halles. The greatest interest of his book comes from the inventiveness and sheer vulgarity of his language, a Parisian that would have brought joy to *'les trois A' (les Trois Argotiers)*. (He also refers, in respect of les Halles, to *les 4 B; boulot, bouffe, bibine* and *baise*, a full programme.) As he states, it is not an elevated language ('les discussions rasaient le bitume'), its centre of gravity often placed at the level of the bottom: 'le pétoulet près du gazon', of someone short like himself. One of his acrobatic partners, 'la mome Andréa', is deliciously described as 'frappadingue du valseur'; in one of their acts, he finds 'son faubourg à portée de ma bouche': *valseur, faubourg, pétoulet* all evoke the bum. 'Pue du cul' is a finely expressive insult. 'La botte de persil' is located on the other side of the female anatomy. Readers will no doubt find their own way with *lope, miro, les schmitts, clille, rider, doul, roupanes, gaspard, surin, lardoire, eustache, saccagne*; the last four instruments frequently carried and occasionally employed rue de Lappe. 'La Maison du Pullman Facile' refers to the police, 'la Carlingue', to the Gestapo, French and German. Here is Lageat himself, 'en titi parisien', greeting one of his Yugoslav wrestling coaches: 'Bonjour René, c'est re-moi.' And he observes, with delicacy, on the subject of the lack of a bathroom, passage

Pecquay: 'je continuais à me laver le cul dans une cuvette'. After the move to the rue Beaubourg, they do get a bathroom, as well as a bedroom and a dining-room set, the latter in the Dutch style, both of which would appear to have been 'signé Lévitan'.

He refers to commercial travellers 'de passage à Paname sapés Belle Jardinière'. And once he starts fishing on the Marne, he equips himself in the full rig-out, BHV. One of his *clilles*, rue de Lappe, he describes admiringly as a 'jacteuse de jar'; there are others he describes less admiringly as 'des qui salivent à la midinette, à la dactylo'. He is a pretty good *jacteur* himself. He is also a *chic type*, a race that, even in the 1970s, has somehow managed to survive.

Apart from the language, we encounter a *fine fleur* of personalities that includes a Monsieur de la Rotule, Président du Club des Culs Nus, who show their bare *valseurs* somewhere on the Marne, Louis le Cosaque (a *fort*), Gédéon Gida and Stan Karolyi, two Magyar wrestlers, Dragan Draganoff, a Bulgarian one, l'Ange Blanc, a Spanish one, Riton la Barbouille, a painter, Le Grand Phonse, Henri Fefeu (a bit easy with his *flingue*), Tonton la Pédale, Poil au Naze, Kid Jonas and Assane Diouf, both boxers, Yan le Gall, a Breton *catcheur*, Baratin, and the brothers Richard, René, Roméo and Raymond Bukovac, who run the Club des Lutteurs Yougoslaves, once situated, along with a boxing saloon, in the Palais Berlitz.

As long as Robert and Thérèse and their son Jacquy and their grandson Phi-Phi are around, there is still hope for Paris and for the survival of a few authentic *Pantruchards*, even if it means going to the XIème to find them. Go East Young Man. *Avancez, Messieurs Dames.*

Jacques Mesrine*

There is something about the appearance of Jacques Mesrine that is familiar. A large, bulky, but athletic-looking man, clearly in good physical trim—this is accentuated in one of the photographs by the fact that he is wearing a track-suit and gym shoes—his wide face and big dark eyes with very large pupils are not without an amused bonhomie and even a certain benevolence, 'l'air nonours'. To sit opposite that rather moonlike face, whether framed with a beard or not—it is the beard that hints at benevolence—at a restaurant table would be to sit opposite an attentive and generous host, with the promise of a very good meal indeed ahead. It is certainly the face of a gourmet; and, given the white cap, it could also be that of a chef. It is hard not to find something rather reassuring in what is clearly the face of an eating man, increasingly so, in his mid-thirties or early forties, with the beginnings of a double chin. The lower lip, often concealed by a curving moustache, is both sensuous and well adjusted to a glass: a drinking man then, too, and certainly a womanizer.

In short, the face of a *jouisseur* of the most straightforward type: food, wine and women, and preferably all three together; there is a happy photograph of Jacques at the end of a meal, the bill paid, post-*digestif*, with a look of sated satisfaction, sitting next to the conventionally pretty, though rather stupid-looking Jacqueline Deraiche, his French-Canadian mistress (with, alas, an accompanying French-Canadian accent—we are told that Jacques made her keep her mouth shut in public places, in case she should give away her origin and thus help to establish his own identity. That is what the *author* says, but one cannot help thinking the reason was that the best way of dealing with *l'accent québécois* is to ask its owner to keep it turned off). 'Look at me', he seems to say, 'there

* This essay first appeared as a review of Carey Schofield, *Mesrine. The Life and Death of a Supercrook* (Penguin) in the *Times Literary Supplement*, May 1980.

is no food I cannot buy, there is no woman I cannot attract and ensnare.' And so it is also the rather naïve face of a man who exults in the display of conventional success and who needs to flaunt that success in public.

I could not at once discover why the face seemed familiar. Then I spotted it: there was a distinct reminder of the Genevan actor and film-star, Michel Simon, though without Simon's famous *moue*, his endearing spoilt boy pout surviving into middle and old age, a clue indicating that 'Boudu' had never grown up and that 'Clo-Clo', in *Jean de la Lune*, still expected to be humoured in his childish cravings. The eyes, though much larger, reflect Simon's alert malice. The parallel may go further than a lingering physical resemblance. For Simon was a natural anarchist, a true *sauvage*, who ended up surrounding himself with a whole menagerie of animal dependents. Both got considerable satisfaction from scoring points against Authority. Mesrine managed to get himself rapidly expelled both from the Collège de Juilly and from Chaptal; and it is hard to believe that any Swiss Protestant establishment would have long succeeded in accommodating an adolescent Michel Simon.

Of course, one should not take the parallel too far. Simon was quite repulsively dirty, his table manners were revolting, he slobbered in his soup and drank wine, *au même le goulot*, like a tramp. 'Clo-Clo', towards the end of his life, no longer needed to act a tramp, he *was* a *clochard*. Mesrine was quite fanatically clean; after each escape he would wash elaborately, as if to remove the institutional smell of prison; he had excellent table manners, and kept the food off his expensive, rather showy silk ties. Yet, as with an ageing and impish 'Clo-Clo', there is something unmistakably childlike about Mesrine. One of the illustrations depicts him flicking through a crime magazine, with his own picture on the cover, reading all about it in one of his many hideouts. There is laughter at the corners of his large eyes. And look at him photographed triumphantly brandishing his police card, Préfecture de Police, a tricolour diagonal through the middle, dated 22 November 1975, and stamped with the seated Republic surrounded by spikes, the very thing, in fact, that he holds up, straight-faced, a trump in his perilous game with M. Broussard, the director of the Police Judiciaire. Both pictures are much more convincing than the one that depicts him staring from behind a pointed sub-machine gun.

There is something in his attitude, even when in physical repose, sitting down at a restaurant table, or chatting to three warders in a courtyard of the Santé, that suggests tip-top physical condition, constant training, and an ability, held in reserve, to move very fast indeed. No wonder the prison authorities got worried when the warders reported that he was doing daily press-ups! Though an unusually large man, he could move with the speed and decisiveness of a puma. Mesrine trained for crime and escape with the assiduity of an Olympic athlete.

We are ready to believe too, if only from a look in those half-humorous yet coldly implacable eyes, that he was also a master at disguise, could convincingly hobble on a stick, could transform himself into a bald and arrogant *énarque*, a timid hair-dresser in his white apron, a plausible student, or, oddly, the double of a recent West German Chancellor. Disguise was absolutely essential to his long survival, especially when his unusual build would pick him out from the crowd, and when, as a naturally gregarious Parisian, he liked to walk the streets, eat in restaurants, do rather careful shopping, or merely linger in his favourite quarters of north-east Paris.

On at least one occasion, disguise seems to have been pushed to the limits of carnival: while holding up the octogenarian millionaire, M. Lelièvre, he had himself photographed wearing a mask representing the enlarged, but unmistakable, features of Georges Marchais, an indication, the author suggests, of his admiration for the French communist leader, though rather an odd way to express it.

It is true that, by this time, Mesrine was going downhill very rapidly, perhaps owing to his increasing isolation and to the fact that he was becoming more and more cut off from the easy sociability of the Paris streets and markets. He was beginning to repeat to anyone who was prepared to listen—and it would have been highly unwise *not* to have been prepared to listen, for it was generally Mesrine who did all the talking—the boring and repeti-tive drivel of *gauchisme* and Instant Revolution. In his last fantasy, he had managed to convince himself that he was in fact a revolutionary; this might have been harmless enough, merely rather trying for his criminal friends and for his mistresses, had he not established contacts with the internationale of political killers. It was just as well that the police caught up with him when they did. *Gauchiste* bores are trying enough; but armed, quick-moving and highly skilled ones are dangerous recruits to the armies of nihilism.

Not that there was anything very surprising about this final evolution of a man dominated above all by his limitless conceit. If the revolutionary left needed him, as, years earlier, or so it is suggested, though the evidence is thin, the OAS had called in his skills, well then here he was, 'frais et dispos', and ready for something really big and that would make the world sit up. What indeed was the difference between a killer of the right, a killer of the left, and just an all-round, all-purpose killer? Only, in the case of the second, the dreary verbiage of mindless fanaticism. There was absolutely nothing funny about the Jacques Mesrine of those last few months.

Carey Schofield has had the advantage, denied to most of us, of having heard Mesrine speak. There seems no doubt at all, from his almost instant success with a great many people: police chiefs, *commissaires*, ordinary *agents*, warders, shop-keepers, bank-clerks, waiters, neighbours, that the Clichy-born Mesrine was a *baratineur* of the top flight, a smooth-tongued charmer in the best Paris tradition. We do not know whether he had a Parisian accent; given his middle-class background, it is likely that he did not. But there is plenty of evidence of his ability to charm, to inspire confidence, to make people feel important and to put them at their ease.

All his numerous neighbours—and he was always on the move across the map of Paris and its suburbs—refer to his politeness, and he seems even to have succeeded in softening the hearts of *concierges*—though, predictably, he was betrayed by a succession of these—and to have introduced an easy-going hilarity in police vans on his way to courts.

One of the photographs shows him deep in conversation with three warders from the Santé, one of whom, a smallish man, can be seen looking up to him in amused ease, in the attitude of a bird waiting to be fed by its mother, his mouth half-open in wait of the *drôleries* issuing from the big man—we gather that Mesrine had a favourite line too in *contrepèteries*, in the manner of 'les Albums de la Comtesse'—the other two appear to be laughing, the biggest with his shoulders shaking. It is a marvellous conversation-piece in an enclosed prison courtyard. Mesrine was talking to a purpose. He was out to establish friendly relations with the three warders and he was talking himself into more time outside in order to examine every detail of the yard and the wall.

The author was clearly captivated by his conversation, as well she might have been—it was an important scoop for a girl just down from Cambridge to get an interview with Mesrine while he was on the run in Paris—but, through the filter of translation, it is impossible to convey the velvet of his voice and the smoothness of his accompanying gestures, the warmth of his greeting, and his rather wry turn of humour. French is the language of flattery and hospitality, of rapidly accessible intimacy and complicity, of comforting admission into a closed, mysterious, fraternal circle. None of this can be rendered in English; and as the author's French is very defective, pedestrian and inaccurate, there is an important element in Mesrine's formidable arsenal that is almost completely missing. All we can say is that he seems to have had a considerable and readily accessible fund of small-talk. He was even able to persuade a French-Canadian lady from Percé that he and his Parisian mistress, a Pigalle prostitute, were Belgians, going on to talk at great length about life in Brussels, one of the few capitals that he had never visited. It is true that a French-Canadian lady from Percé would have few positive notions about 'les bons Belges' and Mesrine may have been feeding her with Mlle Beulemans and similar Parisian lore on the subject of those who live *outre-Quiévrain*.

Nor can it have been very difficult to dazzle the nineteen-year-old Jocelyne Deraiche, just out of her convent school, a *petite oie* from the suburbs of Montreal, with his Parisian polish and *savoir-vivre*. Jocelyne's parents were likewise bowled over, and do not seem to have resented the fact that Mesrine, having made her his mistress, trained her up to be quite an effective—as long as she kept her mouth shut—partner in crime. French-Canadians were not really fair game for a velvet-tongued Parisian; and even a Montreal millionaire—Jocelyne's parents were *petits bourgeois*—was prepared to take Mesrine and Jeanne Schneider at their word, when they answered an advertisement for a chauffeur-chef and a housekeeper. He should have known better. One is astonished by the trusting naïvety and provinciality of *les Québé-cois* when confronted with the pretty run-of-the-mill Parisian Mesrine. But there is no doubt about his charm and his attentive considerateness.

He was also very Parisian in his lively comeback and in his enjoyment of breaking in on other people's conversation (especially on the subject of crime), in restaurants and public places, *à la cantonnade*. It was only in the last year of his life that he began to hector and to preach.

But by then he had been infected by *gauchiste* rhetoric, by a galloping megalomania, by self-pity, and by what appeared to be a growing death-wish. But even when he had managed to convince himself that he was the victim of a cruel society and had taken to ranting and raving, there was still enough residual affability to captivate a young English girl.

Mesrine came from a middle-class family. He was born in 1937, 'l'année Expo', 'l'année Weidmann', in Clichy, where his parents possessed what is described as a comfortable flat. His mother, Monique, came from a village in the Vienne where, in 1940, she still had numerous relatives, mostly farmers. His father, Pierre Mesrine, is described as a textile designer and engineer, running his own business. But we are not told where he came from nor what was the origin of his bizarre and most un-French surname. Mesrine may have been only partly French; and this could have accounted for his almost *gaulliste* self-identification with the great figures of French history—poor Jocelyne was not spared a visit to the Vieux Marché during a rapid tour of Rouen—especially during his schooldays and his early years in crime. During his military service he seems to have acquired all the current racialist prejudices on the subject of Algerians: *les ratons, les crouillas*, and one of his boasts, probably untrue, was that he had derived great satisfaction from torturing captured *fellaghas*.

The Mesrine family were clearly affluent. There was a manor house in the country near Beaumont-le-Roger; and Mesrine was given an expensive private education: the ultra-smart Collège de Juilly (which parted company with him when he was fourteen; but his time there was later put to criminal profit, thanks to his knowledge of the Meaux area) and Chaptal. Nothing could have been further removed from a deprived background.

One suspects that the Mesrines were in fact nouveaux-riches. At one of his trials, Mesrine was described by a counsel for the prosecution as a parvenu. And, throughout Miss Schofield's rather wide-eyed account of *The Life and Death of a Supercrook* one is constantly reminded of the undoubted vulgarity of her dubious hero. He dressed vulgarly: Italian suits and silk ties, track-suits and anoraks, basket-ball boots, woollen jackets. He had vulgar tastes in furnishing and comfort; the author refers to the 'solid rustic' furniture he installed in the inn that he ran near Compiègne.

We can guess what this means: *Vie et Campagne, faux manoir normand*, wagon wheels, red-and-white check table-cloths and little brass lamps. The house in Lower Normandy no doubt had white plastic garden seats. His enjoyments—night clubs, flashy girls, expensive watches and jewellery, bath salts and masculine scents—were vulgar. Like any Frenchman living in an apartment *de grand standing*, he was a persistent and diligent *vacancier*, equipping himself with all the elaborate paraphernalia of the Parisian holiday-maker. Even crime and burglary had to stop in August; he was far too conventional to have considered staying in Paris as an *aoûtien*. Indeed, many of his criminal activities were directed towards financing elaborate holidays in the sun, *bronzage* and meals in fish restaurants.

His odd attachment to Deauville, dating from his childhood, is also explainable in terms of his vulgarity; he liked the make-believe of Norman black-and-white disguising even administrative buildings: a school, a *commissariat*, a restaurant.

He returned to Deauville again and again, not only to rob, but because he liked the place, enjoyed an artificial seaside town devoted to ostentatious wealth. Jocelyne has a flashy vulgarity; we do not know what Sylvie or Janou, the Pigalle prostitute, looked like; but the former, on the day of Mesrine's death, was carrying a miniature white poodle in the car that was to take them—on a Friday, the beginning of the obligatory weekend—to their newly acquired flat in Marly-le-Roi, for which they had recently purchased (closely followed by two detectives) an enormous divan. For a man who, in the last year of his life, was claiming to be a revolutionary, at war with the bourgeoisie, Mesrine seems to have been dominated by petit-bourgeois values and by a vulgarity which grew with affluence.

In other ways, too, he was surprisingly conventional, *routinier*, almost *pantouflard*. His attachment not just to Paris, but to particular quarters of Paris, above all to the XVIIIème, at the northern tip of the city, was both touching and, ultimately, highly dangerous to his clandestine style of living.

His adult life, right up to the time of his death at forty-two, tended to be circumscribed within a predictable topography: Clichy, northern Paris, Orbec, Bernay, Beaumount-le-Roger, Deauville-Trouville, the *grands boulevards*. To these he returned again and again, in an effort, the author suggests, at reassurance. It may have been so. He met his death, Place de Clignancourt, at the end of the *métro* line; and there is a photograph of his body, in a brown leather jacket riddled with holes, lying between the disdainful shoes and trouser bottoms of detectives, on the round *pavé de Paris*, in his favourite *arrondissement*.

He took enormous risks by hiding in Paris, simply because he could not bear to leave the place for long. But he also exploited its complicated topography with masterly skill. There was not a *passage* nor an *impasse* that he did not know—and use. Of the many addresses cited in the book, half a dozen are *impasses*. Like Raymond Queneau, he adored the *métro*; he also used it intelligently, as the simplest channel of escape, after a hold-up.

After getting out of the Santé, he chose a refuge near the Invalides, because it gave easy access to two *métro* lines. And, on several occasions, after a burglary, in broad daylight, in his favourite terrain, he would simply walk off, quite slowly—it was the unflustered slowness of his movements, during and immediately after a crime, that so much impressed victims and witnesses—into the vast anonymity of the Gare du Nord or the Gare de l'Est. At a moment when the police of half of Europe were searching for him, he was quietly queuing in front of the international ticket office, Gare du Nord, waiting to buy a ticket for London. Like la Piaf, whom he greatly admired, Mesrine was *un enfant de Paris*; perhaps, when among his underworld associates, he even called the place *Paname*.

Although totally uneducated, his schooling having been completely wasted, and his favourite reading having been cheap thrillers, he was as quick-witted as he was quick-moving. His ability to escape was unique—it is his greatest claim to a sort of fame—but it was based on very careful observation and minute preparation.

In advance of any operation, he would go over the terrain again and again, would indeed often return to it for a second operation, on the principle that no one would expect a criminal to return to the scene of his crime. Mesrine liked going back, not only out of calculation, but also as a sort of bravado, as a means of testing himself. He realized the importance of detail, and, in the preparation of his operations, he displayed the sort of satisfaction that one might associate with a researcher working in an archive. It was not just that he liked the XVIIIème—and it is indeed one of the few remaining strongholds of Parisian individualism—it was also because it offered, at its northern tip, ready access to the *boulevard périphérique*, death to the motorist and weekender, escape to the bad boy.

Mesrine was ultimately undone by the carelessness of his last accomplice, Charly Bauer, a carelessness and an impudence *signé Parisien*. The police had succeeded in tracing the registration number of the car belonging to Charly's mistress and political indoctrinator (Charly was just a vulgar Marseillais bad boy who rolled his own cigarettes); the car was soon discovered, parked on the pavement, opposite l'église de la Trinité.

Charly and *la pétroleuse* were discovered living in the vicinity soon afterwards. Mesrine would not have made that sort of mistake. A creature of habit, as much as any petit-bourgeois, for his operations he favoured Fridays, especially for hold-ups and burglaries, because, the good Parisian weekender that he was, he was aware that the city would be under-policed in the second half of that day, many *agents* themselves already using the weekend to try out their latest gardening equipment acquired from the bottom floor of the BHV. Friday too had generally been his lucky day. But, on Friday, 2 November 1979, determined, like a million or more other Parisians, to drive off to the country in the afternoon, he was cornered and shot through with twenty-one bullets, at approximately 3 p.m.

Vulgar, banal and big-headed though he was, Mesrine's

attachment to Paris, to the Orbec region, and to the valley of the Lower Seine is touching, almost endearing. The man was certainly a monster, a boaster, a show-off with his silly card tricks, a cold-blooded killer, and a torturer who exulted in the infliction of pain, and who took a particular delight in inflicting it on those who had crossed him at some previous time; but he was also something of a Parisian poet (he liked to compare himself to Lacenaire, the nineteenth-century *poète assassin*). After his dramatic shoot-out in Deauville and his escape, with François Besse, walking through three nights among the Norman orchards in May, he stole a boat moored to the bank, at Jeufosse (the author calls it Jenfosse) and eventually reached a safe house at Port-Villiez, a few miles farther down the river. The next morning, he wakes up, in a comfortable bed, to glimpse, propped up on his pillows, through an open window, the silver river, as it curls round, beneath its steep, chalky right bank, towards the islands off Vernon. It is one of the few happy, peaceful, quiet moments, in a chronicle of violence, cruelty, escape, and violent death. It was to such a scene that Mesrine would have liked, eventually, and impossibly, to retire.

Carey Schofield's book is a rush job, written in breathless journalese and abounding in stage props ('the pale sun was shining through the leafless trees which lined the road'; 'Jacques Mesrine, three and a half years old, sat quietly on his bed'). She does not explain the *phénomène Mesrine*, beyond giving us the bare outline of a career, many points of which still remain obscure (and Mesrine himself was a compulsive *fabuliste*). On page 31, she writes: '. . . the exact nature of Mesrine's involvement with the OAS is difficult to determine'. But on the very next page she states boldly: 'Mesrine's involvement with the OAS marked a turning-point in his career'; and throughout the rest of the book there are recurrent references to his OAS contacts in France, French Canada, Spain, Venezuela. He may have been in the OAS, may even have served in the murder squads of the *Commandos Delta*. We do not know for certain. There is rather stronger evidence that, after his escape from la Santé, he may have been in contact with left-wing terrorist groups in France and in Italy.

Miss Schofield also tries to prove too much: the absence of a father during the formative years of childhood, the effects, on a child of three and a half, of the national humiliation of June 1940, the excitement of the Resistance, the brutal violence of the Liberation. A great many French children must have been born in 1937, many of them had fathers prisoners-of-war in Germany, some of them had spent the Occupation years in the country, where food was easier to obtain, and lived among female relatives, spending some of their time walking in the fields and tending cows; many were spoilt by over-indulgent parents, loved birds and animals, failed the *bac* or played truant from school, enjoyed shooting at targets, did their national service in combat units in Algeria. Yet they did not become Mesrines. Mesrine is a phenomenon. And, if there is any explanation, it must be sought not in his chronology, nor in his privileged background, but in his own monumental conceit and in his craving for fame.

The author is also far too prone to pad out her narrative with long disquisitions on public events, as if the fact of Reynaud's resignation had some effect on Mesrine's three-year-old awareness. Of course he went through *l'Exode*; so did some eight million others. Her historical judgements are crude; Vichy may have been subservient to the Germans, but there is more to it than that. At best, she provides us with a useful framework of derring-do, of killing, escape, disguise, and cruelty. We learn little of Mesrine's many accomplices, even less of those who, without being criminals, took considerable risks—one of them a man of seventy—to give him shelter.

There will be other books about Mesrine. One hopes that they will be better written, less naïve, and more penetrating. Of course, silence would be the best monument to this evil, cruel man. But that we cannot hope for. Already, apparently, he is a cult figure among the punk-rockers of a café in Saint-Ouen, le Rex.

Soon he may be claimed by Genet—at least he won't be claimed by Sartre—as a Saint-Mesrine, a true revolutionary, a hero who waged war single-handed—not quite, he always had chains of people to fall back on—on the French State, on the French police, on the French bourgeoisie, on wealth and property, inequality, capitalism and so on. What is most chilling about the present account is the frequent reminder of the new and utterly sinister *trahison des clercs*, of the willingness of French intellectuals to flirt with terrorism and crime, of the collusion between teacher and gangster, as illustrated by the case of Charly Bauer, and his mistress, a *professeur de lycée*, not even sacked but 'mise en disponibilité', presumably to give her time to indoctrinate her Marseillais full-time crook and provide him with his 'formation politique'.

At least the present book does not disguise the fact that Mesrine was a sadistic monster, ready to shoot his way to fame, even to the extent of humiliating, torturing, stripping and half-killing an unfortunate journalist from *Minute*, and then taking photographs of his handiwork and sending them to the press. Mesrine's rightful place is with a *chronique judiciaire* that has entombed a Weidmann, a Petiot, a Pierrot-le-Fou and a Marie Besnard, rather than with the chilling, grisly fantasies of Instant Revolutionists.

The Homburg Hat

Even to an unpractised eye, it was apparent that school began at Paddington. For here were all the *signes avant-coureurs* of what was awaiting one, all the untold horrors of the unknown, much further up the line. On the departure platform, there were small groups of twos and threes, keeping their distances from one another, perhaps in a last desperate bid to cling on to the family unit, even reduced to bare essentials, in the absence of sisters and elder or younger brothers, and to hold on to the last tiny particle of home, holiday and privacy. Boys, of vastly different sizes, but all affecting a brave unconcern, almost as if anxious to get it all over and settle down in the compartment; mothers, on the verge of tears, a few actually *over* the verge, fathers sharing with their sons, whether tall or quite tiny, a brave indifference and common stiff upper-lipdom. Some of the boys were standing awkwardly on one leg, others were shifting from leg to leg, as if in need to go to the lavatory, or indeed needing just to do that, but unwilling to admit to its urgency. From inside the compartment, I watched the scene, with some trepidation, but glad at least to have got it all over, as far as I was concerned, without witnesses, on the up platform of Tunbridge Wells Central: once in the train, a welcoming tunnel had at once blotted out the sight of my parents, as they disappeared in a swirl of yellow smoke. It was a station fortunately not suited to prolonged adieux.

I thought that I could distinguish between those who, like myself, were newcomers—later, as I was to learn, their correct designation was New Scum—and the hardened old-timers—two-year-olds, three-year-olds—other expressions of a mysterious vocabulary awaiting to trip me up, like so many other things, at the other end—by the apparently unaffected ease and studied casualness of the latter, some of them standing in slightly drooping postures, as if they were meeting their parents at a social occasion, or as if they were holding invisible sherry glasses, or had come together by chance at a race meeting. One tall boy even had his back to his parents, another could be seen handing his father a silver cigarette-case.

The equine illusion was reflected in the manner, likewise studiedly casual, in which all the boys, both tall and apparently fully grown, and diminutive, were clothed: brown shoes indented with complicated arabesques, or, daringly, suede shoes, grey flannels, hacking jackets with wide vents, or furry sports-coats in brownish, grey or green herring-bone, polka-dot ties and wide-striped Vyella collars, all topped, at the command of a mysterious, unwritten uniformity, by trilbies in brown or dark grey—brown was the majority response, grey suggested that of the vaguely *osé* and raffish—the brim pushed well over the nose: Mark One long and solemn, Mark Two snub, Mark Three bulbous—or worn at a rakish angle. An intent group of tall and tiny punters, dressed for Newmarket, Newbury, or the Eridge point-to-point. Had I been better acquainted with that *milieu*, I would have expected to see brandy-flasks emerging from hip-pockets. As it was, the hip-pockets were, like the rest of the outfit, articles of make-believe. Judged from the studiedly informal scattered groups of normal-sized or miniature racing enthusiasts, the contingent from the South-East must have represented quite a considerable fraction of the school. This I found vaguely reassuring; and I was certainly in dire need of reassurance.

There had been no mention of the trilbies on the lists supplied by Matron. Clearly they belonged to some unspoken tradition, a code that one ignored at one's peril. Certainly all had heard the hidden voice, for there was not a boy to be seen whose head (and sometimes his ears) was not covered, or who was not casually holding his hat by the brim, or twirling it around with abandoned ease, as if he had never set foot out of doors without this sign of middle-class self-advertisement. What strange laws are those of English social conformity! for, as I was later to discover, these hats were only worn six—or, counting half-terms—nine times a year, on the journey in one direction or another, on the Paddington to Birkenhead Express.

It had been a stroke of pure luck that I had been forewarned about the hats, thanks to the fact that two brothers, who had been at the school a year and two years ahead of me, lived in Tunbridge Wells. Thanks to them, I was saved the awful humiliation of having been seen at Paddington, or at the station of arrival, or on the drive from the station to the school, BARE-HEADED. It would have been a very bad start indeed, and one that might have dogged me for years: COBB, THE BOY WHO DID NOT HAVE A HAT.

As it was, I was able to tell my mother that, in addition to the reglementary top-hat for Sunday wear—one was provided, already battered, by my maternal uncle, a country doctor—I absolutely needed an ordinary hat in which to travel. As the hat was only to be in use for travel, my mother did not see the need of providing me with a new one. One of my father's hats, no doubt dating back to official occasions in Cairo, was dug out. It was light grey, with a light grey band, and with an embroidered turned up brim in even lighter grey-silk, and a silk lining. Inside it had the name of a Cairo *chapelier*, as well as the Egyptian royal arms, indicating that he was the *fournisseur attitré* to the Court of the Khedive. It was somewhat faded and had certainly seen better days, on no doubt khedival occasions when my father had had to present himself in Cairo. By the Thirties, it was a type of hat already outmoded, though still worn, to go with spats and gloves *gorge de pigeon*, by elderly Dutch politicians of the Anti-Revolutionary Party. Its antique and heavily formal appearance caused me considerable misgiving. If trilbies sat ill on the head of a fourteen-year-old, this stiff Homburg, hinting at a pre-War Karlsbad, could only make me look utterly ridiculous. It was also much too large. But then, I thought, I would only have to wear it for a few minutes, and might even not be noticed in it. I could not hold it, owing to the giveaway upturned brim. And indeed, at Paddington, I had managed to get into the compartment holding the wretched thing against my body, on the train side. I had then hidden it behind my suitcase on the luggage-rack.

It was at Birmingham that the disaster occurred. A grown-up traveller, stretching to put his luggage in the rack, displaced the pearl-grey homburg that, hideously, and as if impelled by familiarity, fell into my lap, witnessed by the whole, observant carriage. There was a dreadful roar of laughter, which even grew in volume when it was discovered that the hat revealed little of me above chin level. The rest of the journey was pure hell, though, by one kind dispensation, none of those who had caught me in this unforgivable social faux-pas was from my House, so that I was never identified there as the owner of the homburg. A few weeks after the beginning of term, profiting from a rainy day, I was able to throw it from the bridge into the Severn. Thus removed from the cause of my social humiliation, I was able to look on the observant world of my fellow-boys with something like self-confidence. Later in the term I profited from a visit from my godmother, who lived at High Ercall, to purchase a new trilby, dark brown in colour. Travelling after that caused no problem, though the approach of my first Speech Day was marred by my trepidation as to my *father*'s choice of headgear. In the summer, my father favoured a boater. A panama would have been all right, but not a boater . . . : To my intense relief, he turned up in plus-fours and a cap. What is more, I noticed that the mother of someone in my house was wearing a leopard-skin coat; and no *lady* ever wore one of these. As soon as I left school, I celebrated my freedom by buying myself, in Vienna, a furry black hat with a wide brim.

Bastille Day 1944

At about three in the morning, just when I had finished running off the English news-sheet and was about to start on the *bulletin* in French, a cow butted against the tent, stuck its head through the flap, upset the table and the heavy army typewriter, and then, withdrawing, its legs entangled in the ropes, brought the whole thing down on top of me. This was almost a nightly occurrence; but that morning it came at the worst possible time. I sorted out the wreckage; but was unable to get the tent up again. Working outside on a table, I had completed the sheet in French by five. I had even decorated it, like a notice of General Mobilization, with crossed flags, to mark the occasion.

At six, I went to the *école communale*, which also served as *mairie*, to await the little messenger sent out, just after dawn, twice a week, by the *maire* of Cottun, a little girl of eleven, dressed in a sort of sack, and wearing *sabots*. She turned up at 6.30, pale, worried, and very polite; I gave her a copy, which the *maire* would have pinned up on the notice-board outside the village café and watched the frail figure clopping uphill, her thin legs striding out with an air of purpose. I then set off on foot for Bayeux, bearing about sixty *bulletins*. There was seldom any military traffic on the dusty, yellowish road, but that morning it was unusually crowded with old-fashioned, two-wheeled farm-carts, rather smart *carrioles* in polished pale wood, with dark green covers turning down forwards, so that one could scarcely see the drivers' faces, cut off at mouth level, giving them a rather sinister appearance like corduroy-covered Teutonic knights. There were scores of them close-packed on all sides of the road, and all heading in the direction of the town, raising a beige-coloured fog up to the level of my middle, so that I seemed to be gliding along legless above the low clouds, though, on each side of the narrow road, the orchards and pastures, the white fences and the black-and-white cows could be seen clearly in the bright morning sun. The road itself looked like an immense, twisting yellow serpent, as it headed towards the capital of the Bessin.

A cart, drawn by a very smart black horse in bright, polished harness, pulling out of the dimly-seen stampede, on to the grass verge, and tipping over dangerously towards the road, stopped beside me. 'Montez, Monsieur le sergent', said a brick-red chin, from under the green cover; and I clambered up the metal step, pulling the cart over towards the verge. Once inside, and so high up, sitting on an upright wooden bench next to the driver, I recognized him as the *maire* of a village near Barbeville with whom I had done a recent exchange of cigarettes for calvados: *Maître* Lecordeur, not that he was in the law, but, as the largest farmer in the place, thus honoured by his fellows. I clutched my pile of *bulletins* as the cart jerked forward at a word from the red-faced driver. We bowled along at quite a pace, soon catching up with the main group—Ben Hur in slightly slow motion—and falling into a rhythmical clop-clop as we hit the *pavé* of the 'route de Balleroy', lined by poplars, on the outskirts of Bayeux. It was already very hot, as it had been ever since our arrival.

We reached the town, past the familiar house of the Town Major, a large place in grey Fleury stone, covered with Virginia creeper, with long, handsome windows, green shutters, and an imposing double-door under a sculptured archway. It might have been the home of a *notaire* or a doctor, or, in this part of the world, a vet: anyhow, a man of consequence. The Town Major had chosen well. Next to it was the small factory of 'la biscuiterie Marie', which was closed for the day; the biscuits, made out of pure butter, were very good indeed, and as the market was restricted by the proximity of the Front, there was no shortage of them. We entered Bayeux in style, high up, like conquerors, amidst a tremendous clatter and jingling. It gave me the agreeable impression of having moved back into a peaceable nineteenth century, or at least into a pre-1914 France. Apart from my uniform, there was no hint of war; nor was any military vehicle to be seen, the red-capped traffic motorcyclists having been withdrawn some time before. Bayeux was already on its way to being a backwater, to the openly stated satisfaction of many of its inhabitants.

The farmer put me down in a large yellowish square, also thick in dust, and surrounded by red-roofed grey buildings with green or cream shutters. All round the square was an irregular but continuous line of *tricolores*. There were similar carts, up-ended, all over the square, the horses tethered to plane trees. The drivers, large men with red necks, in corduroys or black suits and caps, could be seen heading, in small groups, towards the cafés on or just off the square. There were hardly any women to be seen; as it was a *fête*, the farmers had left their women at home. Whatever significance they may have attached to the event, they had decided that it should be celebrated *entr'hommes*.

But there were plenty of women and children (in neat blue or check smocks) in the *Grande Rue*. I walked along it through a forest of flags—M. Ploemakers, the shoemaker, had a huge Belgian one, embroidered at the edges, outside his shop—turning off, halfway down, into a shady courtyard, full of pots of geraniums and nasturtiums, and pushing open a rusty door which ground shrilly on its hinges, under a temporary wooden notice, black-edged, with bold, old-fashioned lettering in red: 'La Renaissance du Bessin', which, as I knew, had been hastily put up, about a month previously, in order to cover over the more affluent-looking and solid brass letters of *Le Journal de Bayeux*.

Even in the deep shadow of the cool room, I could at once pick out the startlingly brick-coloured face and white hair of the editor; and, although it was both irreverent and unfair, I could not help thinking that, however unwittingly, he reflected at least *two* of the national colours, indeed, in more perfect shades, both redder and whiter, than those displayed outside; or, better, all *three*, for, as I drew closer, and shook his rather limp hand across the table, I could also examine—like the much-studied map of a familiar estuary—the broken network of red and blue veins around his eyes and working its way, in an uneven, meandering series of squiggles, down his ravaged cheeks. 'Arborer les couleurs du jour', the triple colour scheme seemed to say; and it was further accentuated by the brilliant, Norman blue of his watery eyes, a shiny electric blue suit, double-breasted, with a red ribbon in the left lapel, and dating back to the mid-1930s.

The editor, a royalist in his mid-sixties, was as devoted to calvados as to the duc d'Harcourt. His assistant, an albino with reddish eyes and red hair, M. Hébert—a name much in evidence in Lower Normandy—was sitting at a little side-table amidst a mass of cuttings, mostly advertisements, in curiously old-fashioned type reminiscent of the Second Empire: 'Hippolyte Lemarchand, Pompes Funèbres du Bessin' was in again, occupying half a page, in the special number. He had been in, twice a week, under the Occupation, and, under the new title, ever since the Liberation; since which the local hospital had been crammed with peasants—mostly small boys and girls with horrible stomach wounds, caused by mines stepped on in long grass, and who lay, dreadfully pale, and with frightened eyes, even in the corridors and on the ground between the beds. M. Lemarchand represented continuity.

On the dusty shelves of the untidy office were little piles of yellowing *Le Journal de Bayeux* tied up in pink *notaire*'s tape. I handed over my *bulletin*, devoted mostly to news of the Eastern Front, to the editor, who took it with a look of distaste. However, he then opened a drawer and pulled out an unmarked greenish bottle, which, predictably, turned out to be a local, and very potent, calvados. The three of us clinked glasses—dusty too —exclaiming, uncommittedly, 'à la bonne vôtre', M. Hébert (who, once, alone, had told me he was a republican) and I drinking silently to the Day, the editor, I do not know to what: not, I think, to a Restoration, for his watery eyes looked as if they had long lost hope of anything so positive. There were sounds of fanfares and cheering coming from the street. I thought I heard 'Sambre-et-Meuse', played too slow, and rather tinnily; but the editor did not seem to notice, plunged in a *rêverie calvadocienne*.

I walked through the town, past the cathedral, which had two huge tricolors flying from the tower—they were flapping northwards, the south-westerly wind bringing the sickly smell of death from the battle area. The Tree of Liberty (the only one surviving in France), still in provocative adjacence to the cathedral (though I think the message had long since been lost) had also a large flag blowing from a top branch. There was a crowd outside the Sous-Préfecture, watching a march-past by a group of ragged firemen, out of step, and little boys in white suits and red side-caps; the *commissaire régional*, M. Coulet, the new *sous-préfêt*, and the old *maire* were on the balcony. I made for one of the straggling suburbs, beyond the silent station, 'la cité des cheminots', where I had lunch with a railwayman, his wife, and two very polite children. The couple were among the rare *CGT-istes* in the little market and cathedral town. They had decorated their grey *SNCF-style* stucco house with 'le grand pavois', including Union Jacks and the Soviet flag. I left them a *bulletin*, and went off to a football match between the Stade Bayeusain and a scratch army team drawn from HQ L of C.

I began distributing my news-sheet to the civilian spectators, but was almost at once arrested by a member of the Provost Corps. I spent the rest of the day in detention, missing the evening fair and the roundabouts, on a great meadow to the south of the town. I was told that I had infringed security regulations by mentioning Bayeux in my news-sheet and my *bulletin*. But I was let out in time for my nightshift, which started at nine. The wind was still from the south-west, bringing a steady low rumble and the same cloying smell. As far as the army was concerned, Bastille Day was an irrelevance; but to the inhabitants of Bayeux—a place suspended in time, cut off from most of France, the railway line silent, deprived of news (the Germans had long before collected all the wirelesses)—it meant something: the promise at least of a return to more normal conditions, the resumption of everyday life, the end to what the Bayeusains referred to, rather ironically, as their little town's 'heure de gloire'; a luxury of brief headiness, but, by mid-July, already in over-bloom, dusty, and beginning to wilt, like the blowsy foliage of the trees. A bit before midnight, I could hear the noise of carts, the clop-clop of hooves, and the drunken shouts of the drivers, as they returned to Barbeville and to the villages beyond. I was rather glad that I had tried to do *something* about Bastille Day 1944.

21 July 1945

Les was on one of his regular trips from Brussels to units in France; but this time it was not to the old headquarters in Roubaix. He was to pick up some small component from the REME people in Valenciennes. As I had never done the stretch between Leuze, through Péruwelz and Condé, to the frontier, I said I would come with him, when he offered me a lift. We roared off, on his big Army Triumph, down the familiar way out of the town, through Anderlecht, then past the sign to Ruisbroek, which always made me think of Brueghel—it was said that he had used the landscape round there again and again, whether for grim battle scenes and a field of gibbets or for a sunny *kermesse* and the lazy stretched-out sleep that followed, the men in a cartwheel, their feet towards the middle. It was already a beautiful day, radiant, dry, with a bright, early morning sun behind us, and the rough *pavé* for once quite an inviting, almost uniform bluey-grey, a hazy ribbon stretching ahead; even so, though it was already hot, I was glad of his broad, leather-jerkined back in front of me, right against my chest, for I only had a tunic over my shirt. Up to Hal, I kept my eyes fixed on the back of his neck, the dark curly hair crinkling over the collar of his khaki shirt; it helped to keep me steady and to prevent me from noticing the breakneck speed with which he always attacked this road, as if the War had still been on and he had been carrying an urgent despatch to Reims, instead of going to pick up a battery. I didn't mind the speed really, as long as I looked ahead at the brown and beige of Les's back—his shirt had gone quite pale from washing after washing, he thought it more fetching that way—it and the noise we made gave me a sense of purpose and importance. But at Hal, as usual, we had to slow down almost to a crawl, the bike swerving to stay up, where the road narrows by the church. The place was covered in huge flags, both national and municipal (yellow and green), and a group of small girls and boys, dressed in white, were marching behind two *orphéons*, the bandsmen in blue and red uniforms.

Once through the little town, Les aimed his bike at France, as if it had been a weapon and he had it in for the Republic (he much preferred Belgium). I could just make out the round signs indicating Ghislenghien and Ath, as we shot through them, eating them up, through a double line of black, yellow, and red. From the corners of my eyes, the uniform gold of the flat, open cornfields was all at once briefly interrupted by streaks of red buildings, green, black, and white shutters, and the curving, undulating line, like a streamer on both sides of us, of the national colours, and yellow and red dots from the flowers in the window-boxes, all running along with us, like a coloured code, the noise of the engine hitting back at us from the walls, then the racing kaleidoscope colours all at once running out, and the brighter, wider gold returning to escort us. Just on the far side of Leuze, on the road to Tournai, past the low white inn *chez Maria* (a very dark Flemish woman) he slowed up, turned left into a courtyard, and propped the Triumph against the white wall of the stables. The Senator and his children, a young married couple with a baby, the owners of the big pink farmhouse and the scattered cream buildings around it, were not surprised to see us, as this was a regular stopping place on our way to or from France. They had brought out a long table into the courtyard, and there were a dozen people, men in shirt-sleeves and girls in summer dresses, sitting on benches and drinking beer or red wine. An outstanding tricolor, edged with a border in the same colours, was hanging from the window above the kitchen door. We had rather counted on the Senator making this an occasion, and he certainly did.

By the time we got back on the Condé road, it was nearly six, and the glow over the huge fields, high with corn and rolling very slightly in the gentle hillocks of this part of the Tournésis, turned to a richer gold, the shadows thrown by poplars and church towers becoming longer and blacker. The yellow fields were full of people: girls in white blouses and bright headscarves, men and boys in faded blue shirts; and in the villages we passed through, there were more blaring bands, and the usual *terrasses* had been supplemented by trestle tables and indoor chairs. In each place, the whole population seemed to be in the street, along with much of their furniture. There was a very old man in an enormous armchair, and some of the trestles had been decorated with checked red and white tablecloths that billowed in the breeze and with plants in brass pots. We turned off the main road before Péruwelz, and dawdled lazily—Les had apparently lost his impulse to take France by storm—in dusty country lanes, beige-coloured in the fading light, the Triumph humming gently. At the top of a slight incline, we could see five bulbous-topped church towers: Baugnies, Wasmes, Roucourt, Callenelle, Brasmenil, each topped with an enormous tricolor, blowing straight out, like the flags in a Dutch print of a seventeenth-century siege; and every village we passed through was covered in outsize flags, some of them extending a couple of storeys. People were on the move everywhere; we could see the upper halves of lines of them, heading through the corn, some of them carrying tired children, the heads of larger children bobbing up and down just above the line of golden yellow now turning a pale beige; and on every tiny village square, brass bands were making a tremendous row with martial music, the young men sweating behind their silver instruments, their peaked caps—*orphéon municipal* and a lyre in silver thread—pushed back from their foreheads. Although only a few miles from the main road to Valenciennes, we seemed to be deep in the country, and it looked as if many of the people had never seen a British soldier before. But Les's bike was the big draw.

In the areas of encroaching dusk, between the comfortable, solid, reassuring ochre, cream, pink, green, and black (to outline windows) villages, the still countryside itself seemed to be *en fête*, the fading gold of the tall, abundant corn—a marvellous harvest—the red poppies dotted in the sighing fields, and the deep shadows thrown by the farm buildings, barns, and lines of trees, rearranging, in vast and unexpected patterns, vaguely discernible, the national colours of the flag-decked villages, as if in silent approval of the mood of collective euphoria. From a hillock, the rich, gentle farmland of the Tournésis, so apparently remote from war, took on the tidier aspect of a child's toy battlefield, with flags atop everything that stood up (there were even some in the top branches of trees) blowing out joyfully in the evening breeze: a child's toy battlefield, but, in this frontier land, a scene of almost idyllic peace and rural stillness, at the close of a marvellous summer day: and to imitate those of a Brueghelian summer scene, Brueghel's *kermesse*, in the villages over the brow of the hill, reaching a crashing, frenetic rhythm, as the strings of coloured lights began to go on, the yellow electric light flooded the narrow streets and squares, and the *orphéons* boomed on, competing with laughter, screams, the explosion of fire-crackers and the noise of hurdie-gurdies. The still tranquillity of the evening had given way to the full-throated roar of the blue-black night, scented with dust and powder. As we turned towards the main road, we could still see the many-coloured glow of village lights, follow the proud ascent of rockets, and pick out the muffled blare of uniformed bands. A little before midnight we left the kingdom, its first National Day since Liberation clearly likely to spill over into the next—the frontier post on the Belgian side was empty, the gendarmes and the high-capped *douaniers* were celebrating somewhere else—and headed for the quiet black night of a flagless France.

The View from the Mont des Arts

Between the rue Ravenstein and the Montagne de la Cour, there used to be a small, unassuming and very friendly public garden, perched, in a series of terraces, on the very steep slope dropping from the Place Royale and cascading downwards towards the rue Haute (something of a misnomer, as it was only half-way up the slope, a frontier between the Upper and the Lower Towns), the Galeries Saint-Hubert and the Ville Basse. Each terrace, like a series of balconies in an opera house, gave a view, from a slightly different angle, of the spire of the Hôtel-de-Ville, topped with a golden, winged statue of Saint-Michel, so that, as one followed the precipitous slope downwards, the spire would appear to settle in, as if to seek warmth, comfort and companionship from the surrounding jumble of buildings. In the evening, the spire and its saint would be silhouetted against the sunset, which lent an exotic, ochre glow to the charming eighteenth-century palace housing the Bibliothèque Royale and its attendant chapel, a Gothic appurtenance which was then the home of the Archives Générales du Royaume.

As I have always enjoyed reading in public places, whether outside in a park, or in a café or a *taverne* (to the accompaniment of Ekla or Stella-Artois) I found that, in retrospect, I would identify a particular locality with a particular novel. No doubt I should have read both *Villette* and *Vanity Fair* in Brussels; but I did not, reading the former at the seaside, the latter on wet and mercifully cricketless afternoons at my preparatory school in Sussex. What I was reading, when I first began to go regularly to Brussels, were the Russian classics, in French translation—at eighteen I was the age for them—so that, in the evening light, it did not require much effort for me to identify the golden yellow buildings and green roofs with St Petersburg or with some imagined provincial capital in South Russia, such was the hold over me of a first exposure to Dostoevsky.

I realize now—what I did not realize at the time, or did not want to realize—that no association could have been more inappropriate, for there can surely be no more *un*revolutionary capital than Brussels, and no more respectable and reassuring part of Brussels than the Mont des Arts and the approaches to the Ville Haute, itself spelling out, in unmistakable terms, a Habsburg outpost, and then a modestly constitutional monarchy. Though, on my return in 1944, I was well aware that a bookshop and picture-shop half way up the Montagne de la Cour had been the scene of the most dramatic political murder of the Occupation years—it had happened, so far as I can recall, in 1943, the victim being the editor of *Cassandre*—such an act of violence seemed completely out of place in a locality designed for prudent enjoyment, modest reassurance, tidy leisure—there were many iron baskets, scattered like sentries at each level, within reach of the seats—and middle-class respectability. In fact, such was its complacent peaceability, the Mont des Arts could absorb and swallow, almost without a trace, save in the memory of its regular *usagers*, an act of such indecent and improper brutality. 'On n'assassine pas à Bruxelles', and *certainly* not on the Montagne de la Cour. Or so it seemed to me.

For it was a very quiet place, almost a provincial backwater, though so very close to the Palace, to the fashionable Saint-Jacques-de-Coudenberg, and to the Parc. One could approach the white, gold-lettered Bibliothèque Royale from a tiny, cobbled side-street, little more than an *entrée*, leading off the Montagne de la Cour, as if the statue of Charles de Lorraine and his pretty, unassuming palace were attempting to hide themselves from the casual passer-by, revealing themselves only as a reward to those with enough curiosity to follow the discreet invitation suggested by green double-doors standing open and by an unexpected perspective, hinted at rather than clearly seen, in the deep shadow contrasting with the sunlit yellows and greens of the Montagne de la Cour. Brussels used to abound in semi-secret places of this kind, unexpected gardens approached by narrow passage-ways, glass-covered *cours*, even ivy-strewn wells surmounted by elaborate ironwork.

To the left, as one approached Godefroy de Bouillon (still about to take off) and the frescoed church, there was a large, rather dowdy London store—possibly Harrods or Fortnum and Mason, specializing in expensive teas, water biscuits, shortbread and marmalade—a suitable and discreet monument to that rather touching, unquestioning anglophilia that one so often encountered both *chez le gratin belge* and among middle-class people. (At times I have had the impression that half the Belgians of my generation or a little older were looked after by English families, as refugees, during the First World War, so often has the experience been evoked in my presence; though, in fact, the experience must have been relatively rare.) Sometimes I have suspected that an anglophilia so insistent may have as its reverse an attitude of hostility towards the neighbour *outre-Quiévran*.

On the other side, on the steep street flanking the terraced garden, there were small, unpretentious, but very neat, rather old-fashioned shops (denoting that sense of *confort* that seems to be the particular trademark of Brussels): stationers, picture and print-shops, photographers, milliners, the inevitable tobacconist, with a fantastic array of colours and aromas, the equally inevitable and succulent *pâtisserie*, none of which ever seemed to do much business, content to sun their façades in the evening light, their interiors dark and mysterious, their owners invisible, dozing like the nursemaids and grandmothers beside their prams, on the stone benches of the garden.

Further still, Egmont and Horn, tiny figures, almost garden gnomes, certainly not looking a bit as if they were awaiting decapitation, indeed anything but heroes, overlooked, from their neo-Gothic bases, an equally tranquil group of female knitters and child-watchers, sheltering from the windy rue Royale in this ivy enclave. To the right, a street ran down past the large Gothic église des Sablons, memorable to me only because opposite stood the Librairie des Sablons, a marvellous bookshop where, in 1945, an attentive assistant introduced me to *L'Etranger*, which he described to me as the best book in French published during the Occupation. Indeed, during the immediately previous years, Brussels—judging from the shelves of this wonderful shop—had clearly developed as a notable publishing centre in its own right, with translations from the Dutch, and Belgian editions of Céline, Rebatet, Laubraux, Montherlant, Drieu and other authors then unobtainable in Paris, and which were published, I think, by Les Editions de la Toison d'Or.

139

I was surprised at the time—and have remained surprised since—at this still visible evidence of the vigour of intellectual life in Brussels between 1940 and 1944; perhaps the existence of an artificial barrier between the Kingdom and France (save the Nord and the Pas-de-Calais) may have had something to do with what appeared to have been an indigenous literary and artistic revival, Paris having become temporarily inaccessible, and many Belgian writers and artists having thus been driven back on their own resources. I was surprised too at the high quality of many of these publications, well printed, on handsome paper. But, in my concern to fill in the gaps of my French reading, I missed an opportunity since much regretted, to have become *au fait* with the specifically Belgian writing of the period.

The Mont des Arts had its regular, daily, even hourly, clientèle. It was not the same as that of the Parc, busier, noisier, crossed by schoolchildren on their way to or from the nearby *athénées*, and by groups of wandering tourists, up from the more recommended sights of the Lower Town. The women with prams came from the tall houses on the Montagne—they could hardly have pushed them up the slope—so did the elderly men, wearing *camées* in their ties, and exercising their dogs, some clad in little tartan coats. Thanks to its westerly prospect, it was also favoured by young couples, on spring and summer evenings, looking over the dark pit of the Lower Town and the green, red, and blue neon lights from the Grand' Place, the lamps of the garden clustering like oranges in the vivid green leaves of the clipped trees.

It did not attract the tramps and drunks from the rue Haute; I think the climb must have put them off, not the presence of the park-keeper, in a uniform of Prussian blue with red facings, and a cap with a long peak, who kept an eye on his little triangle of territory, fanning out as it spread to the lower slopes. There were readers scattered singly on each terrace; most of them appeared to make *Le Soir* last for an afternoon until, on a sudden impulse, they would carefully fold it up and head off purposefully.

The Mont was the centre of my kingdom within a kingdom, my regular place of return, the guarantee that there existed a physical environment that would, if not accept me, at least not reject me, not rise up and angrily throw me out. It represented the early stages of my education *ès Bruxelles* as long as I was quite alone in the city. It was like the backdrop of a theatre, immobile, with only the light changing to indicate the approach of night, and the people painted in, to go with the benches and the shopfronts: a self-indulgent play, without a character, not even a listening post.

But later, when I could indeed begin to fill in the familiar topography of the Upper Town with living people, Christian names and surnames, with the enrichment of friendship and the reassurance derived from regular meetings that gave a more human pattern to the week and lessened the desolation of the weekend, I began rather to neglect this first and trusted companion, in return for new, more varied itineraries, no longer walked, or trammed, alone. When I first came back to Brussels, in the delirious *tintamarre* of early September 1944, it was to a city the entire population of which seemed to be out on the streets or on the café terraces, and in which, to the English soldier, every door was invitingly open, as if the whole place had been turned inside out for a vast collective spring-clean.

Then indeed, for once, could the historian's obsessive ambition be fulfilled: to get inside, to step beyond the door and down the corridor. I saw more interiors even than there were nights, at widely remote ends of the town, following a bizarre and partly vinous zig-zag track; and all I can remember of such an itinerary in the midst of the collective joy and hubbub is the light on a wall with the morning sun streaming in, the warmth of a kitchen, a series of prints of the drawings of Mabel-Lucy Atwell in a bright front-room. Even a few weeks later, I would have been quite unable to retrace my movements in the course of that fantastic week, would not be able to recall whether it had brought me to Saint-Gilles, to Forêt, to Anderlecht, to Laeken, or to Uccle, or down by the Gare du Midi; all I could retain was that the whole town had opened up to me, as if the façades of the coloured houses had been on hinges, to be let down flat, like the fronts of dolls' houses, revealing the size of families, the hints of professional status, taste, wealth and class, embroideries of le Roi Chevalier, photographs of the King or of the Regent, souvenirs of la Panne, and regiments of le Mannequin Pis, in hundreds of variations of his extensive wardrobe. It was not the sort of thing ever likely to be repeated; and, indeed, of all the people who welcomed me in during that week, I never saw one again.

Some time in the following year—1945—coming out of a concert, and in the expansive enthusiasm derived from shared enjoyment, I met Pierre Moulaert and his wife. They asked me to come back to their flat, saying that they lived quite near, rue Mercélès, off the chaussée d'Ixelles. What at once attracted me to Pierre was his gentleness. He had wavy fair, reddish hair, and a very soft, persuasive, patient way of speaking, curiously married to the barely recognizable traces of a Brussels accent; he would be, I thought, an excellent teacher, because he seemed so eager to communicate his own enthusiasms, as well as an immense, affectionate, yet candid knowledge of the Brussels literary scene. He was then the music critic of *La Dernière Heure*, a *professeur de solfège* at the Uccle Conservatoire, writing music for films in his spare time. Though his brother René had long set up as a *décorateur*, in Paris, in a cinema world partly colonized by fellow-Belgians, including the brother of the Foreign Minister, Pierre had never felt the pull westwards, or had resisted it if he had, having, on the contrary, the good sense, or the modesty—I think both—to remain perfectly content with the agreeably circum-scribed parish of Brussels's musical and literary life.

He was, so he often claimed, a provincial, but one who could look beyond the Porte de Namur and the Porte Louise, to take in the many estuaries and the extraordinary loops of the foggy Scheld, the sandy Campine, the forests so close to Brussels, and the impenetrable greenery enclosing Couvin. He guided me through the course of the great lost river, the Zwijn, as well as through the mysteries of the Kredietbank and its many involve-ments with the Congo (about which he was engaged in making a film).

But, above all, he was a Bruxellois, that is to say, a provincial, with fixed habits and regular itineraries. Every Saturday morn-ing, he went to a large café on the Porte Louise to have drinks with a group of fellow-critics, journalists, painters, teachers and writers. I do not suppose any of them was particularly outstand-ing, but I found them friendly and rewarding, and, in the regularity of their meetings, the predictability of their greetings, and the inwardness of their gossip, they seemed to belong to a safer, almost nineteenth-century world, of Leopoldine solidity: *un cercle d'amis*, enclosed and secure in a language of hints and allusions, as well as in an often boisterous *tutoiement*, not lacking in malice, noting, and commenting on, absences, and, in general, like a great many of their countrymen and countrywomen, disrespectful and irreverent.

It is no doubt hard to live behind an impregnable wall of isolation, in a small and very crowded country, most of it urban, a landscape of endless streets and small houses strung along them, and in which, as in the then village of Sint-Niklaas, opposite Antwerp, even the polders gave a view of a town, spread out, as in a seventeenth-century, print, as though awaiting a *siège en règle*, the Steyn, the cathedral, a cluster of towers and churches; and I gained the impression, both from Pierre and his friends, and, later, from others of a very different milieu, that very little went unobserved. Many of the comments were undoubtedly uncharitable, some were envious, but nearly all were funny, and, what is more, lively, with that liveliness that goes with familiarity and visual alertness. It was as if one *knew* the subjects of such repeated commentary; and the likelihood was that, sooner or later, one would indeed know many of them, 'à la fortune d'une rencontre', in the street or in a café.

So much knowledge, so readily shared, is of course both flattering and comforting to the foreign visitor, thus made to feel that he is really being taken in, as if he too were one of the company. Brussels is particularly attractive in this respect; but I have no doubt that Liège or Ghent would have as much to offer; and I know, from many visits to Léon de Nave, at one time a journalist on *La Métropole* (before he moved to *Le Soir*, after difficulties with *la maison Gevaert*) that Antwerp did. What I picked up at the weekly meetings was much better than anything I could read in *Pourquoi pas?* Even now, after all these years, the former Regent, Prince Charles, retains the familiar proportions of a Bruxellois, someone one might conceivably meet in the rue Haute. Pierre Moulaert and his wife supplied one of the keys to this pleasingly provincial world. I soon acquired several others: from a Socialist Senator in Leuze, from an artisan family in Ixelles, from my old friend de Nave, from a banker, from a university teacher.

'Et maintenant', said General René Willems, taking a key out of his pocket, 'voici les MAUVAIS Belges.' He was conducting me on a private tour of the Musée Royal de l'Armée, and we had just been seeing the good ones: *Grenadiers du roi* and so on in their nineteenth-century uniforms, officers and soldiers of the last two wars (as well as the sumptuous plate and silver of the Preobrajensky Guards). He opened a door, and we were in among the black uniforms, the VNV, the Rexists, the dress uniform of Staf de Clercq, other black-clad Fascists, Flemish and Walloon SS, *la garde noire*. They were not for public display; but at least they had been included, and the General thought that I should see them. I did not even find them particularly sinister; but then they were only dummies. In a country so small, and where so much was known by everyone about pretty well everyone else, concealment was difficult; and it would be hard to find a people more firmly protected against myth.

I was not even entirely convinced about the true acerbity of the linguistic problem. As far as I could make out, people married right across the linguistic board—at least, the people I knew did—and, in this respect, the country was less *cantonal* than Switzerland. But, like Switzerland, much of its charm resided in its unaffected parochialism. Even *Le Soir*, which had an impressively international look about its front page, rapidly relapsed into an unashamed localism as one worked steadily towards the middle. It was much more interesting to read about a crime in Hal, a poisoning in Braine-le-Comte, an accident in Vilvorde, than about Berlin or Vietnam. It gave one a reassuring sense of domesticity. I liked the way in which people in the middle 1940s referred to the then Prime Minister, Achille van Acker, as 'notre Acille national' (*Acille*, because, so it was said, he could not pronounce *ch*). *National*, in Belgian French, or at least in Bruxellois, meant: ordinary, familiar, unpretentious, unmysterious, open to inspection. I doubt if things have changed very much, despite la place de l'Europe, and although the Mont des Arts has gone, and Pierre and most of my other friends are dead. Anyhow, I hope not.

Bourgeois Ladies from the North-East of France*

'Madame va descendre à l'instant: elle vous prie de l'attendre,' said the neat servant, in her immaculate black and white uniform, as she showed me into the *salon* of the enormous red-brick house. It was a familiar opening, almost a ritual; and I knew, from previous experience, that 'à l'instant' could be extended to ten minutes or a quarter of an hour, while Madame tarried in the mysterious rooms upstairs, engaged in whatever strongly feminine activities that kept her on the higher storeys of the silent house.

Preparing for a long wait, I took in the details of an equally familiar *salon*: a heavily waxed and polished parquet floor, covered in rugs, on which were placed a semicircle of identical *faux*-Louis XV chairs, lined in silken floral patterns. I sat bolt upright on the edge of one of them towards the end of the semicircle, so that I would not have my back to the door when Madame eventually came down.

Everything seemed to be in place: above the mantelpiece there was a recess, painted in blue and edged in white, that contained a small statue of the Virgin holding the Child Jesus, both in white. A huge clock in a glass case ticked loudly in the silence of the still house. On side tables and marble-topped *consoles* there were nine photographs in heavy silver frames of children, five girls and four boys, the former in white dresses and white floral arrangements in their hair, the latter in black suits and Eton collars, with large white bows on their right arms, all holding white-bound missals, a range of *premières communions* extending over a dozen years. There were three more photographs, framed in dark wood, two

* This essay first appeared as a review of Bonnie G. Smith, *Ladies of the Leisure Class: The Bourgeoises of Northern France in the Nineteenth Century* (Princeton University Press) in *The New York Review of Books*, December 1981.

of them of nuns, the third of a rather startled looking young priest in heavy glasses.

A glass-fronted corner cupboard, well stocked with coloured bottles bearing familiar labels, the Dubonnet cat to the fore, seemed to smile at me, spelling out a message less austere and more laical. And on a small and highly decorated round table, placed in the exact middle of the motionless semicircle, was the usual talisman of local rank and hierarchy, a volume bound in rich red *marocain* and carrying in golden letters on its spine the proud title: *Les Grandes Familles de Roubaix-Tourcoing*, a volume, always as prominently displayed, with which I had filled in the gap of a great many 'à l'instants', up and down the boulevard de Cambrai, the boulevard de Paris, and the leafy avenues off the Parc Barbieux.

It was a volume that gave much greater weight to the second half of the alphabet than to the first, as if there were more virtue in a name beginning with an M or a P or a W (unique to this area) than to one beginning with an A or a C or a D: Masurel, Motte, Prouvost, Tiberghien, Toulemonde, Wibaux. The book was like a pack of cards that, constantly reshuffled, endlessly turned up the same variety of combinations: Wilbaux-Prouvost, or Prouvost-Wibaux, Motte-Masurel, or Masurel-Motte, Glorieux-Pierrepont, or Pierrepont-Glorieux, Tiberghien-Toulemonde or Toule-monde-Tiberghien, Wibaux-Florin, or Florin-Wibaux, the male always taking precedence over the female. Better still were those that left it open to doubt: Prouvost-Prouvost, Wibaux-Wibaux, Toulemonde-Toulemonde, or Motte-Motte. The book spoke elo-quently of the endlessly repeated patterns of intermarriage be-tween a dozen or a score of families of the Roubaix wool barons. I would still be plunged in these wonderful combinations, this or that way round, or the same both ends, when a light step would bring me to my feet: 'Quel bon vent vous amène, Monsieur Cobb?' asked Madame. It was only a matter of time, and after the usual formal verbal sparring, until the glass-fronted corner cup-board would be opened.

This was in 1944 and 1945. Professor Bonnie Smith, an Assistant Professor of History at the University of Wisconsin, Parkside, has enjoyed a number of similar *entrées*, often no doubt to the same ladies, thirty years after my visits, though her territory has also been extended to include the cotton families of Lille, the sugar merchants and industrialists of Valenciennes and Douai, the biscuit manufacturers and ship-owners of Dunkirk, a range well beyond the carefully limited horizons of the Roubaix-Tourcoing marriage network. But to judge from her abundant and intelligently used statistical evidence, it must have been the Families of the Book that provided her with the most eloquent examples of a society already enmeshed in innumerably repeated marriage links, and constantly reinforced by battalions of children (an average of eight) throughout the second half of the nineteenth century, at a time when patterns that till the 1950s, at least, remained almost immobile, were in the process of being established.

Already, in her book, it would have been almost unheard of for a girl from a Roubaix mill-owner's family to marry into one from Tourcoing, although the two towns ran into each other: to have married into a family from Lille would have been a sin against collective solidarity. And there was consternation when a Roubaisienne married into one of the leading silk families of Lyon, even though it was of equivalent wealth. It was something even worse than marrying for love. For nearly all such marriages as described by Bonnie Smith were arranged, generally through negotiations between both sets of parents, sometimes through the *bons offices* of a priest or a monk, the brother or the uncle of the bride-to-be. Girls would be married off, in strict order of age, at twenty-one; four months after marriage there would be some alarm if there were no signs of pregnancy.

During the period of engagement, the two future partners might write to each other, addressing each other as *Mademoiselle* and *Monsieur*, and in the second person plural. Equally, when the female children were sent to the Sacré-Coeur, or to some other convent (and after 1905 it would be over the border in Belgium), it was quite likely that they would be taught by nuns who were their aunts, their first cousins, or one of their elder sisters, and would be watched over by a Mother Superior who was likewise a great-aunt. It is not surprising that those who had been through the convent, and had come out of it with recollections so loving, so affectionate, and so marked, when questioned in extreme old age by Professor Smith, should have described the Sacré-Coeur simply as an extension of family and home. It often was both.

It is unlikely that *any* other society, at least in Northern Europe, could have offered a better example of narrow clannishness and parochialism (in the most literal sense: *paroisse Saint-Jacques*, in Roubaix, *paroisse Saint-Maurice* in Lille) and of 'keeping it in the family'; and certainly no other society could offer better opportunities both for the study of a matriarchy and for the reconstruction of the domestic world of the woman, the *maîtresse de maison*, in the home. The author has been particularly well advised in her choice of terrain and milieu. Having worked for long periods in the main towns of the Nord, she is well aware that she is dealing with family structures that are unique and that the *bourgeoise du Nord* of the second half of the nineteenth century, far from witnessing for the general condition of the married woman in the home, can only witness for herself and her female compatriots of the same social background in their often architecturally identical, enormous, brick-built homes.

A great deal more of what she has to say about the ladies of the upper-middle class of Roubaix-Tourcoing and of Lille in the period 1800–1914 would apply with equal vigour to the same milieu at the time of the Liberation. As Professor Smith stresses on a number of occasions, we are dealing with a domestic society immobilized in its ways, rites, and symbols, fixed in a sort of timelessness that separates it from the strident calendar of public events, and responding to a more intimate and ancient calendar of family pressures and responses. We encounter in the 1940s the same intense and yet unostentatious piety, the many family links with the clergy, the monks, and the nuns, the daily, weekly, and monthly routines of visits, pilgrimages, charitable activities, and domestic chores, the discipline, routine, and teaching methods of the convents (though carefully approved reading would certainly have extended from the accepted trio of entirely 'safe' novelists —Joséphine de Gaulle, the General's industrious and pious grandmother, Mathilde Bourdon, and Julia Bécour—to include a much wider range of improving novels emanating *de chez Mame*,

Editions de la Bonne Presse, in Tours, or from Desclée & de Brouwer, the Franco-Belgian Lille and Tournai religious publishers).

In the 1940s, as in the 1900s, girls would be sexually innocent at the time of marriage. An active and sincere engagement in private charitable works, organized through the parish, would still distinguish the well-to-do womenfolk of the Franco-Belgian border from those of other parts of France; and the recipients of such charity would still have to prove themselves morally worthy of such help. Unmarried mothers and women whose homes were untidy or dirty would still be likely to be excluded from such solicitude. Here too godliness and cleanliness would still be firmly allied. Indeed, in the Nord, as in Belgium, the obsession with domestic cleanliness had long been communicated to the women of the working classes, the bright door-step witnessing for a virtuous interior as much in the rue aux Longues Haies as in the boulevard de Cambrai.

Likewise, an intense regional pride, coupled with a deep suspicion of Paris and its inhabitants, and even more of the Midi, would still characterize the *chtimis* (the slang word for the inhabitants of the Nord) of all classes and both sexes, even up to the present day, when M. Mauroy makes a point of spending more time in his Lille fief than in Paris. The wool barons might often possess subsidiary mills in Mulhouse or in Mazamet which they would have to visit at regular intervals, but they would not be accompanied by their wives.

For holidays, even the richest textile families would play it safe, opting for Wimereux and other places on the nearby coast of the Pas-de-Calais. When, for some exceptional reason—perhaps preparing a trousseau, with a visit to the Printemps or the Bon Marché—the womenfolk had to go to Paris, they would cling prudently to the Hôtel Terminus, at the Gare du Nord, or would stay with relatives in the quartier de la Trinité, a quarter regarded as relatively 'safe' since it contained a sizeable colony of Northerners. There was no question of such visits to the capital being *enjoyable*; and they would confirm and reinforce the accepted views on the subject of Parisian frivolity. On the other hand, it is unlikely that the descendants of Professor Smith's bourgeoises would still be attached to the hopeless politics of royalism; and possibly even the maternal unity of these massive families may have been somewhat eroded since 1968.

Professor Smith's research has been carried out with considerable care and imagination, including a series of personal interviews with ladies, most, one suspects, from Roubaix-Tourcoing, though some from Lille—in their seventies and eighties, as they evoke, always with nostalgic affection and in minute detail, their own childhoods, their mothers, and their grandmothers. This is an area of France in which family memories are particularly intense and in which knowledge of genealogies is fully shared between the sexes. Bonnie Smith's book is a convincing contribution to the still little explored history of the family and the home, as illustrated by the experience of women, and as measured in the private calendar of female domestic and biological cycles.

Perhaps some of Professor Smith's conclusions are overstated. As she shows, both in the late eighteenth and in the early nineteenth centuries there still survived in this part of France some quite formidable *femmes d'affaires: Madame Veuve Une Telle*. But I do not think that they entirely disappeared, as it were at the command of Professor Smith, from 1850 or thereabouts, though there may well have been a general retreat into the more stable, more feminine world of domesticity. Nor would I follow her when she emphasizes the contrast between female piety and masculine impiety, religious indifference, and anticlericalism. That women received more consolation than did men from the ministrations of the clergy cannot be doubted; but in the 1900s there were a number of very pious wool barons, and before 1914 Lille-Roubaix-Tourcoing offered the most promising terrain to *le Sillon* and to Social Catholicism.

Often the *patrons* seem to have been as pious as their wives. Indeed, with their direct encouragement, *Jocisme* spread downward, at least in Roubaix, to bring in a broad section of mill workers of both sexes. After the Liberation, Roubaix represented one of the most promising growth areas of the newly founded MRP. And I do not know on what evidence Professor Smith bases her assertion that, while husbands will now read *Le Monde* or *Le Figaro*, their wives would fall back on *Jours de France*. I think it much more likely that both would read *La Croix du Nord* or *Nord-Eclair*.

Professor Smith has an excellent subject, and she has made the most of it. However, her book often makes very hard reading. It is extremely repetitive, sometimes long-winded. She is at pains never to leave the reader to his own devices; and he is lectured to at great length even on such subjects as Myth. An attachment to sociological jargon continually intrudes between what is perfectly obvious, what could be expressed quite simply, imposing a language both obscure, ungrammatical, and wooden. Her quiet, well-organized homes drip with 'artifacts' and swim steamily in 'symbolism'. Even the simplest acts are heavily 'symbolic' of something or other. Sometimes one has the impression that she is dealing with a tribe and that she is borrowing the crude tools of the anthropologists. In her text, there are seventy-five references to the 'women *of* the Nord'; 'women *in* the Nord' score twenty-one, 'northern women' get eight points, 'business women *of* the Nord' get two; '*ladies of* the Nord' get only one (a bit hard), so do 'women *from* the Nord', and 'girls *in* the Nord'. The bludgeoned reader might well end up feeling rather like old John Knox when he evoked the Monstrous Regiment of Women.

It is in Part II ('the Domestic System'), and more especially in Chapter 4, 'Domesticity: The Rhetoric of Reproduction', that Professor Smith displays herself at her most tiresome, particularly in the elaborate illustration of the absolutely self-evident. She seems to have made it a rule that when faced with a choice between what is simple and clear and what is obscure and complicated, always opt for the second. It is a shame, for the chapter gets off with a brilliant start:

By 1870 her portrait is finished, revealing a carefully corseted lady in a plaid taffeta dress, slightly gathered across the stomach, full in back, her lacy shawl arranged to display a white collar attached with a cameo; a small veiled hat on her head, a plush purse dangling from her gloved hands. She is about to make her afternoon visit—in fact, several of them. The children have been dispatched, some to school, some to the care of servants; she has drawn up an *ordre du jour* for the household staff, attended mass, written letters and entries in her diary, presided over the noon meal. In the evening she will sit with her family to listen to one of the children read from the Comtesse de Ségur's *Evangile d'une grand'mère*; while listening she will embroider a cushion and eventually summon the servants for evening prayers. This daily routine is punctuated by visits from the seamstress, knitting for the poor, mending, making lists of repairs, purchases, and projects, and preparing an occasional lavish entertainment at which she and others of her female guests will play the piano and sing.

It all seems plain sailing and one awaits the rest with interest and the promise of enjoyment. But Professor Smith is a stern teacher. Enough of *that*.

She is going now to take us into the home, and the home, she relentlessly reminds us, is 'the arena of reproduction'. 'Arena' does not suggest fun, and, sure enough, we are in for bad time, a proper trouncing. We are reminded, not just once, that women are biologically different from men and that their biological time cycle is not the same as that of men. As she hammers away determinedly on the subject of the reproductive role of women, she manages to reduce the whole varied and comforting area ('arena'?) of domesticity to the single function of reproduction —fair enough perhaps when applied to mothers of eight or more, and with possibly a couple of children stillborn or dying in infancy, but nevertheless almost comically restricting. Women employ 'a language of reproduction', not of course in so many words, for they have been well brought up, as by gesture and hidden signs. The house glitters and glimmers with 'domestic symbolism'.

'The bed', she informs us gravely, 'lay down hallways, under canopies and drapes, and behind closed doors. Women sought to erase that centrality of the natural by placing water closets severely out of view.' (Did they indeed!) 'Sexual life', she pronounces, 'was confined to the central bed, in a specified room. So too the water closet had its own fixed location.' Well, she must *know*, for she has been inside, and must have noticed things that I failed completely to spot: 'As we enter the Northern bourgeois home', she says, adopting the voice of an Intourist guide to the Hermitage, 'and observe its daily life, we can regard its operations as part of a symbolic system.' (She certainly seems to have somewhat abused the proverbial hospitality of the inhabitants of the Nord, in such earnest sniffings upstairs and downstairs and in my lady's chamber; one would have to think twice about having her again.) Where *should* the marriage bed have been? In the *salon*? Would it not have been more 'natural' to have the water closet in the hall?

But this is only a beginning. Every object is exclusively designed to express woman's reproductive function, her domestic power, and her fragility and imprisonment (under house arrest in 'the arena'). Women 'saw themselves in the glazed salmon and in the carefully chosen strawberries that graced the table'. Professor Smith has a thing about 'glazed salmon', as well as about 'truffles', for both turn up several times. 'Reproductive contours distributed themselves . . .' (all over the place, you could not escape them, they turned up even in table legs and velvet cushions); 'the dining-room contained a buffet along the walls with the table and the chairs at the center . . .' (well, I *have* met that sort of layout, and not just in the Nord; it had seemed to me a perfectly reasonable arrangement for eating in comfort and talking to one's neighbours; but I have missed the point, it is designed of course to emphasize reproduction.

'A bed [here we are again] occupied the focus of a bedroom'; and, later, she observes sagaciously, and apparently quite unaware of the suitability of the phrase: 'our women of the Nord [speak for yourself, they are not *mine*] led lives *embedded* in reproductive functions'. The bed, in her account, certainly does not seem to offer much fun. But even minor objects—indeed *all* minor objects—are regimented to illustrate her implacable thesis. Women 'saw themselves in a waxed buffet'. Is this why it was waxed? Did they literally catch their reflection in it?

Fashion, too, has only one function: 'the higher waistline . . . metaphorically accommodated the elongated and impregnated uterus . . .' (*not* the sort of remark, to judge from my own experience, that would have gone down well on the boulevard de Cambrai).

If a woman favoured a floral design, it was because flowers too symbolized reproductive functions. A woman could not just be allowed to *like* flowers; and if she preferred green to pink, brown to blue, yes, you can see it coming: the old functions. Even when she indicates, either by pressing an electric bell under the table, or by a sign with her lips, or by a look, that it is time to bring in the next course, the lady of the house is expressing herself in 'preverbal signs'. 'Women saturated the social space with the color and volume of their clothing'; and there is a further reference to 'the symbolic refurbishing of the female space'. We hear too of 'the undifferentiated encapsulation of the self in nature'; we are informed that 'the notion of fashion in any genre of domesticity could only arise at the intersection of reproduction and the market'. *Which* market? *La halle aux poissons?*

Even the poor domestics are dragged in. Servants of course are to be pitied, because they are victims of exploitation. 'The personal nature of the bonds sometimes alleviated the worst features of this authoritarian structure,' primly states Professor Smith, resuming her Intourist tone. Of course it would never do if servants actually became attached to their mistresses. But she has not finished with these poor victims of capitalism yet: 'The household staff projected her presence in all their activities, including their incapacity in the sexual and reproductive sphere. The servant, in the long run, was not just functional; she served as the negative metaphor for reproduction.' I do not know what we are to make of this bold statement. It would be unlikely that living-in servants would have children, for part of their duties would be to look after the younger children of their mistress. But this surely does not imply that these healthy peasant girls from the villages of French Flanders *could* not have children? And, no doubt, the dailies, such as the cook or the washerwoman, often had children of their own.

All in all, there does not seem to have been much joy in the Roubaix bourgeois home. Or perhaps, if the *maîtresse de maison* really did derive great joy and contentment from the domestic scene, from her children and her relatives, from the comforts of her home, and from the regular and reassuring routine of a private calendar, she was merely displaying her ignorance of her unliberated state. That is what Professor Smith seems to imply, in a throwaway remark that comes at the end of her book: 'the story of the reproductive past is unpleasant for its revelation of women's primitivism and antirationalism'. I found this chapter both unpleasant *and* vulgar *and* crude.

It is a pity, for elsewhere she writes well and displays a very sharp insight. She has a brilliant chapter on the family novel of the Joséphine de Gaulle vintage: a moral tale in a straight fight between good and evil, in which the heroine often has an alter ego, a female doppelganger, whose role is to lead her into temptation, and in which men are generally dangerous intruders. Such stories are motionless, entirely predictable, and so boring, but reassuring. They were not to be read for enjoyment, but for edification. Elsewhere there is a wealth of information and observation.

Perhaps Chapter 4 is just a lapse into some ill-digested pseudo-science that excludes *all* human qualities. Certainly, elsewhere, Professor Smith re-establishes women both in their dignity, their simplicity, and their diversity. She offers some marvellously evocative accounts of how the *ladies* of the Nord were likely to spend their day (once they escaped from the 'arena'), hour by hour, when they would go on visits, how they would behave, what they would say, and where they would sit on visits, what they would do on Saturdays and Sundays, how Mondays would be employed, what would be the correct attitude to adopt towards an older woman, how to design a menu, when to spring-clean, when to change the covers, how carefully to walk, amid tight social conventions, in order to retain *respect*; and respect was everything in this private world.

This is a major contribution to the history of leisure; it also represents a very original incursion into the still largely closed areas of private, as opposed to public, history. What a pity Professor Smith could not have omitted all the sociological twaddle! Perhaps it is too late. One fears so, for, in her last paragraph, she pays a tribute to Simone de Beauvoir as to one 'who breathed new life into twentieth-century feminism'. She certainly has not breathed *any* life into anything else.

The Period Paris of
René Clair

Historians and examiners, for professional or educational reasons, will favour one set of great divides; private individuals, when concerned with the remembered past, will opt for a variety of others, depending on age, experience, and national origin. For myself, recalled French history will fall into two quite distinct periods, with a gap in the middle: 1935 to 1939, and 1944 to 1958. During the 'years between' I was absent from France; and, after 1958, as far as I was concerned, nothing could ever be quite the same again. I have returned frequently to France since then, but more and more as an observer, who was beginning to lose his way in unfamiliar territory, and who was no longer able to read the new signposts or even always to understand the new language. I know few French people under thirty-five; and those I do know are the children or grandchildren of friends. Nor am I by any means alone in dating the transformation of Paris, from what it was, to what, unhappily, it now is, from 1958.

In my personal textbook of contemporary French history, the opening year would be 1935, for that was when I first went to Paris; but I do not think it has any other significance. The real dividing line, for the later history of the Third Republic, would be 1934. There is no need to emphasize the political importance of 6 and 12 *février*; but the great divide is provided by the *affaire Stavisky*.

It is not just a matter of public history; it is also the gap between a Republic that was still curiously light-hearted, even in its amiable cynicism and humorous, but shameless self-examination, and a Republic that was becoming sombre, divisive and increasingly frightened. M. Alexandre belongs to the sunnier side of that gap; and his mysterious death in Chamonix is the end of something more than the fantastic life of a generous, pleasure-loving, fashionable Russian adventurer. There was a *style Stavisky* which was also that of a period.

Put in another way, it might be said that I had come in at the tail-end of the last great period of French *insouciance*. The death of Serge-Alexandre was like the untimely and quite unsuitable end to a party. I was in time for the overlap: the mystery surrounding the death of the *conseiller* Prince, his body discovered on the line from Paris to Lyon, at the evocative la Combe-aux-Fées. Another event of the previous year, the assassination of Alexander of Yugoslavia and Louis Barthou, had much less impact in Paris; what most people seem to have retained from it was that it had happened in Marseille, and on the Canebière to boot. An almost loving indulgence in the ever-widening ripples of the *affaire Stavisky* seemed to represent a lingering, sentimental attachment to a period of relative optimism, as well as to the desire to exclude anything from outside that might jar a comforting sense of continuity. Even *le Canard* was both more light-hearted and much more amusing in 1935 than it would be in the following four years. The departure of Jean Galtier-Boissière may have had something to do with this change of tone.

Of course, much of the *insouciance* was mere affectation. The first half of the 1930s were years of bitter social conflict and often brutal police repression. Nevertheless, 1934 *does* seem a watershed. There was nothing frivolous about 1936, 1937, *l'année Expo*, did indeed have hints of a partial return to fantasy. Much of the fantasy was provided by the Exhibition itself, particularly by the twin spectacle offered by the German and Soviet pavilions, as they faced one another, over a narrow channel, in competing ugliness. But a direct outcome of the *Expo* was the *affaire Weidmann*, a one-man, artisanal, precursor of the massacres to come. Weidmann murdered only half-a-dozen people or so, nearly all of whom he had met—for they were a disparate lot: a taxi-driver, a seedy commercial traveller, a *demi-mondaine*, an American ballet-dancer—while acting as a guide at the German pavilion. When the young German was finally arrested at the famous villa—*faux manoir normand*—in la Celle-Saint-Cloud the house was found to contain all the clothing, handbags, shoes, luggage, jewellery and so on of the meaningless victims: even the red and black G7 taxi, with an R numberplate, was in the garage. The *affaire*, as it

gradually unwound, was rightly seen as an unscheduled prolongation of the *Expo*; and many people at the time consoled
themselves with the hope that *tant que durera l'Expo, il n'y aura pas
de guerre*. It was a pity that it could not have been carried over into
the following year; but this Weidmann, right up to the time of his
public execution in Versailles, succeeded in doing. With Weidmann gone, there was the chaos of the mobilization of 1938 and
the ugly panic of the Parisian well-to-do.

In their portrayals of Paris and its inhabitants, René Clair and
Georges Simenon stand on different sides of the 1934 divide, the
cinéaste on the sunny one, the Belgian writer on one almost
wholly sombre. But it is not just a matter of chronology; Maigret
had made his first appearance in 1929; but he seems almost to
have gone out of business in the second half of the 1930s; and
unlike Queneau's Valentin, he even missed the opportunity of
taking a look at *l'Expo*, perhaps because his creator was inside it,
as an exhibit. The difference is both in temperament and in the
choice of an observatory. Clair is always light-hearted, tender,
sentimental, full of fun, wonderfully inventive, and wholly optimistic; he is also in a hurry, and his characters have to move very
fast; there is not time for philosophizing. They are also always
redeemable, even bank managers, industrialists and politicians,
even *Immortels*; and bearded senators may all at once be taken
with the itch to sing and dance. There is always a way out: prison,
or the open road; suicide may be contemplated, even attempted,
but a girl in a short black velvet dress, a *bandeau* and enormous
made-up eyes will arrive just in time. It will end in song; even
concierges and villainous-looking *surineurs* will join in. Taxi-
drivers are light-hearted poets of the night, even the *agents*,
buttoned to the neck, like presidential chauffeurs, externally
waving their hands outwards to the cameras, at the assassination
of Doumer or at that of Alexander, even *agents* are *bon-enfant*.
Nothing could be farther removed from the self-searching, the
sense of guilt and failure that seem to dog most of Simenon's
people.
   For the urban decor, there are five constant favoured compo-
nents: the attic with a sky-light, offering easy access to the roof,

the chaotic, jagged geography of roof-top Paris, chimneys and stove-pipes, chasms and drops, the staircase climbing to the seventh floor, the café, blazing with lights, open all night, and the dark street, its *pavé* gleaming liquidly like dark treacle. Clair is *the* poet of the Paris night: a bluish sensuous night of dark velvet, carrying a whiff of powder and the promise of adventure, indeed, a perfectly convincing evocation of the Parisian night of the 1930s, at a period when the night was still democratic and *à la portée de tout le monde*: areas of impenetrable black, picked out by the yellowish headlights of the black and red G7 taxis, contrasting with the brilliant milky-white lights of a café: curtainless windows, dimly lit, silhouetting a woman undressing, and adding a further shade of yellow. A café in which *le père la Tulipe* and *Jojo la Terreur* might encounter, at the bar, a *noceur*, in white tie, a runaway accountant, or a love-sick *monsieur décoré*, not a flight of fantasy, but an accurate representation of a limitless sociability that did exist, especially between midnight and four in the morning, in the 1930s, and that even partially revived in the 1940s.

Nor is the *chambre de bonne* or the studio beneath the roof an object of poetical creation. In the 1930s, as they had been ever since 1914, rents were so low that the poor artist or the *grisette* could indeed live sparsely *sous les toits*, especially in a central *arrondissement*. And the *pneumatique* does arrive within two hours, the post *is* delivered on Sundays, the newspaper *does* come out on Sunday (but not on Monday), taxi-drivers *do* wear peaked caps, *mauvais garçons do* wear checked ones and black and white shoes, senators *are* fat and bearded, important personages *do* wear stocks, artists and *instituteurs do* wear *lavalières*, and Parisians of both sexes *are* more likely to be dark than fair, so that their eyes will dilate in the light and dark of the city night, their brilliantined hair will glisten under the white lights. It is still best to keep away from the *Zone* at night. Nor is the Bastille yet entirely safe; and the rue de Lappe could still provide unpleasant surprises in 1930. The accordion and the *appareils à sous* still hold their own. Clair's villains, decked out in conventional *mauvais garçon* rig, all appear to be French; indeed, they readily talk Parisian, like everyone else, including the elderly *boulevardier* or the *aristo en rupture de ban*. Perhaps we are indeed still a little ahead of the Corsicans, well ahead of the Tunisians; the Yugoslavs have not even been thought of.

There are students; but they are in the conventional Murger tradition: artistic, but unrecognized, torn between two girls, or sharing a girl with their best friend. They live on the top, in conventional fear of the *concierge*, who, when things are really bad, proves indulgent and even generous. Professional people are professionally dressed: hard collars, dark hats, black over-coats, spats. The PJ wear long belted macs and grey hats with dark bands; elderly and sweet-natured *poivrotes* wear black straw hats with artificial violets; *bistrotiers* are moustached, and wear caps and aprons, they have curly dark hair, a variety of trades still sport peaked caps. All the men, and most of the younger women are constantly lighting up—an action that illuminates their faces in the dark—and then have cigarettes hanging from the bottom lip while they talk. Small boys wear smocks and berets. Fringe characters—their identity and occupation not at once revealed —will wear berets too; in Clair, the beret gives nothing away, and it is of the modest variety, not the fascist floppy kind. There are more berets about in Clair than in the second half of the 1930s, far more again than in the 1940s. Indeed it might be argued that the death of the beret coincides with that of a Paris of human proportions.

For the abiding attraction of René Clair is not merely a matter of nostalgia, though there must always be plenty of that, because he *is* a period piece. He evokes the easy, unsuspecting sociability of a city the inhabitants of which share a common slang and most basic assumptions, and enjoy a wide area of mutual encounter: the café, the street, the market, the staircase, the shop. No one is especially afraid of anyone else; and nearly all can converse in an imaginative and briefly expressed irreverence. The common ideology is scepticism, softened by friendship, understanding and habit. There is also plenty of love, spring-like and un-ashamed, infectious and encouraged. The function of the news-paper is to carry *petites annonces* and the *chronique judiciaire*, as well as news of Longchamp and Vincennes, to furnish a covering to the floor during house-painting (and a friendly *peintre en bâtiment*, wearing a newspaper in the manner of the Carpenter, will help out, in return for some other service) and to envelop meat and vegetables. The function of the *hauts personnages* is to be ridiculous; but if they step down from their plinth, they will be forgiven. Urban society is geared to the modest aspirations of routine and habit of individuals and individualists; the enemy is loneliness, and the remedy is companionability and verbal exchange. French is for speaking. Everyone is really all right, if approached in the right way. The burglar has his job to carry on just like anyone else, the counterfeiter is an artist who has retained an artist's pride in the quality of his production, even the *gigolo* is perhaps more comical than cruel.

It is, of course, also *le monde à l'envers*; for, in Clair, there is nearly always more satisfaction in coming down than in going up. The room is only at the top physically and there is a sort of release in the gambler cleared out, in the cashier who has gone off with the cash, in the banker who has taken to the quays or the Halles, in the industrialist who has headed for the open road. The only allowable success is in love; and if you do win the lottery, you give it all away, remembering all your friends and neighbours, organizing a splendid repast, champagne, *vins de choix*, in which all, even the *agent* and the *entrepreneur des pompes funèbres*, will readily join in.

Join in what? A celebration, even a way of life aimed at the satisfaction of simple enjoyment, conversation, food and drink, the spring, sunshine, and of course, the cadre, the *only* cadre for personal and collective fulfilment, PARIS. Clair's Paris no doubt sometimes *sent le carton-pâte*, quite a number of his streets look as if they had been put up in Epinay (they had), the roofs and shop-fronts especially often seem overdone. Yet they *are* recognizable. Of course Clair is an artist and an urban poet, of course his films are delightfully light-hearted fantasies. But there is much more to him than that. He is as convincing a witness of place and period as Carco or MacOrlan. But, surely, it will be objected, people cannot all have been so *nice*? Well, I think, on the whole, they *were*. We are now a *very* long way from the 1930s. Clair's attics are now converted into studio apartments for university teachers, antique-dealers (who never feature in Clair's films, in which we only encounter modest and picturesque *brocanteurs*), technocrats, *énarques*, the staircase has been deadened by carpeting, the doors do not open readily and are protected by electrical alarm devices, even the *concierge* has been disposed of. Many of the shops have gone, most of the cafés have been replaced by bars.

Paris by night is no longer a reality lived by its inhabitants, no longer a place for the lonely, in which they may feel drawn by the inviting blaze of a café; it has been reduced to a jaded round of tourist night spots. Much of the city is dead at night; some of it is dangerous as well. Clair's characters have mostly been expelled from the city, following the unfreezing of rents, the destruction of the Halles and of enormous areas of the IVème, to Rungis and elsewhere, taking with them a friendliness and a ready irreverence now only available in daytime, and already running out on the *métro-express* in the early evenings. It is no longer a place where people of all conditions may meet regularly, informally, in the endless excitement of the chance encounter. Where would they meet? There is no longer any common ground, and much of the old centre has become a single-class stronghold, shuttered, selfish, uninviting. Those cafés that have not become bars, have been converted into branch offices of banks. The long yellow-lit windows of Clair's films, silhouetting a young man in shirt sleeves or a young woman in a summer dress, no longer have anyone leaning out to take in the street, for there is nothing to take in, just a dark trench, between rows of silent cars parked on the pavement; and the yellow light has been replaced by a discreet table-lamp, *la lumière tamisée*, the shouts across the street have given way to the filtered sound of elaborate record-players. Paris has largely lost its human dimensions; René Clair's Paris really *did* exist; but it doesn't any more.

The Bon Marché*

One should not be put off this fascinating book on the Bon Marché department store in Paris by the litanic style of the introduction, which hammers home again and again the distinction between *gemeinschaftlich* and *gesellschaftlich* (I have not the faintest idea what these cumbersome teutonic adjectives mean, nor do I know what possible bearing they can have on good M. and Mme Boucicaut, the founders of the store, the one a Norman, the other a Burgundian). Nor should one be put off by the author's obsession with the word 'culture' (which makes twelve appearances on page three and thirty in the introduction: an awful lot of 'culture' in fact, though not the brand that made Goering reach for his revolver). Moreover, throughout the book, the author refers to the 'bourgeoisie' as if it were a physical being, endowed with an overriding sense of purpose and a great deal of guile. Professor Miller's 'bourgeoisie' is a busy sort of bee, always up to something or another, or merely 'pulling itself into the nineteenth century'.

The reader should plough on through these insistent litanies, discarding the code as he goes; and then he will discover, behind these cardboard frontages, that there coyly lurks a very good book that does full justice to its title and that, only here and there, in occasional genuflections and furtive gropings at the beads of a sociological rosary, brings the author back to his votive subtitle. It is business history with a difference: social history has been added in. Professor Miller is an imaginative and compassionate social historian who writes about people—most of them faceless and nameless, most of them infinitely weary, with fallen arches, bad feet, bunions, and disintegrating socks—with sympathy and sly humour.

* This essay first appeared as a review of Michael B. Miller, *The Bon Marché*: *Bourgeois Culture and the Department Store, 1869–1920* (Princeton University Press) in *The New York Review of the Books*, July 1981.

The Bon Marché is certainly the most famous of the Paris *grands magasins*. It was also the limb out of which grew the Louvre, the Printemps, and the Galeries Lafayette. The Samaritaine, the Belle Jardinière, and the Bazar de L'Hôtel de Ville do not really belong in the same family tree, since they deliberately catered to a humbler, lower-middle-class or even working-class clientele. The Bon Marché was not the oldest Paris emporium: the Ville de Paris, the Pauvre Diable, the Coin de Rue, and les Enfants de la Chapelle (which the author fails to mention) were all older. But the Bon Marché was the biggest of the lot, came out first with all the most original ideas, put on the most stupendous sales, and represented the summit of the sad, stuffy, weary, endlessly deferential profession of shop assistant.

To get into the Bon Marché was to fulfil one sort of timid ambition. To *stay* in the Bon Marché until one was expendable at fifty was an even more fantastic one. Few made it that long; 40 per cent at least were out after five years, perhaps with a reference, certainly with bad feet. Such was the grind that there does not seem to have been time for a pause to assess and to contemplate; as far as I know the Bon Marché has secreted no Kipps, no Mr Polly, no Hoopdriver, or any of the other characters H. G. Wells wrote about in his stories of commercial life. Perhaps there would have been none of these either had Wells worked in a vast machine such as Harrod's or Swan & Edgar's, rather than in a haberdasher's on Bromley High Street.

We know only the bare facts about Aristide and Marguerite Boucicaut; the spur of their commercial genius eludes us. Aristide was born in Bellême, in Lower Normandy, in 1810. He took to the road in 1828, and only reached Paris in 1835 at the age of twenty-five. He worked as a shop assistant at the Petit Saint-Thomas, using his evenings to learn English. Marguerite Guérin was the illegitimate daughter of a peasant from the Saône-et-Loire who had come to Paris, with the usual letter of introduction to some vague cousin, in the 1830s; like thousands and thousands of provincial girls, she worked first as an apprentice laundry-woman, escaping from the steaming laundry boats to take up a small job as a servant in a restaurant. It was there that, in 1835, she met Boucicaut. They were married the same year. Both early careers continue to illustrate absolutely classic eighteenth-century patterns; both appear to have walked to Paris, Boucicaut pausing on the way.

But almost at once the nineteenth century takes them both over: Boucicaut learns English, he is soon a partner, then he buys out his partner. And the rest of the two careers are part of the public history piously chronicled of the House, the *oeuvre*, the *grande famille*. What distinguishes both the founder, the foundress, and a chain of continuators (one is struck by the unconsciously Stalinist vocabulary of House handouts) from similar entrepreneurs and members of the managerial class was their apparently sincere piety. The Boucicauts were ardent Catholics —and the author does not suggest that their ardour owed anything to the fact that the Bon Marché set up shop in the most clerical quarter of Paris, though this was at once to prove a fruitful combination—and they appear genuinely to have believed that they had a moral duty towards their ever-increasing staff. The Bon Marché was an *oeuvre* in which moral values were constantly emphasized and from which moral failings would result in instant dismissal. Boucicaut was a Pétain under a glass and steel roof. Madame Boucicaut lingered on as the guardian of the tomb. Both were sincere and simple Catholics. The *vocabulaire-maison*, especially after the death of Boucicaut, apes that of the parish bulletin, the words *loyal* and *loyauté* forming the core of a Bon Marché anthem.

The author offers some telling examples of career patterns at a less exalted level too. Here is a young man born in a village in the Calvados; he moves to Rouen, spending one year as a shop assistant in the local branch of the Belle Jardinière; once in Paris, he spends eleven months at the Pauvre Diable, ten at the Coin de Rue, eight at the Louvre, before entering the Bon Marché, whence he moves steadily upward, from *premier* to manager, through *la caisse, la batterie de cuisine*, via *rideaux*—not to be curtains in his case. (Would one go from *baignoires* and *bidets* to *literie*, or would it be the other way round? There is an element of mystery in the vocabulary of these Brief Lives that certainly has nothing to do with the grinding monotony of the reality.) Another example the author provides is of a peasant born in the Basses-Pyrénées who starts as a shop assistant in Pau, moves on to a slightly better job in a large store in Bordeaux, before spending four years in military service, after which he reaches Paris, eventually landing a job in the Bon Marché, not a place, as far as employees were concerned, that one walked into.

Both case histories, indeed like the early stages of the careers of the Boucicauts, retain an eighteenth-century pattern of geographical mobility, despite the railways that, one might have thought, would have tempted people to come straight to Paris and to make the great city in a single leap. Not at all, so it seems. *La montée à Paris*, on the contrary, is taken in several, prudent stages, like an early nineteenth-century Tour de France. So there is a period of acclimatization in the nearest provincial capital: Rouen, Pau, or Bordeaux. The only change is that they would now come up, *seated*, by train, in the hope eventually of landing a job that, after years of standing, twelve hours a day, might eventually offer the supreme luxury of being once more seated. The Bon Marché offers a dramatic contrast between the standing and the seated: the latter a tiny élite.

Most such employees remain poor, faceless, nameless young men, dressed like mannequins (look at all those starched collars in the group photographs from the *Livre d'Or*), deferential, endlessly patient, of careful and studied gesture, and sweet breath (no garlic was served, one supposes, in the vast House restaurants), and well-brushed hair.

The author allows himself the brief fantasy of wondering how, in their weary sleep, they may have had nightmares about infuriating female customers, trying on dress after dress, fingering article after article. But where did they go when, at the end of the day, they escaped from the public stage, the electric glare, and the stifling heat and litanic noise (*la caisse, la caisse*) of the monster shop, in order to let off steam, to display their bourgeois clothes and their middle-class airs, and, above all, no doubt, to SIT DOWN, legs outstretched under a marble-topped table on a café terrace, while they fingered their moustaches? What was the private face of the meagre existence of these young men, or not so young, clothed in black and white?

Some, we are told, rushed off to enjoy the noise of *café-concerts* and music-halls; and this would be a bad mark against them. Could they ever escape the prying eye and the minute intelli-

gence service of an insistent and fussy Moral Order? Did not the
Boucicaut information service (which relied on *concierges* for the
distribution of catalogues) trace them down to their little hotel
rooms in the Xème, the XVIIIème and the XXème, scout out their
compagnes, scrutinize the dubious sheets, break into their patheti-
cally exiguous, fragile privacy? This seems likely, for mistresses
and drinking habits are noted down on dossiers, along with
rudeness, insolence, and answering back—the deadly sins—
among causes for dismissal.

   What an *awful* life! Surely much worse than the relative freedom of the factory or the harvest. And yet, and yet, one can
follow the author in being convinced that a great many Bon
Marché employees readily adapted to the Boucicaut ethos, that
they clung, with dogged desperation, to the outward garments of
middle-class respectability, as if, like the Naval & Military Tailors,
Gieve's, Clothes Make the Man (and Gieve's Make the Clothes),
the uniform, the deference, the good manners, the careful politeness (*Madame désire?*) really *were* a ladder into bourgeois respectability. They were even, we are told, prepared to give up precious
leisure, the poor secrets of privacy, to stay on in their immense
prison in the evenings, in order to learn fencing, a virile sport, or
to take Spanish or English lessons. Perhaps some even trailed
behind them, once outside the immense portals, the odour of
incense, and the rancid smell of Left Bank clericalism.

Certainly the most astonishing aspect of the Boucicaut achievement is that so many of the employees seem genuinely to have
adopted the House spirit and indeed to have felt quite filial
gratitude toward their Father and Mother on Earth, *carrefour de
Sèvres-Babylone*, the latter perhaps the most ill-named street in
Paris. Of course, these are the ones who managed to stick it out to
honourable retirement and a generous pension scheme. The
wastage rate was colossal; but many who were dismissed were
sorry to go. In a way, the Bon Marché really *did* look after its
people, provided, that is, that they conformed to House rules;
and these were both elaborate and strict.

   The author refers briefly to the proletariat of the House: the
garçons, working in the basement and in the parcels and delivery
departments, most of them in fact grown men, dressed in uni-

form and given numbers, who slept anywhere they could: on shelves or on counters—and the *demoiselles de magasin*, more easily scrutinized than the male employees, and more readily exposed to disgrace: seduction, the weekend picnic, pregnancy. Professor Miller remarks shrewdly: '*Demoiselles* and the ladies they waited on were not all that far apart.' For the Bon Marché served a number of purposes *not* advertised in its beautifully produced catalogues: it provided writing rooms in which married ladies could write to their lovers, showrooms in which they could make discreet rendezvous, unnoticed in the immensity of a constantly moving crowd. There is a brief reference to the *frotteurs*, not, as one might expect, polishers, but, in the *vocabulaire maison*, men who used the shop to brush against harassed and certainly sweaty (they had to wear long black dresses) *demoiselles*. Clothing provided other opportunities, in this age of ample fashion: there seems to have been a steady percentage of shoplifting, mostly by carefully dressed women.

The top level of administration, the rare success stories, *gérants*, managers, chairmen, the continuators of the Boucicaut *oeuvre*: Morin, Fillot, Ricois, Caslot, Chambeau, Dru, Lucet, Plassard, reveal a boring succession of patient, prudent, yet enterprising men, nearly always one step ahead of fashion, and in fact dictating its shape in the immediate future, totally imbued in the ethos of an organization in which most of them had spent the whole of their adult lives—few came in from outside, save one or two *familiers* of Madame Boucicaut, including her solicitor—steadily promoted from the ranks of the head cashiers or the *premiers* of this or that department: *blanc*, furniture, silk, ready-mades, toys (toys, especially, could offer a way up), sports equipment.

Here they are, little more than names, sitting in their assigned hierarchy around the boardroom table, beneath the portraits of Aristide and Marguerite. Some of them are intermarried; and in their manner of life and their very success, due to hard work, probity, commercial acumen, and advertising inventiveness sometimes amounting to genius, they seem to have taken the House rules and the annual catalogues as the guiding lights and twin catechisms of their heavily ornate style. Their solid, over-furnished homes—XVIème, VIIème, banlieue Saint-Lazare—are crammed with Bon Marché furniture and linen, carpets, curtains, clocks, paperweights, bronze gladiators, table lamps, dinner and cutlery services. They may be presumed to push their devotion so far as to wear Bon Marché ready-mades, gloves, hats, boots; and they eat Bon Marché food.

They invite one another, their social relations are confined mostly to the world of the great emporium. They do not seek social recognition, though honours, when they come, are accepted as a tribute to the *oeuvre* rather than to themselves. And so their private lives are quite unobtrusive and colourless. The musical evenings and the other social occasions held in the shop itself are an indirect and effective form of advertising. Deputies, senators, academicians, writers, industrialists are not cultivated for their social enjoyment, but for the greater glory of the Bon Marché. In their slightly vulgar houses hang the portraits of M. and Madame B. They are not aspiring to rise further in the world, do not seek admittance in the Tout-Paris, content to be *honnêtes commis*.

Even the grandchildren of some of the pre-1914 *gérants* and chairmen, interviewed by the resourceful and indefatigable author, speak with genuine affection of the founder and of *la grande famille. Famille, Travail, Patrie* could be as much the motto of the House, in its golden heyday between 1890 and 1914, as later it was to become that of the Pétain regime, a triple formula that the Bon Marché was much more successful in promoting than the incoherent regime of the Marshal and his motley adherents. There is a sort of symbolism in the decision to open a branch of the Bon Marché in Vichy towards the end of the last century; its slightly dowdy, 'safe' image seemed well suited to the hepatic population of the various *Sources*.

All those engaged in the service of the House, especially the *gérants*, seem to have taken themselves as seriously as those who, forty years later, enrolled in the Marshal's campaign of Redemption, Atonement, and Moral Renewal; and such monumental absence of humour will occasionally produce a similar bathos. In a letter addressed, from the front, to the management, by a former employee serving in the First World War, the soldier writes: 'I will do everything within my weak means to throw back the invader for the honour of France and the Grands Magasins du Bon Marché', a *jumelage* of such majestic proportions as only the French can offer: *Grand Hôtel des Cyclistes Stéphanois et de l'Univers*.

Note too the meekness-*maison*, the copy-book humility: 'my weak means'. The soldier had got the spirit of the place, so imbued was he in it indeed that, even from the trenches, he could fall faultlessly into the *style* Bon Marché. Of course, he may too have been hoping for something in return. In a language so formalized, so treacly with unction, so heavily dripping in gratitude, it is sometimes difficult to distinguish between a sincere expression of feelings and that of a formalized conformity. Bon Marché public pronouncements sound positively Pecksniffian in translation; to get the full flavour of them, it is necessary mentally to translate them back into French, in order to recapture the echo of standardized rhetoric. Anyhow, one hopes that the soldier, having won the war for France and the Bon Marché (not to mention Joan of Arc and Sainte-Geneviève), got his job back on demobilization.

This excellent and original study brings to mind related questions of topography. Each of the Paris department stores was carefully sited physically, in both communications and potential clientele. The Bazar de l'Hôtel de Ville, looking to the eastern suburbs for its specialties in fishing and gardening and kitchen equipment, is admirably placed on the east-west line Vincennes-Neuilly, with its own entrance on to the metro station Hôtel-de-Ville at the rue Lobau exit. The Printemps and the Galeries Lafayette are constructed like a great net in which the teeming commuters on foot from Saint-Lazare are filtered through: a better class of customer than perhaps the staider client of the Bon Marché, and much better than that of the Bazar de l'Hôtel de Ville.

The Belle Jardinière and the Samaritaine, competing at much the same level as the Bazar de l'Hôtel de Ville, are almost equally well placed for both eastern and northern suburbs within walking distance of the Châtelet, the square also best known to every French provincial. Their immense rectangles mark the silhouette of the Right Bank riverside, they cannot be missed. The Louvre lies at the intersection of the avenue de l'Opéra, the place du Palais-Royal and the rue de Rivoli. Both the store and the hotel had been carefully sited with a foreign and provincial public in mind. But the Louvre could also be reached directly from the shallow metro station Palais-Royal on Vincennes-Neuilly (or, more likely, Neuilly-Vincennes, the Parisian appeal of the shop lying strongly to the west to Auteuil, Neuilly, and Passy). Les Enfants de la Chapelle catered, as its name implies, to a peripheral, locally based, and very modest public.

In its catalogues, postcards, and publicity handouts of the Eighties, Nineties, and the 1900s, the Bon Marché was in the habit of depicting the emporium and its annex as being in the dead centre of Paris; indeed, sometimes in its pictorial maps of the Paris region, it would be the only building in the capital, vying with the château of Ecouen, the basilica of Saint-Denis, the palaces of Versailles, and the cathedral of Chartres. In other maps, Paris consists of the Bon Marché, Notre Dame, the Invalides, and the Eiffel Tower, a far from discreet reminder of its Catholic affiliations, its appeal to the military families living a little to the west (in fact, Army, if not Navy), and of the fact that the immense iron galleries had been the work of Eiffel himself, chosen personally by Boucicaut. But, of course, it was *not* in the centre of Paris, being, on the contrary, the only department store on the Left Bank. But, within the Left Bank, it was strategically placed at an intersection of a boulevard and of four streets, directly opposite the prestigious Lutétia hotel, and served by a metro station that was a junction of two busy lines (a station much used, in the 1970s, by the gangster Mesrine while on the run).

For an enterprise that gloried—some would say wallowed—in its piety, its good works (there is still a prix Boucicaut for vouched-for respectable young virgins about to get married), its high moral tone, the store was quite magnificently placed, on the very frontier between the quartier Saint-Sulpice, the centre of religious bookshops and trinkets, of *bondieuseries*, seminaries, and hotels that catered for the special needs of priests and seminarists, the fashionable churches of Saint-Ferdinand and Sainte-Clothilde, and the convents and religious establishments of the rue de Sèvres. Even the residence of the archbishop, rue Barbet de Jouy, was within easy walking distance. And if Vice stalked on high heels not too far away, on rues Bréa and Vavin, at least it was Vice discreet and ostentatiously pious: Bretonnes with crosses around their necks, patronized by equally pious *pères de famille* who were parishioners of Saint-Ferdinand. Furthermore, it was an area thick with *lycées* and *collèges* that would provide a steady clientele for the stationery department and for sports equipment and clothing.

One wonders in what order things came about. Did the Bon Marché set up shop where it did because it was already a clerical quarter, well served by the clerical Gare du Montparnasse that linked Paris to a clerical West? Or did the quarter become *more* clerical because it had been chosen by the pious M. and Mme Boucicaut? The answer would seem to be a bit of both. Certainly some of the churches in the vicinity were built years after the Bon Marché as if to facilitate a ready transfer from shopping to spiritual uplift (though the Bon Marché could provide plenty of that, too; it was not the place to go for pornography). The provincial lady, there to provide for her daughter's wedding and setting up house—the store had a special section for marriages and was especially well adjusted to supplying the entire needs of a *jeune ménage*, from bedding to cutlery and leather-bound books that would look well in a glass-fronted bookcase (from internal evidence, and the discovery in the country home at Samois of twenty years of pre-1914 Bon Marché catalogues, it became apparent to me that the entire contents of Madame Thullier's two houses had been provided, in one vast order, by the store) —could combine an extensive tour of the various departments with a confession or two thrown in at the end (all the more piquant if the writing room had been used for illicit correspondence or for a rendezvous). There seemed no doubt that the founders of the shop had considered the quarter as suitably solid, anyhow less likely than the Grands Boulevards to endanger the virtues of the hundreds of young people employed in the enterprise. The *quartiers de plaisir* were at a fairly safe distance.

Certainly, one of the reasons that the Bon Marché put such a gigantic and, at the same time, imaginative effort into the production and distribution of its annual or seasonal catalogues was to familiarize a provincial, foreign, and colonial clientele with a location that would not immediately spring to mind for the tourist and the visitor. Its success in thus fighting against a location that, for the traveller by train, was much less accessible from the main stations than the other great stores, can be gauged from the fact that the *carrefour* Sèvres-Babylone was converted, in a matter of years, into one of the best-known sights of Parisian topography, familiarized in the shorthand of *au carrefour*, or 'let us meet at the main entrance', as one might have said 'under the clock' at Waterloo or the Biltmore, to the inhabitants of Roromantin and Rocamadour, Brussels, Berlin, Rome, Saint Petersburg, London, and Madrid, as well as to those of Algiers (where a branch was opened), Casablanca, Oran, Tananarive, Saigon, and Hanoi.

Like the Army and Navy, the Bon Marché had early acquired a firm stake in colonialism, the catalogue circulating throughout the French empire. A colonial clientele represented a particularly good catch, because they tended to buy in bulk. And was not the role of France in Africa and in Cochin China to convert the heathen? An enterprise that would have appealed to the founder. One suspects that the catalogues of the Bon Marché circulated as far afield as the less exalted *Chasseur français*. Both would seem like links with home to the official sweating it out in Douala or Pointe-Noire. The colonial appeal is perhaps the only aspect of Bon Marché imperialism that the author has neglected. And, of course, the annual catalogues were translated into English, German, and Spanish (though South Americans preferred the more alluring Printemps). Personal reminiscences of the Russian Revolution allude to the fact that to be found to be in possession of a Bon Marché catalogue was taken to be an indication of bourgeois origin—as indeed it was.

So by 1900, the Bon Marché had indeed acquired *droit de cité*. By then a great many provincial children would have been easily persuaded that the Maison Boucicaut was indeed Paris itself; a visit to Paris was a visit primarily to the store, to be fitted up with bathing costume and summer clothes in early July, before the holidays (which, in French primer society, always began on 15 July, the day after the prize-giving), and with sailor suit, overcoat, strong shoes, thick stockings, pencil box, satchel to be worn on the back, and black *blouson* with long sleeves, in time for the *rentrée*.

Of course, such an operation could just as well be carried out in a branch in Rouen or Bordeaux, but a visit to the *maison mère* would be a major treat. Such a visit might also take in the Théâtre du Châtelet, a great favourite with the provincials, but little else. As for little Parisians the neat, brightly coloured delivery vans, driven by uniformed *garçons*, to be seen in every quarter carrying the Boucicaut flag up the heights of the XXème and the XVIIIème, would be a reminder of a Thursday afternoon excursion to the shop, followed by a visit to a *pâtisserie*. For such, the Bon Marché signified half-holidays, holidays, and the approach of Easter and Christmas. It was both a family shop and a children's shop, but children of course accompanied by elegant, well-dressed mothers, themselves well-behaved and grateful.

In an imaginative passage, the author asserts that the Bon Marché was not just a shop, but a way of life, designed to meet—and indeed to provoke—every middle-class need and craving, to equip its customers with every visible status symbol—new ones were being discovered all the time—and to enable the Hulots of prewar days to walk out in self-confidence, even with a jaunty air and the light flicker of a bamboo cane (purchasable in the umbrella department, from the umbrella salesmen who, in the *Livre d'Or* photographs, gaze out at us with most distinguished *hauteur*, above their high collars), aware that they were properly clothed and fully equipped, and that, if dressed up for *le cyclisme*, one did not tuck the bottoms of one's trousers into one's socks.

How much less ill at ease would poor Hoopdriver have been had he had access to a suburban Bon Marché! It was the apparently immobile, changeless, frozen world of the French primer, of a type which was still in use in English schools in the 1920s, as though the Great War had never been: the band—the *garde républicaine*, is always playing in the bandstand, the little boy in sailor suit is always sailing his boat in the *grand bassin*, the little girl is always pursuing a butterfly with her butterfly net, a tiny boy is always rolling his hoop, elegant ladies are always sitting, in decent bathing costumes, under brightly coloured parasols, languid ladies are always reclining in hammocks, reading edifying literature (*chez Mame*), family groups are always having tea on the open balcony, the formal fountains are always playing, little girls in straw hats are always batting their *cerf-volants* across a net, artistic women in loosely fitted print gowns are always sitting at their easels, painting, girls and boys, well wrapped up in coats with fur collars, are always engaged in snowball fights, Nanny is always pushing baby in an elaborate pram with a white canopy, young men in white trousers and blazers and boaters with bright ribbons are always lounging, dangling their tennis rackets, the game is always about to begin, the *bonne* (Alsatian or Breton) is always laying the table for a grand dinner, the napkins laid out with their fantails in the air, the elderly, white-haired, deferential gardener is always watering the flowers, gentlemen in white gloves are always dropping their visiting cards in silver trays, the family home is always faux-Henri III with crenellations, as in Larousse, under 'Maison'. For, in Larousse, too, everything is eternally immobile, solid, well-made, long-lasting.

Everyone knows what to do, to remove gloves before shaking hands, how to kiss a lady's hand, slightly bent over it, when to advance a chair, when to sit down, how to retain the crease in tight trousers in the act of sitting down, how to light a cigar, when to open a door, how to blow one's nose, when to raise one's hat, and to whom. If in doubt, go to the Bon Marché, the academy of *bon ton*.

Professor Miller, who is a sociologist, perhaps overemphasizes the deliberate imposition of the middle-class ethos, as a form of 'social control'. The Boucicauts were concerned primarily to sell goods, to ensure a constant and rapid turnover; they were not consciously attempting to construct a safe class system. But he is undoubtedly right in pointing to the resultant strengthening of middle-class conformism, from one end of France to the other. In this respect, Bon Marché catalogues had much the same unifying effects as the advance of literacy and the consequent spread of a sense of a national identity as described so brilliantly by Eugen Weber.* The Bon Marché, too, could keep abreast of diplomacy and foreign affairs, providing dolls dressed as Russian as well as French soldiers (or, rather, officers). The shop did not cater to a

* Eugen Weber, *Peasants into Frenchmen: The Modernization of Rural France, 1870–1914* (Stanford University Press, 1976).

closed, immobile middle class, but rather to a wide-open one. Even its own employees could gain access to its lower ranks; and the point of the musical evening was to display its own salesmen exercising middle-class skills. Through its catalogues, middle-class values spread further and further down, to be emulated, at a still lower level, by the catalogues of the Belle Jardinière, the Samaritaine, and the Bazar de l'Hôtel de Ville.

It was not just a matter of outward appearance, of clothing suited to a score of different occasions—and for the Boucicauts, the more changes of clothing in the course of the day, the better. Suitable leisure occupations were evoked, because leisure was a middle-class commodity. Fencing was encouraged, because it was regarded as a manly, very Gallic, sport. The Bon Marché was quick to realize the vast possibilities of the bicycle, the motor car, and the airplane: each would provide for several layers of elaborate protective clothing. Bon Marché people went on family holidays, forty or fifty years before the *congés payés* were ever heard of, and at a time when three-quarters of Parisians never ventured far beyond the Valley of the Marne on Sunday outings. Bon Marché people went skating in winter, went to the opera, the theatre, dances, children's parties, were to be seen at Longchamp and Chantilly (but not at Vincennes). Bon Marché people travelled first or second, took sleepers, took the waters, went to church (the shop does not seem to have made any special bid for Protestants and Jews, perhaps because there were not many of them, and it is permissible to suppose that the Bon Marché salesmen were ardent anti-Dreyfusards), had Christmas parties, gave and received presents.

The true test of the durability of a way of life is when it imposes its own calendar. There was a Bon Marché year which began with the early-January sales and extended to the Christmas sales in December. Early February was the time for *la Grande Semaine du Blanc*, a prodigious display of linen; mimosa, perfume, lavender, gloves marked 'late February', the *nouveautés* made their appearance in March, summer fashions crept in in April and early May, winter ones, in October. July might mark a spending spree on holiday clothing; *la rentrée*, in September, would see a run on the stationery department, with the kitting-up for school for the next academic year (Bon Marché children *always* got prizes).

November could be expected to see a run on flowers, artificial and real, especially chrysanthemums, as well as to reduce accumulated stocks of black (like good Catholics, the Boucicauts were very funeral-conscious and cemetery-orientated, though the Bon Marché never had a line in coffins). There was always a brisk winter trade in black crêpe, black silk, black armbands, and lapel-bands. It was an easy journey—all at the same floor level —from death, from black-edged cards, notepaper, and *faire parts* (the black borders would not be too ostentatiously thick, for that would be vulgar) to First Communion: complete outfits in white silk, small suits in black, with white silk armbands, never to be worn again, white missal, silver-framed photographs. Carpets and Oriental rugs for some reason favoured October. Each month had a Bon Marché identity though August must have had rather a jaded one. Until the 1880s, the shop was even open on Sundays, though only after mass.

Everything about the Bon Marché was designed to reassure, as expressing continuity as well as solidity. One annual catalogue would follow another—though I do not know whether any appeared during the First World War, while, at the same time, each year would be given a specific pictorial identity, some of them beautifully designed. It provided a world in which death was decently, respectfully acclimatized, and in which revolution was inconceivable—Boucicaut and his successors may have missed something there, not having discovered that clothes would also make the revolutionary—and in which middle-class values went unquestioned. It would never have occurred to the directors that the unity of the French family could be fragmented or that children could question the authority of their parents. So the great days of the Bon Marché coincide with the lush years of the Third Republic. The author is right to stop in 1920.

This is first-rate social history. But Professor Miller is equally at home in the intricacies of business organization, accounting, advertising, delivery, mail order, salary scales, pension schemes, employee shareholding provisions. This is also very good business history. What is unique perhaps is the combination of such

177

different skills. For the author never neglects the human element, and though the personnel dossiers that he has used give only the barest facts of employees' biographies, he supplements such sparse documentation with an imagination vivid enough to take in the fallen arches and the tired feet, the high rate of firing, and the long, long slog to relative success.

The Bon Marché was probably a better employer than most of its rivals; certainly more attempted to enter its great portals than were ever received. But the work was grinding, the espionage invasive and minutely organized. In many ways, the Bon Marché was a trap for ambitious young men, many of whom would have been much better off employed in some small shop in an un-fashionable part of the city, where they would have time to chat with customers and where they might even end up by marrying the boss's daughter. But then they would not have acquired a middle-class veneer. And some even seem to have *enjoyed* the Bon Marché and really to have believed that they were part of a team.

The Bon Marché is special. But so is Harrod's, or the Army & Navy, or l'Innovation, or the Bazar Hôtel de Ville, which, at least in the kitchen section, runs to a rough sort of camaraderie. Professor Miller has set very high standards indeed for others to emulate. Apart from his teutonic and litanic introduction and conclusion, there is little that one could quarrel with. The famous school is in Juilly (not Jouilly) and '*A* Dr Lacassagne' is rather hard on the famous Lyon criminologist. *The* Dr Lacassagne would have been nearer the mark.

The View from the Promenade

It was something of a wrench to move straight from Paris to Aberystwyth in the autumn of 1955, after spending eleven years in France and Belgium, mostly in Paris. When I first arrived, I was so disheartened by the forlorn aspect of Welsh urban architecture and by the feeling that I was literally 'at the end of the line', in a very small town right in the middle of the great bight of Cardigan Bay, that I spent my first weekend alternately reading *Lucky Jim* on a sofa in the utterly barren residents' lounge of a small hotel, and taking trips to the station in order to reassure myself of the visible presence of the Cambrian Coast Express, the guarantee that there did exist a physical link with London and beyond; but as my second day in Aberystwyth was a Sunday, even that sparse consolation was denied me! It was the first time in my life—I was thirty-eight—that I had taken up a regular job, and I had been on only very brief visits to England—once a year, or once every other year, since 1944.

My mood remained one of deep gloom for several weeks, in fact till the annual November fair, when I was enlivened by a steam organ that blared out with tremendous gusto and at breakneck speed 'The Yellow Rose of Texas', so that I listened to it every evening of that week. By then I had made several other discoveries: that, if one looked hard enough, there were a few quite handsome early nineteenth-century shops in small streets away from the promenade; that, over the other side of the small harbour, there was a row of whitewashed fishermen's cottages, and that a family of five was living in what had been a double-decker Crosville bus; that, very early in the morning or at the turn of the tide, a regular group of elderly men, some wearing peaked nautical-looking caps, others bowlers or cloth caps, scoured the three beaches for drift-wood—a coaster carrying pit-props had sunk in the bay some time previously—or any other treasures offered up by the sea (there was a persistent rumour about a leather purse, greenish from immersion, containing thirty

179

sovereigns); that, on most days, one could see the big, black cormorants diving for fish; and that, during our Thursday departmental meetings, my professor, who had certainly never heard of Kingsley Amis, and indeed had little interest in anyone who had lived later than Simon de Montfort, would answer the phone: 'History Speaking'. By then, I had also discovered that it was possible to drink on Sundays by joining the Marine Club, and that the surrounding countryside, both inland and along the coast, was of quite biblical beauty and innocence, and, well inland, of weird abandonment.

But my most surprising discovery was that I thoroughly enjoyed lecturing, in conditions that, throughout winter, meant competing with the crash of the sea, the roar of the westerly gales and the screams of the gulls. My audience—large because it was a first year: the pretty South Walian girls, and those from Llanelli outstandingly so, in the front rows, a fairly passive middle-ground, the last tiers to the back dominated by the solid forms of the rugger club—had both to be made to hear me against the competition from outside, and to be kept interested. A single attempt to lecture on the Sublime Porte ended in chaos at my first evocation of the Black Eunuch (I was unable to carry on to the white one); and I quickly abandoned any attempt to cope with Russian institutions. My lectures were in the nature of a circus act and owed much to audience participation. After less than a term, I was *em*phasizing certain words on certain syllables, pausing instinctively to do so. I had, quite unconsciously, acquired a Welsh cadence: a teaching device I suppose almost as admirable as spoken Russian.

My pupils were completely unpretentious, pleasantly irreverent and egalitarian, and very quick to spot fraud or showmanship. In fact, I could not have had better masters. Jokes were a matter of very fine calculation, as they would have to carry a double appeal to the front-row flowerbeds and to the rugger rearguard; the middle would always follow. Inward jokes, involving some knowledge at least of Welsh topography, were the most successful; and, like Claude Lévi-Strauss in his years at São Paulo, I had to be able to cope with at least two sets of Christian names: Hywel Wesley Jones, Griffith Craig Evans, and so on, in order to address my pupils individually.

UCW was a small, tight, but varied community. There were over forty pubs in Aberystwyth, even more pubs than chapels, and each one had its specialized clientele: there was one, run by a very old untidy lady, whose three bars were always empty; another sold evil-smelling 'scrumpy', producing its own extensive Saturday-night network of vomit, sometimes reaching almost to the station. A number *sang*, in Welsh, a sound as beautiful as the waves of the angry sea. The rugby club had generally to penetrate farther and farther inland: when I first went there, a *zone interdite* had just penetrated as far as Lampeter. But, as I was a resident, at different times, in four hotels, I was sometimes able to accommodate the rugby club at least in drink; and, as a result, was asked to leave two. It gave me a feeling of warm satisfaction to know which of my students would be in which pubs on which night. I am a provincial and enjoy the reassurance of habit.

I also greatly enjoyed the finely chiselled malice that staff, students, and locals all displayed in talking of one another. There is nothing more discouraging than discretion; and here discretion was out of the question. Artistic malice and intense curiosity are not only forms of friendship, they also furnish lives that might otherwise be rather dull. And a seaside town with a curving promenade, three beaches, offers a marvellous social observatory; one of the professors, placed strategically in the middle of the Promenade, was in the habit of socially observing through powerful marine binoculars. As a historian, I was further fascinated by the minute ramifications of 'cousinage'—an information service readily available that could easily take in its stride great-uncles and 'my second cousin's mother-in-law'. Attempts to escape detection were engaging: two professors, the one a bachelor, the other a widower, living in lodgings, were in the habit of keeping their whisky in a tea-pot, pouring it out into cups, for fear of being discovered by their landlady, who told me that she found academics *very* strange: 'Would you, Mr Cobb, drink whisky out of a tea-pot?'

At first I missed Paris very much. Then, gradually, I felt myself more and more enfolded in a comforting community of gossip, elaborate and often exquisite malice, a stunning demolition of pretension, a community in which almost everything could (and would) eventually be known. I have never enjoyed any place so much and account most of my enjoyment to the fact that the vast majority of my students were from South Wales. I learnt from them the importance of simplicity and clarity, of simply being myself and of expressing my own prejudices and enthusiasms, and above all the shared joy of a lecture on a good day, when lecturer and audience were on form. The Welsh have done as much for me as the French; indeed I think they have much in common, and I used to marvel at the wonderful French cadences that Welsh female students would acquire as the result of a year spent in France. What they especially have in common is respect for education and delight in *la chose parlée*. But I must not carry this too far. My great good fortune was to have started my teaching career when and where I did: in 1955, in UCW.

Brassai's Paris*

Brassai, the *Hibou Nocturne* of the velvet blue-black and brilliant, liquid white of the Paris nights of the Thirties, was entirely fortunate in his period. It enabled him to command a wider, more varied spectrum than that offered by the much darker eighteenth-century night of Restif, the original Night Owl. The Hungarian photographer was working at a time—1931–2, and so a Paris still recognizable in that of three years later, when I first went to the city—when the electric night had long replaced the softer gas night of the July Monarchy and the Second Empire. He is as skilled in looking out on to the street below, on to the bright lights of the fairground as seen from an upper window, as looking in, penetrating the much-used intimacy of a brothel bedroom on the fourth floor, or the still dangerous sociability of a ground-floor *bal musette* in the rue de Lappe, some of which were still the rendez-vous of the really bad boys in the flat, long-peaked caps and the long points of their shirt collars, *cols Danton*. He is at his best as a miniaturist, with a wonderful eye for significant detail—detail that, at times, places his visual chronicle firmly in the early Thirties, and that, at others, illustrates the remarkable continuity from the Thirties to the late Fifties, eliminating the Occupation years altogether, as if they had brought no significant changes at least in the outer aspect of things. The lurid pattern of a wall-paper, the texture of a bed-cover (which will not be removed), the simple, summary architecture of a *bidet*, the regulation fringed towel, handed over at the moment of payment for the room in the brothel or *hôtel de passe*, hanging on the edge of the washbasin, having served its purpose to clean up the man, following his brief moment of pleasure: the continuity of a reassuring sordidity.

The *lack* of continuity is more striking. Here are girls with carefully curled fringes of their very dark hair, four or five

* This essay first appeared as a review of Brassai, *The Secret Paris of the 30's* (Thames and Hudson) in the *Spectator*, July 1983.

adjoining curls, like a row of cedillas facing the wrong way, the now lost, distant race of working class and lower middle class Parisiennes of the 1930s, their eyes bright with excitement, drink and invitingness. The brilliantined and well-brushed hair of the men, the neat parting to the side, the men apparently as dark as the girls, like the characters in a René Clair film, speak as eloquently of the Thirties as the curled fringes of the girls. Both seem somehow more French than the chlorophylic inhabitants of the *Hexagone* of the 1980s, as though, at that time, no blonde French had existed. It may of course all be the effect of the night lights. The bad boys, too, look very bad indeed, as though they meant business with their *eustaches*—their knives—ready to hand, famished and rat-faced, as they stand, feet insolently splayed out, caps to one side, with their hands in their pockets. Equally menacing is the waiting group of *la bande du Grand Albert*, silhouetted against a brightly-lit long peeling wall somewhere near the porte d'Italie. All—fringed girls and stony-eyed men —have limp *gauloises* hanging provocatively from their lower lips, as if further to emphasize their Frenchness. Here are the broad lapels of the jacket, in loud check, the made-up bow-tie over a pullover that comes up to the collar of the shirt, the bow-tie like a toy stuck on, a burly man, pleased with himself as he stands squarely at the counter of a café, *bal musette*, in the rue de Lappe. It was as if Brassaï's characters, caught wide-eyed by his flash-bulbs, were consciously acting being French. Were the French more French then? They were certainly more joyful, more uninhibited, more eccentric, less conformist.

The choice is as varied as was the intensive night life of a still living, socially varied Paris. I particularly like the sailor and the petty-officer, with the fringed girl between them, and in front of them a rising pile of saucers. The girl is paying more attention to the sailor, turning towards him; the petty-officer is too far gone, he will never make it. Then there is an amazing lateral shot, through a glass panel, of a *bal musette*, an elderly man in a hat, such a one as could have been described in the happy Thirties as a *noceur*, his mouth wide open, in laughter or in song, supporting himself on two girls, rather like the elderly gentleman described by Guilloux in his *Carnets*, who, when it was proposed that they make an outing to a brothel, says: 'Wait while I put on my *Légion*

d'honneur.' Among the strange creatures of the night collected by
Brassai the strangest is *la môme Bijou,* rippling with cheap jewellery, rings and bangles, hatted, gloved, wearing a moulting fur,
many scarves and floating draperies, a sort of dotty elegance gone
to seed, her eyes bright and slightly mad, as she stares at the
camera, holding a glass. She is said by some to have been the
model for *la Folle de Chaillot.*

A police cycle patrol—*les hirondelles,* some of the police with
1914-style moustaches, accompanied by two burly inspectors,
heavily muffled, their breath visible—are waiting expectantly at a
brightly lit corner, staring into the night. On the facing page are
five men of *la bande du Grand Albert* looking in the direction of the
patrol.

Before and after: a couple, reflected in the long horizontal
mirror beside the bed, the man still in tie and waistcoat, his hair
unruffled, his jacket thrown carelessly over the chair, the woman
partly beside him, both lying on a bed-cover decorated in a flower
pattern, the clothing soon to be removed but not the bed-cover.
Then the woman sitting on the *bidet,* her broad and sagging
bottom protruding over the rim, as she washes herself in front,
her feet in flowered high-heeled shoes, the man balanced on one
leg while putting on his trousers. Stage three: the woman, still
naked save for the shoes, her broad back marked by the red line
left by her brassière, reflected in the mirror, the man, now in his
shirt, adjusting his tie and brushing his hair in the mirror of the
heavy wardrobe that, for some reason—for this was a place for
unclothing, not for keeping clothes—so often cluttered the bed-
rooms of brothels and *hôtels de passe.*

There is a bizarre picture of three short girls lying on a couch,
like dolls, their faces heavily made up, against a huge flowered
wallpaper, two little dogs lying at their feet and looking like toys.
The outside girl is wearing net stockings and black buckle shoes
that accentuate her doll-like respectability. A well-dressed lady in
a saucepan black straw hat is showing her hand to a voluminous
cartomancienne, the tarot cards spread out fanwise on a table
covered with a heavy cloth, against a corner background of
wallpaper samurai. The grotesque gorilla-man, in a heavy plaid
dressing-gown bends over the little naked blond boy, Peter-
chen, in a Montmartre hotel bedroom that houses gymnasts and

circus people. Or the benevolent, child-like face of the old tramp beneath his shapeless beret, heavily bearded, sitting holding his little black cat, his overcoat tattered at the cuffs and held together by a large safety-pin, on a winter night on the quays beneath the Pont-Neuf, his female companion lurking in the offing, having refused to be photographed. Brassai is as compassionate as he is observant; and he warms to the independent and rather well-spoken *clochard*, the denizen of a lost age, when the quays were still free of traffic and the home of tramps and lovers. But he can also be merciless, as when he portrays, twice, the triple-chinned *taulière*, queening it, in black dress and heavy necklace, over her own establishment: once, when she is seated playing cards with two of her girls, one looking very bored, and a customer, his hair brushed back; then when she is standing commandingly in front of a heavy mirror, her three chins sagging beneath her blotched face.

Brassai's album is a nostalgic one. It depicts a Paris still vibrant with life, throughout the night hours, and when it was still possible, at the café *au carrefour de Buci*, to meet *le père la Tulipe*, a misnomer, for, top-hatted, he sold violets, bought at the *Halles*, standing at the counter, from four every morning, for a round, or several rounds, of *canons*, most of which he was offered by customers grateful for his familiar presence.

As Louis Chevalier has written, and as Brassai might have said, something of the wonder and variety of the Paris of Balzac and Eugène Sue had survived into the Thirties, and, indeed, beyond, into the early Sixties, before the *Ville-Lumière* began on its slow death, early to bed, burglar-alarms set, all doors bolted and barred.

The Assassination of Paris*

Architects, town planners, and specialists in traffic circulation are much more dangerous than sociologists, who, so often, have merely served to complicate what might have seemed self-evident and simple to the historian. The errors, assumptions, and miscalculations of the former are both durable and visible: solid contributions to human misery, whereas, while sociologists may attempt to bypass history, or to render it unintelligible and unreadable, they do not seek to destroy it altogether.

What virtually all architects and urbanists since Haussmann have had in common is a loathing for the past and an overriding desire to erase its visible presence. Like sociologists, they have little time for individuals and their trying, quirky, and unpredictable ways, tending to think only in terms of human destiny: so many units in the formation of a Grand Design (or a *Grand Ensemble*, to use a modish French expression), as if people, in rectangular blocks of a thousand, or ten thousand, were to be assimilated to a gigantic set of Lego. There is nothing more remote from humanity and more devoid of the human scale than an architect's model plan for a new urban development. Even the trees are puny and plastic, and of a sickly green (*chlorophile*); the cars, lined up in their *parkings souterrains*, are gaily coloured, but the people to be assigned to the new Alphavilles are not even dots.

One of the few, wry, consolations to be derived from Norma Evenson's well-researched and implacable record of architectural insensitivity is the realization that the horrors that architects and planners were actually *able* to perpetrate were as nothing to those that they had *meditated* and that, for one reason or another—often a war, or an economic recession (both concealed blessings for the urban dweller)—they had not succeeded in getting away with.

* This essay first appeared as a review of Norma Evenson, *Paris: A Century of Change, 1878–1978* (Yale University Press) in *The New York Review of Books*, February 1980.

Consider Le Corbusier, in his forty-year campaign against the beauty and variety of Paris. How he *hates* the place! With what sovereign contempt does he treat its mindless inhabitants! Here he is already in 1925 obsessed with his *grande croisée*, a swath of huge expressways cutting through the centre of the city, east-west and north-south, marking Paris like a hot-cross bun. And here he is again back in the 1920s, with plans to uproot Les Halles and most of the old street system between the rue de Richelieu and the rue Saint-Martin, and to erect on the vast quadrilateral of the old Right Bank thus devastated a series of tower blocks, the first of many versions of his alarmingly named *Ville Radieuse*. And here he is in 1931 proposing a grandiloquent entry into the projected *Voie Triomphale* (the triumph of inhumanity), either at the Porte Maillot or the Pont de Sèvres.

The implacable Helvetian is tireless in his assault on Paris, doggedly determined to line both banks of the river with an aligned barrier of dragon's teeth. What is the secret of his hatred of the place? Is it the rancorous provincialism of a twentieth-century Girondin? Anyhow, right up to his death, he submits plan after plan for the dehumanization of the city, and appears as constantly surprised by the rejection of his overtures. It must have been only a minor consolation to him to have been given a free hand in Marseille, or rather outside it, for the erection of what the locals at once nicknamed *la maison du fada*—the idiot's house.

What distinguishes Le Corbusier is the sheer persistence of his war against the French capital. As the years go by, and conceit and rancour take their toll, the black lines on his maps, criss-crossing the city at its very heart, get blacker and thicker and more impatient, the ordered rectangular cubes of high-rise blocks become heavier and more febrile. The main assault is still on the Seine and its vicinity; but, with each year, the pencil of potential destruction moves inward, mapping out further swaths of de-molition, as he greedily eyes the tempting fruit of the once plague-ridden pockets of the city known as the *îlôts insalubres*: Saint-Merri, Sainte-Avoye, Saint-Gervais, Saint-Paul, the Gravil-liers, and the promising space left by the destruction of the old fortifications on the northern rim of the city.

Others do not quite last the pace thus set. But the awful Eugène Hénard, working at the turn of the century at the municipal office in charge of public works, could tote up at least twenty-five years of anti-Parisian dream-drawings. By 1903, long before the Swiss *marchand de soleil*, he is already obsessed with a *grande croisée* of his own, provided, in this instance, by a widened rue de Richelieu, leading to an avenue de Richelieu on the Left Bank, forming the main north-south axis, and intersecting an enlarged avenue de l'Université. His east-west axis would have actually cut through the courtyard of the Palais-Royal, while a further swath, the avenue du Panthéon, would have obliterated the rue Mouffetard, which, being narrow, and warmly human, has attracted persistent assaults from several generations of planners. If Le Corbusier reserved his most persistent loathing for the old Right Bank centre, Hénard was primarily out to destroy the quartier Saint-Germain-des-Prés.

He was not alone in his distaste for the jumble of narrow streets stretching from the carrefour de Buci to the rue Mazarine, the rue Guénégaud and the rue de Nevers. The architect André Ménabréa, writing in 1932, looked forward to the razing of the whole area, in order, so he said, to erase the memory—somewhat remote—of the September Massacres of 1792, when, so he claimed, the rue de Tournon, the rue de Seine, the rue de l'Abbaye, and the rue de l'Echaudé had 'run with blood'. Why not, then, tear up the rue de la Grande Truanderie and the rue de la Mortellerie, because they commemorated long-forgotten killings and ancient violence? Why not raze the cloître Saint-Merri, because it too had been the scene of a more recent massacre?

Even as late as 1937, urbanists were still toying with plans to prolong the rue de Rennes (the most desolate, inhuman street in Paris) to the level of the Seine, either at the Pont-Neuf or at the Pont des Arts, or at both, knocking off a wing or two of the Institut de France in the process (it was in the way). As in 1913, when similar proposals had been made, so in 1939 the advent of a providential war saved the integrity of the old Left Bank. The architects and planners and the technocrats of public health not only followed one another in their hatred of a human past and of a human street plan; they copied one another, from decade to decade, handing down, from 1900 to the 1960s, schemes for the assassination (an expression used by Professor Evenson) of Les

Halles, the clearance of the riverside areas to the east of the
Hôtel-de-Ville, the brutal invasion of the tranquillity of the enclosed Palais-Royal—a safe paradise for lovers, *flâneurs*, and
children—and the cutting of a huge swath through the quartier
de Buci.

From 1900 to the 1960s, all such plans were dictated by a false
priority, an obsession with the improvement of internal circulation, east-west and north-south, at the expense of a long-
established human geography. Paris for the automobile, rather
than Paris for the Parisians. This is what Paul Delouvrier, urban-
ist and prefect of the Seine, had in mind, in the typically pretentious phrase written in 1963: *Paris doit épouser son siècle.* One can
see what this *mésalliance* signifies when one contemplates the fate
of what had once been the Right Bank quays until they were
converted into roadways.

So, indeed, it could have been much worse. The unfulfilled
blueprints of destruction, the firm red lines of the planner's pencil
are even more chilling than the visual—and aural—evidence of
what has actually been achieved by the combination of urbanists,
architects, and building speculators. Had M. Pompidou, who
also liked to talk of Paris being forced to marry her century (which
did not prevent him from living on the agreeable tip of the île
Saint-Louis), lasted a little longer, the canal Saint-Martin would
have gone, covered over to carry a semi-circular highway which
would then have roared through the lower slopes of the Mon-
tagne-Sainte-Geneviève. And the quays of the Left Bank would
have gone the way of those of the Right, and the Seine would
have become as unapproachable as the majestic Hudson River.
President Pompidou *did* get his *trou*, his hole, officially designated as *le plateau Beaubourg*; and he is commemorated by a
strange building that rises above the modest levels of the old
houses of Saint-Merri and Sainte-Avoye and that looks like a
gigantic *paupiette de veau*, with all its innards displayed on the
outside. Others have compared it to an enormous, multicoloured, and very venomous insect.

Most of the worst horrors, the vast mushroomed, domed follies
of the 1960s, are well away from the centre. Except for the
unfortunate people who must live or work there, no one needs to

go anywhere near the convention centre and shopping complex at the Porte Maillot, much less to the vast complex of high-rise apartments and office buildings at la Défense; the glass and concrete apartment blocks at the Front de Seine are only visible if one approaches Paris from Versailles by car. It is possible even to avoid the immense uniform towers of the new Porte d'Italie; and only a few elderly enthusiasts of a little-known XIIIème will recall, with nostalgic affection, the small streets and courtyards, the low-lying houses, and the warm and varied sociability of the rue Nationale and the rue du Château des Rentiers, now mere names derisively harking back to a vanished topography that was still quite recently genuinely working-class and that tightly enclosed a shared fraternity and a confident *esprit de quartier* that was sure of its environment and was content to stay put. This was the Left Bank equivalent of Belleville and Ménilmontant and managed successfully to combine a population of XIIIème-born French—many of whom had only left the *arrondissement* to do their military service, and some of whom, among the older female inhabitants, had never crossed the river, indeed, had never *thought* of crossing the river—with sizeable groups of Algerian immigrant workers. Now the factories and workshops have gone, along with the two-storeyed houses; and so have those who worked in them. The new inhabitants of the vast Porte d'Italie complex are young, middle-class couples, with no memories of the old XIIIème, and nothing to attach them to a recent, but vanished past.

The Boulevard Périphérique circles Paris with the constant roar of tyres, the screams of sirens, and the presence of sudden death. But, as its name implies, it is well outside the city proper, and may be only briefly glimpsed from the comfortable safety of suburban overhead railways like the *ligne de Sceaux*. The horrors of the huge high-rise complex of Maine-Montparnasse, constructed during the 1960s, and the Tour Zamansky, it is true, cannot be disguised: the one sticks up like a threat from another planet, at the end of a neat line of trees in the Luxembourg gardens, the latter dwarfs the beautiful proportions of the tip of the île Saint-Louis. What, one wonders, did M. Pompidou make of *that*? The white hulk of the vast District de Paris building stares arrogantly across the river at the stilted cement and glass jungle of the Faculty of

Science, as if defying the old-fashioned and familiar barges in between making their way to or from the equally familiar sand port of Paris.

But, since the 1950s, the greatest damage to Paris has not been architectural so much as human: a process that might be described as the de-Parisianization of Paris, as a result of the removal from the city of much of its traditional and characteristic population. Since the turn of the century, Professor Evenson tells us, the balance between Parisians and *banlieusards*, or suburbanites, has been steadily reversed. In 1901, the population of Paris stood at 2,700,000, that of the *banlieue* at 955,000. In the following year, nearly 200,000 people are stated to have been living in *meublés*, a form of cheap furnished flats that persisted through the 1930s and that survived at least into the early 1950s, enabling both the provincial newcomer and the foreigner to live comparatively cheaply in the city.

The exodus from the city seems to have begun in 1919, as a result of the introduction of the eight-hour day and the extension of the suburban railway network, and, between 1919 and 1939, by the formation of *cités jardins* on the model of the suburban English Garden City of Letchworth, designed by Ebenezer Howard. Because of the *octrois*—the toll houses on the outskirts of Paris where a tax was collected on goods entering the city—which were still in existence in the mid-Thirties, food was cheaper beyond the municipal barriers, inducing many people to move just beyond them, into overcrowded *communes* such as Vanves, Pantin, Aubervilliers, Malakoff. In 1926, there had been as many as 40,000 people living in the old military zone beyond the obsolete fortifications built around the city in 1845; all these *zoniers* had been cleared out by 1932, when on the former *zone* were built a series of HBM blocks (*habitations à bon marché*, quite literally, cheap housing), apartments accommodating up to 120,000 people along the northern edge of the city.

By the previous year, 1931, the balance between Paris and the suburbs had narrowed to 2,900,000 and 2,100,000; and on the eve of the Second World War the two populations stood about equal. However, because of the enormous influx of young provincials to Paris following the Liberation, the figures were temporarily reversed; and during the terrible winter of 1953–4, many were found to be living in temporary edifices, minor *bidonvilles*, or shanty towns, within the limits of the city. Two years later, a quarter of a million families were officially listed as *mal-logés* within the Département de la Seine. In 1970, the population of Paris had declined to 2,600,000, that of the *banlieue* had reached 5,600,000. Since then, this trend has certainly been accelerated.

For instance, following the clearing of the Marais, and the re-development of the area as a predominantly middle-class quarter, 20,000 of the original inhabitants were resettled in the suburban *grands ensembles*, complexes of high-rise apartment buildings, schools, and shops built during the Fifties and Sixties. This process of alienation has been sensitively described by Simenon in his novel *Le Déménagement*—the 'move' from the warm and closely observed sociability of the rue de Turenne to the bleak anonymity of one of the *grands ensembles* south of Paris: Arcueil, Orsay, or Antony. One would be quite hard put to encounter, as one used to, Algerian workers in the small hotels of the rue du Roi-de-Sicile, or Yiddish- or Polish-speaking Jews in and around the rue des Rosiers at the present time; and both the small workshops that cluttered the courtyards of seventeenth-century town houses and palaces and the wholesale establishments, button manufacturers, shops selling *articles de Paris*, garment depots, and even the old clothes' trade, once the stable activities of the IVème, have almost disappeared from the quarter. A few kosher butchers and *one* kosher restaurant in the rue des Rosiers are the sole reminders of what had been until quite recently the oldest Jewish settlement in the city. A little further to the west, the rue des Lombards, the rue de la Verrerie, the rue Saint-Merri, and the rue Quincampoix, once the beat of the most antique prostitutes in Paris, since they became pedestrian precincts (*voies piétonnes*) have lost their *hôtels de passe* and their tiny cafés, and have gained—if that is a gain—*couscous* restaurants, antique shops, bars, and discos. The odd Algerian café may be found still surviving—but not for long—on rue François-Miron.

Of course, it would be hard to lament the clearance of the old plague spots, the *ilôts insalubres* of the IVème and the IIIème;

and, architecturally, the church of Saint-Gervais, released from a clutter of low-roofed hutments, now stands out to full advantage, above its steps, while, with courtyards cleared of the many huts that had invaded them at the time of the Revolution, the *hôtels particuliers* of the Marais can be seen in something of their original splendour. From being an area of small manufacturers and independent artisans, the quarter has been transformed into a balanced mixture of museum and luxury middle-class residence. It is nearly all there to be seen and appreciated. But it is as well to remember that the transformation was made at enormous human cost. The Marais, as an area of social mixture and of varied occupation, is now dead. In 1979, walking to work along the Quai Henri IV, I was stopped by a patrol of the CRS, the riot police, who had blocked off a rectangle of streets between Saint-Paul and the quays with four huge police vans, a punitive operation that lasted a whole morning, the aim of which was to clear three families of squatters, each consisting of a mother and two or three small children, from a group of houses designated for improvement, in the rue des Lions Saint-Paul. The Marais has been recovered as a tourists' paradise. But the quarter has lost all warmth and originality.

Long-established artisans, small shopkeepers, café-owners, coal-selling *bougnats*, the employees of the Sorbonne, taxi drivers, typists, and white-collar workers living in hotels or *meublés* have likewise had to abandon the VIème and the Vème; and a present-day Jean Rhys would now be hard put to afford to spend even a single *night* in one of the small streets off the quai des Grands Augustins. There will be no more novelists of the VIème, for there is no life there any more to write about. The *arrondissement* received its official death warrant as a *quartier populaire*—or at least a *quartier mixte*—with the final destruction, after a long campaign carried out by the locals against the planners, of the old marché Saint-Germain. In June 1980, in the rue de Tournon, where I had lived for twenty years, and in the rue des Quatre-Vents, I could only find *one* tradesman, a *marchand de couleur*, who had been there since the Liberation. All the others had gone, their food shops and small restaurants replaced by boutiques and shops selling Asiatic knick-knacks.

In the neighbouring *arrondissement*, the rue Mouffetard (or what has been left of it), once the most popular market of the Left Bank, and a street of intense sociability, has been given over to tourism, bars, and pornography. Only a few old inn-signs—an oak, the Trois Sergents de la Rochelle—hang as sad, limp reminders of what had once been a triumphal gulley of small shops, barrows, over-hanging clothes' lines, and popular eloquence. *Les gens de la Mouffe* have been spirited away, as on a magic carpet, to Sarcelles or to another of the New Towns of the Paris region. Only the big gendarmerie barracks and the convents and monasteries behind their tall green *portes cochères* are reminders of the odd mixture that had once constituted the peculiar flavour of the quartier Maubert-Mouffetard: monks and nuns, gendarmes, and a population of long-living small shopkeepers, many of them widows, according to Louis Chevalier the oldest female age group in the city. Their place has been taken by young *pied-noir* couples running pizza bars and by elegant antique dealers.

Following the destruction of Les Halles, the rue Saint-Denis, the most authentically Parisian of all streets, and for two hundred years the academy of *l'esprit parisien*, has likewise entirely lost its traditional population of people in the food and drink trades, of *les forts*, people who had been in the same work for generations —and of their concomitant: inexpensive prostitutes. What is left of the quarter is rapidly undergoing a total social transformation, similar to that of the IVème, the former *hôtels de passe* and *meublés* having been converted into high-priced middle-class residences. The old Ier *arrondissement* has by now lost all artisanal character so that the population of the central markets, as depicted successively by Zola, Georges Arnaud, and Simenon (in *La Mort d'Auguste*), would now seem as remote as the memory of the all-night café *Le Chien qui fume*, and the lecherous and potentially violent population, as depicted as late as 1966 by Louis Chevalier in *Les Parisiens*. Even the title of his book would now represent an archaism. The once noisy night streets are silent and almost empty, save perhaps for Gaëtan and Marie-Claire, exercising their poodle and out for a midnight stroll in order to purchase *Le Nouvel-Observateur* and *Charlie-Hébdo* at the nearby revolutionary bookshop-cum-pornography.

Of course, there are still pockets of *les petites gens*, of Parisians

People and Places

recognizable to Eugène Dabit and to Raymond Queneau and to other populist writers, in parts of the Xème and at the eastern end of the XIIème. But the Left Bank XIVème and XVème have been totally recolonized; and there is no longer any hint of the transport workers who once inhabited the rue des Favorites, off the *métro* Convention. The Javel quarter has, thanks to the Front de Seine, jumped up several classes as well as several levels. No place any more for the humble and eccentric characters of Mac-Orlan's *La Tradition de minuit*. The XIVème at the present day would suit Lenin and his petit-bourgeois tastes even better than it did when he was living in the rue Marie-Rose; and he would have as neighbours the widest possible choice of university teachers of various Marxist persuasions.

Only the XIXème, the XXème, and the XVIIIème have retained something of their original character, and Eugène Dabit's Belleville-Ménilmontant of the 1930s (*Banlieues de Paris*) can still be vaguely recognized, at least in accent, impudence, independence, and ingenuity at *bricolage*—every sort of repair and fixing —in the rue Ramponeau, or off the Place des Fêtes, or on both sides of the Boulevard de Belleville. *La Vie devant soi* was written in the mid 1970s, and still described a mixed population of poor Jewish tailors—mostly from North Africa—of Algerians, and long-limbed Sénégalais. But even here the high-rise flats are beginning to point up menacingly on the heights and halfway down the steep slopes. It does not seem very likely that Belleville-Ménilmontant, the Paris of the Commune, and la Goutte-d'Or, the Paris of the FLN, will remain for long undisturbed. The middle-class armies from the north will soon be spilling down the hill, engulfing the little artisans' two-storeyed houses of the rue des Amandiers, the rue de la Mare, the rue les Partants, and the rue Soleillet. When these north-eastern areas are engulfed, the traditional Paris, based on the *esprit de quartier* and on a series of villages, thriving on familiarity and gossip, and in which even shopping represents a social function, will be quite dead. Paris will have become more or less a single-class city, reserved for the very affluent and the very ambitious.

Where then have the Parisians gone? The older, the more recalcitrant, the most intractable have *died*. The rest have gone, reluctantly, to Alphaville. Professor Evenson does not attempt to disguise the full horror of Sarcelles—the biggest and most conspicuous of the *grand ensemble* projects which has become a symbol of both the physical and social shortcomings of these suburban developments. She describes the alienation, loneliness, monotony, and despair that French journalists have called *la sarcellite*, as if it were a disease, and she quotes to great effect Christiane Rochefort's eloquent novel, *Les Petits Enfants du siècle*, an account of growing up in one of the *grands ensembles* as described by an observant sixteen-year-old girl.

What she does not state *en toutes lettres* is amply conveyed in the horror of the photographs: the vast concrete coils of the development called la Grande Borne, with its enforced walking precinct, dominated by twenty-foot stucco statues of ducks and geese, of huge wall-paintings of cuddly animals, of immense wall-portraits of Kafka (of course) and Rimbaud (such a homely couple), a *panachage* of a French Disneyland and of a sociologist's *ville radieuse*, the rectangular blocks painted in bright colours. They are all there: not only Sarcelles, an initiative of the Prefecture of Police, but also Cergy-Pontoise (rewarded with a prefecture), Saint-Quentin-en-Yvelines (which also gets a prefect, a very eighteenth-century concept of giving an identity to a town) —particularly sad, as it rises on the edges of the jumble of small individual houses and villas that had once been the railway town of Trappes—Melun-Sénart, Marne-la-Vallée.

The social cost of Alphaville can be gauged from the high teenage crime rate in Sarcelles, with its rare café and its lack of an identifiable centre, in the *chronique judiciaire* of the Paris dailies and weeklies. No doubt any roof is better than none, any *grand ensemble* is preferable to a *bidonville*. Yet, time and again, Professor Evenson returns to the preference shown by the Parisian artisan, ever since the 1900s and the 1920s, for the single house, the tiny villa, even a converted railway wagon or an old bus or green tram, pathetic grabs at privacy and individuality that mushroomed along the main lines, often on quite unsuitable terrain, and denied most of the amenities, on the wide steppes north of Paris, and in sight of the Warsaw express and *l'Etoile du Nord*: a jumble of irregularity, of artisanal fantasy, turrets, minarets, grottoes, plaster cloisters, Gothic towers in yellow bricks, that may be seen flashing by, in irregular lines, interrupted by the solid cubelike blocks of the *grands ensembles*, as one approaches Paris by train, from the north or the east. Life in the unfinished villa, in Drancy or Garches, as depicted in Queneau's *Le Chien-dent*, was pretty uncomfortable; but at least one knew one's neighbours living up the muddy, waterlogged lanes; and there was even a wooden café that specialized in *bifteck-frites*. There is, after all, quite a rich literature of this chaotic type of *banlieue*, the scattered *bicocques*, or shanties, of the 1910s, the 1920s, and 1930s, in the valley of the Orge, in the Pays de France, in the valley of the Marne, from Landru to Queneau, from Dabit to Ben Barka, from Simenon to Sarrazin, from Weidmann to Fallet, from *faux-manoir normand* to crenellated Maison Larousse, the literature of individualism, eccentricity and of do-it-yourself, the jumbled styles of *le facteur* Cheval and his many suburban imitators, and the tiny Follies below the railway viaduct at Viroflay. But, apart from Alphaville and Christiane Rochefort, what can one expect of the *Grands Ensembles* other than inarticulate despair, vandalism, and teenage violence?

Evenson's study is equally informative on the development of the Paris transport system. The suburban railway lines came surprisingly early: Sceaux, in 1846, Bourg-la-Reine and Orsay in 1857, Boissy-Saint-Léger, in 1859. The Invalides line to Versailles was electrified in 1900. The Petite Ceinture was started in 1851, the Grande Ceinture, in 1875. Predictably, ever since the 1930s, the Gare Saint-Lazare has remained far the largest point of entry and exit. There is an evocative section on river transport, the *bateaux mouches* and the *hirondelles*, the former starting as a Lyonnais venture. The author states that the *bateaux mouches* were suppressed in 1934, but I can remember taking one from the Pont de Sèvres to the Pont des Arts in the following year.

We move from the trams to the familiar snout-nosed buses, with their open rear platforms, an invitation to sociability, conversation, and verbal fantasy on the part of inventive *contrôleurs*, one of the few places where one could encounter Paris police on terms of affability, and the stage too of Queneau's wonderful *Exercices de Style, Ligne 24*. But Evenson is best of all on the *métro*, and this is as it should be, for it is the most poetical form of

The Assassination of Paris

Parisian transport. The *métro* was carrying 400 million passengers by 1914, 761 million by 1938, over a billion by 1941, 1.5 billion in 1946, its peak year. Her account is one of steady advance and improvement, from grinding *rames* to the silent rubber-tyred trains of the present day. It would require considerable nostalgia to regret the passing of the old, clanging scalloped coaches of the Nord-Sud, as they emerged from under the Seine. But how I wished that she had evoked the little Dubonnet-man, and the flickering Dubo, Dubon, Dubonnet, the emblem of the late 1930s and the insistent accompaniment to the packed *métros* of the Occupation years! And how I wished that she had quoted the advertisements and *métro*-poems of Raymond Queneau! Generally, her account is so accurate and so well researched, one hesitates even to question it; but the Gare d'Orsay did *not* connect up with the Gare de Lyon; it was the prolongation of the line from the Gare d'Austerlitz, so that, at one time, the Sud-Express, from Madrid, terminated in the centre of Paris.

I wish too that Evenson had made greater use of literary material in her descriptions of the city and its suburbs. Zola is all very well. But why Sartre? Why the boring, self-indulgent Gertrude Stein ('*we* lived', 'in our time, *we all* . . .'). What of *Poil de Carotte* and *Bubu de Montparnasse*, of Jean Galtier-Boissière and of Jules Romains? I wish too that she had taken greater care of the spelling of French words, especially in her bibliography, from which, unaccountably, she omits Louis Chevalier's powerful and angry *L'Assassinat de Paris*. For *that* is the subject of her own careful, beautifully illustrated, compassionate and very human book, the work, surprisingly, of a professor of architecture.